EARTH

EARTH

Pleiadian Keys
to the Living Library

BARBARA MARCINIAK

with

KAREN MARCINIAK
TERA THOMAS

BEAR & COMPANY
P U B L I S H I N G
SANTA FE, NEW MEXICO

LIBRARY OF CONGRESS CATALOGING-IN-PUBLICATION DATA
Marciniak, Barbara, 1948–
  Earth : Pleiadian keys to the living library /
Barbara Marciniak.
      p. cm.
  ISBN 1-879181-21-5
  1. Spirit writings. 2. Spiritual life. Pleiadians—
Miscellanea. I, Title.
BF 1290.M266   1994
133.9'3—dc20   94-31534
                                                        CIP

Copyright © 1995 by Barbara Marciniak

Bear & Company, Inc.
Santa Fe, NM 87504-2860

Cover illustration: Peter Everly
Cover and interior design: Marilyn Hager
Author photo: Bill Touchberry
Editing: Gail Vivino
Typography: Marilyn Hager
Printed in the United States of America

5 7 9 8 6

To the grace of Earth and the seekers of her keys.

CONTENTS

Acknowledgments ix

Introductions xi

Chapter 1: The Game, the Codes, and the Master Numbers . . . 1

Chapter 2: Redreaming the Living Library 29

Chapter 3: Earth Speaks 55

Chapter 4: Earth is Your Home 75

Chapter 5: Galvanization of the Goddess 89

Chapter 6: Landing of the Light Body 113

Chapter 7: The Dimensions Dance 141

Chapter 8: The Gift of the Gods 161

Chapter 9: Riding the Corridors of Time 181

Chapter 10: The Heavens Speak 197

Chapter 11: Earth's Initiation 219

Chapter 12: Awaken, Dear Friends, Within This Dream 239

Epilogue 251

About the Author 253

ACKNOWLEDGMENTS

A joint collaboration in faith produced this book, and recognition is due to the mighty and valiant players involved in the process. With love, respect, and deep appreciation, I offer my thanks to both my sister, Karen Marciniak, and Tera Thomas, co-creators and co-conspirators of *Earth*. A special tribute to the faith of Barbara and Gerry Clow, and to their reliable and responsible guidance and support, as well as the entire staff of Bear & Company, who do an impeccable job of working with and holding the energy. The meticulous skills of copyeditor Gail Vivino brought new meaning to the word "clarity," helping to create a smooth and readable text, and the finesse of Marilyn Hager created the final elegant and splendid form. A special testimonial to the remarkable talents of artist Peter Everly, whose work once again graces our cover. Peter gave us an exquisite image from which *Earth* would evolve.

Loving thanks to my parents, Ted and Bertha Marciniak, and my entire family, who have always been there for me.

A thanks to the pioneers of thought, you adventuresome souls, who so eagerly embrace the world of spirit, and to Earth herself for giving us all a place to be from.

And, not to be forgotten, a loving tribute to the Pleiadians, whoever they may be, who so effortlessly stand by, offering steadfast and undaunted faith in our process as human beings. Their unrelenting love is a marvel to me, and in turn serves to give me the daring and courage to persist and persevere.

It is my intent that this work serve as a catalyst for an emotional cleansing on a mass scale, calling forth a profound realization of spirit and triggering relief and freedom from the old dungeons of our making. May Earth reflect our healing. Blessings be to all who share these probabilities.

INTRODUCTIONS BY THE AUTHORS

Barbara Marciniak

I am an interpreter and conduit for spirit because I am willing and able to grasp the invisible and translate it as best I can. I hear, feel, and experience the web of existence, the universal source. I am inherently connected to it and perceive the whisperings, impulses, and revelations of cosmic forces as I use this source to guide and sustain me. For me, this force individualizes itself as the Pleiadians. Naturally, the experience is colored by my beliefs. This is an operational principle of existence, where the participant/observer determines the event. I have developed great reverence for the power of spirit and a deep trust in the significance of life and the ever-unfolding purpose of people, places, and events.

The process through which I directed the creation of *Earth* involved, at the core, the issue of faith and trust. All of us involved in creating *Earth*—Karen, Tera, and I—believe in and work with the invisibles, whomever they may be. Each of us is a unique individual agreeing to play with a new manual for life. During the process of pulling *Earth* together, we were each challenged to make a leap in faith in our own special field of limitation. Only later would we marvel at our own miracles.

It is no easy task to bring the Pleiadian channelings into written form. The P's, as they speak through me, teach through humor, paradox, innuendo, contrast, compassion, and a masterful use of confounding statements and ideas. They convey their energy and essence of intent so well in the spoken form. Our challenge was to take a vast array of information and technique and use it as the foundation of the

Living Library teachings—as a book in concrete form—when not much of what the Pleiadians teach is concrete.

Fortunately, the format for this book was clear from the start. It was to contain twelve chapters and would be designed to deliver the reader deeper into the experience of the "influence of twelve." The Pleiadians maintained that we were bound within twelve, so to discover more, we could use the binding itself to evolve. The main body of information was to come from thirteen sessions delivered in 1991 and 1992. Five channelings were from trips abroad to sacred sites in Mexico, Egypt, Greece, and two visits to Bali; and eight from specific three-hour sessions offered around the USA.

At times, if I stopped to logically think about doing this book, I would feel overwhelmed with the enormity of the material. However, I had accomplished so very many things without the slightest knowledge as to what I was about, that now, this faith in the process of not knowing sustains me! It is so much easier to live this way. This faith, held by Karen and Tera as well, and a belief in my commitment to bring the book into form, kept me going. The P's, of course, were at the helm, guiding and intriguing the entire free-will process, notching their subtle signature on life's events—dignified, understated, and always there.

Early on, I divined that this book, which was to be about the Living Library and still had no title, was indeed in existence somewhere in the future. After all, I had committed to do it, so somewhere it was complete, on a shelf, waiting to be reviewed. My idea was to find that future edition and use it to create the original, now. The idea gave us great peace, and seemed a whole lot easier than facing the monumental stack of papers containing transcribed Pleiadian potpourri.

I always knew that once I had a cover for this Living Library story, the book would follow and the pages would fall into line. The cover was conceived of in due time by Peter Everly, while simultaneously the title was received by us— *Earth: Pleiadian Keys to the Living Library*. We were immensely impressed with both the cover and the title. Now it was up to us to put something behind it.

The remainder of the process involved a complex series of synchronistic layers, with time and life's events adding a deeper richness to the unfolding story. We dove into the stacks of pages, and for months we were all immersed in another world where our primary intent and purpose was to create *Earth*. The book was coming together in our dreams, where night after night we all dreamt of its formation. I would write on my "to do" list: "*Earth*, create yourself," and so it did!

As I continue to work with this material, I am challenged to further explore the invisible and examine the nooks and crannies of my beliefs. As invisible friends with a personality, the Pleiadians beckon me to experience an endlessly expanding picture of life. They present the neutrality of the force and web of existence, defining it as an expression of love—the essence of existence for all to use—conscious and unconditionally available as eternal fuel to create anything desired. It was from this force that we created *Earth*.

I oftentimes feel as if I'm here as an observer when my galactic self peers in and perceives Earth life with much less attachment than I. This view is expansive, and I "know" in those moments that I am here to experience and affect the *great shift*, as it is referred to by my galactic consciousness.

We each create a different world for ourselves, of this I am keenly aware. However, the subtlety with which this knowledge intersects life can hardly be recognized, let alone awarded its own acclaim. My life choice has been to safari to the undetected and hidden mysteries, to gather some sort of meaning for myself, and ultimately to gather a reason for being.

Life for me is a series of chapters, and it is no great task to picture myself the heroine of my own novel, vaulting from episode to adventure, crisscrossing worlds both inner and outer. With each segment of life I assign meaning, and like a history book with eras and epochs, each phase is recognized for its seemingly sequential happenings in grand procession, offering a unique sense of order and purpose. It was never a great stretch to accept that life and all its component parts had great meaning. For me, everything that we were told to attach great meaning to seemed so meaningless—that the opposite just had to be true!

My personal reflection on the material is this: Don't kid yourselves—not one of us knows anything for sure! Everything can be true and probably is, because as you think, so shall it be!

Love, clear intent, and a sense of humor are powerful ingredients. Coupled with reverence, compassion, and inspiration, they can make all the difference. May this work serve to further your own freedom. Blessings!

Barbara J. Marciniak
Raleigh, NC
19 September 1994
Full Moon in Pisces

Karen Marciniak

On January 11th of 1994, with the new moon in Capricorn, Barbara, Tera, and I signed the contract and committed to writing this book. I fluctuated between a state of excitement and one of despair. I thought to myself, "This book is something I really want to contribute to. How will I find the time to immerse myself in this project and juggle all the pieces of my already-very-busy world?"

A month before we started *Earth*, my husband and I ended our twenty-two-year marriage/partnership. We sold the home we owned, and my seven-year-old daughter, Laurel, and I moved into a rented house. I was busy unpacking, keeping business at Bold Connections moving along, processing orders, answering mail, and feeling I had to do it all at the expense of free time for myself. Many times I seriously doubted whether I could be part of this book process, and I found myself in a panic, visualizing all the slices of reality I would be dealing with in the first six months of 1994, knowing full well the book would command a large slice.

Finally, I realized that if I didn't participate, a major probability for growth and change would pass me by. I forced myself to come face to face with one of my biggest issues: control. Control was behind the challenge of my never having enough time. I saw with clarity how control had limited me in so many areas of my life, and I decided the only thing I could do was surrender, give up control, get some help with the day-to-day stuff, and trust!

Trust. The whole book was a process of trust. Early on, when the three of us were overwhelmed by all the material Tera had transcribed, when we didn't know where to start to make sense of all the mounds of paper, we did know enough to trust. Barbara, Tera, and I had formed a bond, a triangle of energy, and worked as a team in producing *The Pleiadian Times* and other projects. We had mastered the art of accepting constructive criticism from each other, putting egos and hurt feelings aside, and knowing we were never victims. This allowed us to go a long way in what we were able to accomplish. We trusted that when our energies worked together in harmony and clear intention we could do anything we set our minds to.

Over and over again we visualized pulling the book from the future into the now. We had the cover painting by Peter Everly long before we had the completed material to go inside that cover! The painting magnetized and mesmerized us. We were drawn into that reality time and time again. I cried the first time I was able to really stare into it—it felt like the P's were beaming the book information through the painting. Oh, those foxy Pleiadians, they were at it again!

Today, as I sit on my back deck writing, with the book process behind us, feeling the rays of a mellow Carolina September sun, my mind wanders down some of the avenues of reality that I have created for myself. I sit here and smile, recalling events that helped to land me in this particular now, being ever thankful that I was magnetized years ago to the words "thought creates."

Back in the late 1970s, Jane Roberts and the Seth material were a guiding force for Barbara and me. In those days, I was living in Rochester, New York, and Barbara was in Los Angeles. I was settled down with a husband and a job and lived in a beautiful old Dutch Colonial home with a yard that I had turned into my own Living Library. Barbara, on the other hand, was your typical free spirit of the times, always in search of something new to expand her perspective, moving often, and absorbing the new thought that California and the world had to offer.

One year for my birthday, Barbara sent me two books with a card saying something like, "There is so much thought-provoking information out now, I can't read it all myself. You check out these two books and let me know if they're worth getting into." The two books turned out to be *The Seth Material* and *Seth Speaks* by Jane Roberts. Reading these books was a definite wake-up call from the universe!

We spent the next few years reading and absorbing all the available Seth material. We reread it, highlighted it, talked about it, and attempted to live it. I flash back to those days and realize how I immersed myself in the realities of Jane Roberts and Rob Butts as I read page after page. I would picture their realities so very clearly. I would agonize over the slow and meticulous note-taking and transcription that Rob challenged himself with—if only he would work faster then maybe we would get the next book quicker! I pictured Jane with her stacks of unanswered mail and felt her total frustration at never being caught up. Looking back today, I can feel the force that guided me back then to take note of everything they did. Now, as I run the business of Bold Connections and look at the stacks of unanswered mail—the requests for a new Pleiadian book!—I find myself in a situation similar to theirs of the 1970s, with some of the same joys and challenges to deal with.

It was in April of 1988 that Barbara took a trip to Egypt and Greece, laying the foundation for the Pleiadians to enter her reality. I was now living in Raleigh, North Carolina, and the foundation for my new home was being created at the same time, a home that for five years the Pleiadians used as a classroom to impart wisdom, make us laugh, scold us, play with our heads, and teach us about ourselves.

When Barbara returned from her Egypt/Greece adventure, she called me from Boston and said, "Guess what?" I said, "You started channeling." She said, "How did you know?" We always knew. It wasn't something we talked about very often; however, there was a deep unspoken knowing between us that we would be involved in some sort of psychic adventure some day. We had a staunch loyalty to each other; on some level we knew that we came into this reality as female siblings to anchor in a new paradigm of thought, and that we couldn't do it without the love and support of each other.

I was eager to meet Barbara's new friends who called themselves the Pleiadians. We still didn't know how we felt about them. I mean, Barbara was expecting a nice, proper discarnate like Seth, and what did she get? Extraterrestrials! I remember that first time Barbara came to my home and called in the Pleiadians. Their voice was very weak and hard to understand, and I had to strain to hear the words. They gave me some information about who they were and why they were working with us. They told me they were going to call me Moley because I was like a mole who liked to keep her head underground and stay out of the limelight. However, they said, the time was now for me to embrace and live all these ideas that I had been collecting and playing with, that my life would change in profound ways, nothing would be the same. "Interesting," I thought, as I sat there in my comfy home with a husband I loved, a job I was satisfied with, my two-year-old daughter asleep down the hall. I felt so safe and secure; I had no idea what kind of changes they were talking about!

Well, six years later, my life certainly has changed, and not necessarily in all the ways I would have imagined. If I could have envisioned the future back then, I know I would have been too chicken to go forward with it. So, I give great thanks to the P's for all their love and guidance—even the times I didn't think it was love and guidance—and for their persistence in always pushing me to the next level of challenge. I thank Barbara for her love, support, and loyalty, for her dedication to this work and for her penchant for living the Pleiadian teachings and making it look easy. And a thank you to Tera for being a friend that I trust and grow with, a fellow Sagittarian that I can relate to, and a great editor. A special thanks to my daughter, Laurel, who from a very young age was able to integrate watching her Aunt Barbara—or "Cioci" as she calls her—tune into the P's every other week at our home, and for allowing me to travel with Barbara and the P's free of guilt for not always being there; for taking her parents' opposing views of reality, and merging them in her world and finding a unique balance.

As I reflect in this moment, I can truly say I am in a peaceful and harmonious state of being. Trusting myself and knowing I create every aspect of my reality in order to teach myself the lessons I need to experience has given me a great freedom. As September comes to a close and as the splendor of autumn ever so gently unfolds its magic upon this land that is called "The Triangle," I find myself purchasing my own home, taking back my maiden name, and giving up the nickname Moley. I look forward with joy and excitement to the next segment of reality that I find myself playing in.

Karen J. Marciniak
Raleigh, NC

Tera Thomas

I have known Barbara and Karen since Barbara began channeling in 1988. We have worked together, played together, laughed, cried, fought, and developed a deep level of trust with each other. Starting *The Pleiadian Times* newsletter in the spring of 1993 solidified and deepened the relationship between the three of us. We are all strong, opinionated women who have learned how to merge our power to work with spirit, to support each other, and to create something greater than the sum of its parts. So, when Barbara proposed that the three of us work on *Earth* together, I was excited.

Working with the Pleiadians is not the same as working with other channeled information. Rather than a lecture on any given topic, the teachings don't come in a specific order, and some of them are confusing or contradictory—they're meant to be. Those of us who work with them regularly know that the P's rarely hand us something on a silver platter, because they want us to learn to use their teachings in our lives, and to learn to trust ourselves in the process. So, the Pleiadians do not sit down and dictate a book. Working on a book with them is the same as going to one of their workshops. You have to dig inside yourself to pull the information into 3D and into your life.

Having worked on *Bringers of the Dawn*, I knew the process of pulling a Pleiadian book together. First, selected tapes are transcribed, then the information is divided into specific categories, i.e.: "DNA," "Reptiles," "Blood," "The Game Masters." This creates pages of information bundled together in neat little Pendaflex files. The next step is weaving all the pieces of information together to form chapters that make a coherent story in rough form.

When Barbara, Karen, and I work together, we always begin with a small ceremony to solidify our energy and let the P's know we're ready to work. We state our intentions, then ring the Tibetan bells twelve times, once for each chakra.

After that, we're ready to begin working in "no sense," letting spirit guide us.

Our portable file was chock full. The number of categories we had, and the number of pages in each, looked intimidating. We knew there would be twelve chapters, so we got out blank astrology wheels and labeled each house as a chapter. Then we began calling off the names of the categories and slipping them into houses that seemed to fit. We decided that each of us would take four houses, or four chapters, and pull the information together. We each chose a color and colored in our charts. We now had a rough blueprint to weave the information together. When Karen's seven-year-old daughter, Laurel, came home from school, we held up our colored charts and asked her what she thought they were. Without hesitation she said, "It's the book." Well, someone had faith!

Organizing the various bits of information into chapters required a big letting go of control and a profound trust in the process. Of course, in the beginning, we each attempted to do it the old way, by reading and absorbing each and every word on the many typewritten pages and making some sort of sense out of it all. That didn't work well with Pleiadian material. We started getting fuzzy and confused and nothing made sense anymore.

Fortunately, Peter Everly's painting for the cover arrived and gave us all a focus. That painting led us in a way I can't even fathom. I just know that each time I was attempting to control the process, I'd take a deep breath, look at the painting, and I'd be right back where I needed to be—in "no sense"— knowing that the book really did exist in the future, and all I needed to do was trust in that and let the information organize itself.

After we had each pulled together our initial four chapters in rough form, we began exchanging chapters to smooth, reorganize, and fill in the gaps. My chapters went to Karen, Karen's chapters went to Barbara, and Barbara's went to me.

We did this dance of shuffling chapters over and over again so we each had our input in every chapter. When we got stuck or confused, Barbara Clow guided us back on track. Miraculously, or so it seemed, *Earth* was born.

The Pleiadians constantly talk about effortlessness. If something is not effortless, you're on the wrong track. Working with their material *is* effortless; however, that doesn't mean no work is involved. The effortless part is that if you trust, take one step at a time, and don't ask how or why, everything will come together. It still involves a lot of energy, a lot of concentration, and a lot of 3D hustle. You don't get to make intentions and sit back and watch them happen; someone has to do the physical work. And, I can tell you, Barbara, Karen, and I worked hard.

I learned a lot working on *Earth*. Of course, I got to see a lot of my old patterns come to the surface: wanting to control the work instead of letting go, feeling I needed to work really hard and wear myself out or I wouldn't be appreciated, worrying about deadlines and how it could all possibly get done. I made work a burden for myself, subscribing to that old belief that if it's not difficult, it's not good. It's interesting how clear your issues become when you're working in relationship with others. On your own, they're ingrained patterns, part of who you are. When you're in a relationship, it's as if there's a mirror held up in front of you saying, "Look at this!" I was able to recognize my pattern of burden and let go of it. Phew, it felt good!

I also learned a new and deeper way to work as a team, and gained a deeper respect and love for Barbara and Karen, and for myself. We were able to solidify our energies so that we could work as a unit, bringing into play all our strengths without competing with each other or overshadowing each other. And I can see that it's our relationship that created this book. Yes, it was all the physical things we did, the intentions we made, the bells we rang, Peter's art, but those things alone would not have created *Earth*. It was the deep bond between

Barbara, Karen, and me, the love we share between ourselves and the Pleiadians, and the combining of our energies with a profound trust in the process.

I'm now understanding how this level of respect and trust and love can be brought into every area of my life. And, I have a profound thankfulness for the teachings I received while working on *Earth*, for the relationships I have developed with the Pleiadians, with the non-physical realm, with Barbara and Karen, with my family and friends, and most particularly, with myself.

Tera Thomas
Pittsboro, NC

EARTH

ONE

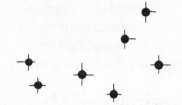

The Game, the Codes, and the Master Numbers

All we do is create imagery from which you can evolve.

Greetings, dear friends, we are here. It is our intention to assist you in creating a new vision—a vision that inspires you to live and love on planet Earth. Like a priceless jewel, buried in dark layers of soil and stone, Earth radiates her brilliant beauty into the caverns of space and time. As a value yet to be realized and discovered, she patiently awaits her coronation by her people. She creates you and sustains you, and without her, as you now know yourselves, you could not be. We ask you, as seekers of the great stories, to proclaim an allegiance to Earth. Pledge the transformation of yourselves, which is the journey through light and dark, and honor Earth's momentous role in setting you free. As threads unravel to reveal your celestial heritage, do not become entrapped by a glamour from the heavens, for you too are on a star, reflecting and radiating light to worlds seeking the solutions to their own creations. Your task at this point in time is to activate the Living Library of Earth, to restore Earth and the human version of life to the forefront of creation. This is the journey you are on.

There are many versions of reality—each viable with its

own purpose and intent. Time, space, and the existence of worlds are amorphous, only as real as the attention you put upon them. There are many Earths to choose from: many timelines from stories that have been forgotten or were perhaps purposely diverted from your awareness and development.

We ask each of you to open your mind and heart, for within your body and Earth herself lie the answers to the great mysteries you seek. Although we appear to exist from without, as a collective of Pleiadian energies calling to you from the future, we also exist within you. We are your ancestors, existing within you as well as without. *We are you*, on the golden spirals of time, cycling the epochs of existence, calling to you yourselves to reconsider all you thought holy. We ask you to reevaluate the purpose of your life, to redefine the forces that rule you, to resurrect the codes of consciousness stored in your being. It is time for you to reclaim your knowledge as a creator through thought, to recall the purpose of the Living Library of Earth, to restore beauty through value of life, and to remember who you are. Journey with us now through the mysteries of your world.

Picture yourself on an excursion through the image of twelve and lay the concept of twelve out in your mind. The material in this book is designed to decode you through the very system that structures and defines you: the twelve. Imagine yourself experiencing the numerical symbols of one through twelve, as in the twelve months of a calendar, the twelve movements through the signs of the zodiac, or the twelve hours around the clock, and then add to these symbols your own personal avenue of twelve. Imagine you have twelve strands of DNA and that these activate and connect to your twelve chakras, which are energy doorways through which you access your spiritual heritage. Herein lies a key: your challenge is to know yourself through your imagination, accessing your inner networks and bulletin boards of reality, which are invisible to your eye. In pursuit of your spirit, you will perhaps consider many new things to enhance your current world with a grander view.

We are here for the game, the codes, and the master numbers. It is part of our karma to deal with Earth at this time, for what we set into motion is what we must dance with. Our ancestors created events that presently stifle our development on the Pleiades, and, as Pleiadians, we are seeking to discover the solutions to this grand dilemma, a predicament that you share with us.

Our civilization, in a future from where you are, is in peril, so we have been impulsed to go on a journey to find a solution to what has been chasing us. We are in your future and, in order to discover what is going on, we went further into our future to meet our teachers, the Keepers of Existence, who can also be called the Keepers of Time. As they taught us how to traverse the various sectors of time, we were enticed to journey back in time to discover where events were stored and locked away. We examined where storms were brewing that were affecting our past, as we were viewing it from the future of our future and, as we view it from now, from your moment of reality.

Our ancestors came from a universe that had completed itself and understood universally that it was Prime Creator, as the journey of Prime Creator in time. They came from a universe that had discovered its essence—creativity. By discovering that essence, they found out that they were the creators. They came into the Pleiades because that star system would someday be able to help you at a most challenging time, a time when you would be ready to reconnect with Prime Creator. Our ancestors were some of the Original Planners of Earth, orchestrators who seeded worlds and civilizations with light and information through creativity and love. Our ancestors are also your ancestors. They gave their DNA to the Original Planners, and this DNA became part of the DNA of the human species.

The plan was to create an intergalactic exchange center of

information within your planet, Earth. It was an extraordinary plan, involving a beautiful place, for Earth is located on the fringe of one galactic system and is easily reached from other galaxies. Earth exists close to many way-portals, the highways that exist for energies to travel throughout your space zone.

There was much scurrying and shuffling to bring individual representatives of all the galaxies to Earth so that they could have their likenesses here upon this planet. Some of those in charge, called creator gods, were master geneticists. They were able to create, discover, and tie molecules together, encoding them with identity, frequency, and electrical charges in order to create life. Many sentient civilizations gave of their DNA willingly in order to have a semblance of their genetic line and coding upon this planet. The master geneticists designed varieties of species, some human, some animal, by playing with the varieties of DNA that sentient civilizations contributed to make this exchange center of information, this light center. The design for Earth was a grand one. Since these creator gods did not exist in time as you know it, a few hundred thousand years or a million years in their terms was nothing.

There have been other species of humans who looked similar to you, whose DNA was intact at one time, and who developed very highly evolved civilizations on your planet. They existed long ago, more than half-a-million years ago. We are not speaking of the civilizations that you call Lemuria or Atlantis, whose epochs refer to a time we call the modern human. We are referring to civilizations that are ancient, like the ones buried under the ice caps of your far southern continent, Antarctica, or under layers of sand in the Gobi Desert of Mongolia.

Energies that you have called gods created everything on this planet, and they put great intelligence in all of their creations. There is consciousness in all that exists on Earth, down to the molecules in your fingertips, and it is all meant to work together. Consciousness communicates continuously by vibrations of electromagnetic frequencies. These frequencies connect and have a cooperative investment in working together so that each benefits the whole. The difficulty with Earth at this time is that humans believe they are separate from all the energy that is here to work together. Your current belief in separate parts prevents you from seeing and accessing the wholeness of existence.

It is our intention to assist you in coming to a greater understanding of the Pleiadian experiments that have influenced Earth. During times of chaos and confusion, times when the human species was suppressed, various factions from our home system came to different locations around your planet and made very subtle openings. They worked with small clusters of consciousness to leave a glimmer of energy upon your planet, for many in the cosmos knew your planet was headed toward tremendous calamity and great suppression.

Earth is in dire straits at this time, there is no doubt about it. Yet, great opportunity lies within this state of confusion. You each have been tapped upon the shoulder to answer a call. Many are tapped, yet few are willing to go into the unknown and feel comfortable being renegades, standing up for something that perhaps the crowds may not support. We applaud your intentions and honor each of you for choosing yourself to go into the unknown. We honor you for being willing to look at the portions of yourself, female and male, that for all practical purposes you have not understood at all. We are quite pleased that you are willing to explore a different possibility, as well as embellish and enrich what you already have. It is time for each of you to be noticed in your own way, to magnify energies as they pass through you, and to make these energies available to multitudes of others as you casually pull light rays into your body and onto Earth.

We always like to laugh and have a good time, and through this playful approach we uncover what is perhaps preventing each of you from going further.

There are families of consciousness that cluster together based upon evolution, intent, and a particular plan. The Family of Light, to which you belong, comes from such a lineage of consciousness. Who *are* light? Who owns light? What is beyond light? Feel this for a few moments and realize that in your human minds you always make a myth, a little story, or a fairy tale about what you think is going on in the cosmos. Your version is minuscule in light of what exists, so we are asking you to consider colossal changes to your stories and imagine bigger versions of existence.

The Family of Light is a collection of entities coded to bring information to this planet. The coding is inside each individual. Once you are able to question and see beyond the current interpretation of reality, you are guided to create thoughtforms to fire the codings in others. We are one group of energies igniting human codes of consciousness at a certain point of planetary development. This process will evolve as you evolve, and there will be a tremendous amount of instruction involving untold teachers who will emerge to assist you.

The Family of Light is vast. Its members gather wherever information needs to be disseminated; they are like renegade special forces, called on in an emergency. Members of the Family of Light are able to integrate and survive reality shifts without destroying the bodies or life forces they occupy. As a member of the Family of Light, the ability to change reality exists innately inside you. You must create the belief system whereby you can do this, because your mind is structured to evolve and form your experience based on what you command, no matter what paradigm-platform you spring from.

The Family of Light acts as a stabilizing factor for dimensional shifts, and its members serve as carriers of a frequency being used to awaken many. Some of you will be frightened of the possibilities and that is OK. Each of you will take the new knowledge and changes as far as you are able. You are coded with this possibility, and deciding to go for change or not is your free-will choice. Whether you think you can do it or not is based on your own free will. The initiation process that has taken place on Earth in many of the mystery schools over the last several thousand years exemplifies our point. Members of the Family of Light have pushed themselves past the laws of third-dimensional reality—through to another dimension, so to speak—by uncovering the coding inside themselves.

Many of you may have the feeling that you have done this before. You have. This is your multidimensional memory of when you have gone to other systems and done the same thing. It is a very familiar process because, characteristically, as members of the Family of Light, this is what you do. You inform systems. You go in and reconstruct realities, and you are experts at it.

You lost your memory of this process because you came here to operate under the same laws as everyone else. Therefore, you came in as human with your memory completely erased. You knew before you arrived that losing your memory was part of the process, and you specifically picked the moment of time and the parentage that would give you the best connection to energetically and genetically bring about your purpose.

When you incarnated into the Earth plane, you received certain matched and paired recessive genes holding light codes that gave you the highest opportunity to develop psychic and intuitive abilities. In addition, these genes carried some memory that separated you from others, even though you could not name it. With these powers and talents, it has been your task to build on your life and allow the momentum to lead you into something different than most humans.

As an extensive mutation occurs on the inside of humans, also stimulated from the outside by those who are assisting you in this genetic upliftment, you must act and integrate what is awakening within you.

Let us give you a scenario here. Picture yourself as a member of the Family of Light, not looking anything like you look right now. Click into your cosmic identity. You are in a classroom, and an instructor is speaking to you, giving you the highlights of the assignment of returning to Earth to become part of the system in order to change it. You are very much at the top of your profession; you believe yourself to be an impeccable systems buster. In this class, you are in great humor because the professor is explaining something to you: "When you go down to Earth, believe it or not, you are going to need to have us come and instruct you because you won't remember any of this." And all of you systems busters laugh because you know that, as cool as you are now, once you sub-merge yourself, you will not remember this classroom. The professor says, "Watch this. We will show you pictures. See, there we are coming through a vehicle, and there you are in your human disguise, and you act as if you don't know what is going on. This is part of your assignment." You are briefed on all of this, you understand?

In that classroom, you were coded to respond to us as Pleiadians, and to many others. As you open to your greater identity, be receptive and willing to go beyond your bound-aries, because this is what we are striving for. We intend to implant new images in your mind to take you further. It doesn't matter how we do it. It doesn't matter if it is true. It simply matters that we create new images for you. One day you will find the groove yourself, and then you will under-stand what we have been after all this time. You will under-stand that sometimes we have completely made things up in order to trigger something inside of you in order for you to grow as a human being. We are very crafty teachers.

It is time for you to make a commitment to create joy, creativity, and love for yourself. Only then will you benefit others, for if you do not evolve yourself, you do not serve others. By becoming a living example, by following what is in your heart, you show the way for others to follow with courage what is in their hearts.

We are not here because we have nothing else to do. We are here to assist the transformational process that is now beginning to bubble and create steam around your planet. In the past few years, multitudes have awakened, remembering a grand and significant purpose to life.

If you knew as much as your higher self knows at this time, you would be very impatient with this assignment. It involves incarnating as a human, thinking you are a human, evolving yourself into something more than a human, and then realizing that you were more than human in the first place! Though this may seem backward, it is necessary in order for you to go through the evolution of your conscious ness as a human being. The transformation requires a mass awakening, spurring you on to consciously evolve as a life form. This process involves choice as a key. You are going to do it step-by-step, and others will watch you do it and have the courage to follow.

Humans are considered by some in this universe to be priceless, though in actuality you yourselves have no idea of the value stored in the human body. Your human body is the most valuable thing you will ever own and encounter. *You are priceless.* Battles have long been fought over Earth, and as a result, you have been purposely enticed away from discover ing the wealth of data stored inside of you by controlling or limiting forces. You are purposely taught that you are insignificant and valueless so that other forms of intelligence will not come and tap into you. Those who control you cannot get the formulas out of you, so they keep you hidden away, quarantined and isolated. In this way, others who need what you have cannot get to you. You are taught the dance of disempowerment, which you choreograph as a species.

You are now learning to find your own value, a value we intend to share, teach, and encourage you to discover through an ongoing process. The value you discover about yourself will grow and grow as you wonder at these formulas inside of you, which we call the codes for other civilizations.

Earth is a microcosm of the macrocosm, a miniature version of what is happening all over, except that Earth is a trigger point, what we call a kernel. You know that a kernel is a seed. We have come back to Earth to assist the members of the Family of Light, who have been seeded here, in this essential time when events can be altered. Time is greatly misunderstood in third-dimensional reality and is much more flexible than you realize, allowing simultaneous movement into realities by stretching, distorting, curving, and twisting itself around. You have been born on Earth to change the course of history by inserting yourself from the future into the past. In this way, you reshape the past. You are a seedling for change.

We are going to share with you some concepts that are going to push you beyond how you define yourself. Many of the things we suggest to you are mind benders and twisters. Why do we do this? Why do we wish to confound you? Well, if we can confound your current view of reality, perhaps we can get you to perceive other realities, and it is our intent to confound you into clarity! You have become so locked into the paradigm your mass consciousness reproduces that it takes great effort and determination for you to step out of your current belief system. Your current beliefs are based on what you call linear time, and on a limited knowledge of historical events.

You have been sold a version of reality, and through your overly valued educational systems you prize and reward yourself for the ability to repeat stories as fact—never questioning the content and method of learning. You have been told many stories, and we are about to tell you a few more. Learn to use the wholeness of your body to read beyond the words we share. For though we gladly remind you that we are storytellers, somewhere in the antiquity of your being lie tools of truth—and it is for you to discover how and when to use them. Words are more than they seem.

Your language is encoded, and sounds create reflected images that stimulate and structure consciousness. Spoken words carry different vibrations than written words. We like to play with both forms of language. When we speak, our intonation has its own signature to it, and we use subtle variances with emphasis on particular sounds. We select with care what we intend to express, and we have certain ways of using each word. We know that you hear one thing but that the sounds we make carry an entirely different meaning to your body. When you come into our vibration, you are getting many, many instructions, triggering layers and layers of knowledge. There are the words you hear that you *think* you understand, and there is the space that occurs between all words, which is another teaching in and of itself. And then there are sounds we make that echo in your cells, that tell you a Pleiadian story. The inner and outer workings are coming together to speed up your evolution.

In the beginning there was the word, and the word was sound. This is how creation sprang into being. Sound affects all of you and is changing your planet. Yet, you do not realize the subtlety behind the process. Our words printed on a page are also arranged and coded to give you many layers of reality. Have you ever read a page of our words and felt they meant one thing, only to read the same words again later and discover a new meaning? Sometimes you may even feel as if what you are reading at present wasn't there before, and perhaps it wasn't.

The words *we are here* can be broken down into another language basically announcing a greater identity of who we are. The word *remember* has to do with claiming the source of who created you, the same as the words *we are here*. The words identify the source of your creator, and when we come to speak to you, the words we use proclaim through sound that we come from the source of your maker in the Pleiades. Your cells hear this and call your body into remembering in its own now.

We have suggested that approximately half-a-million years ago tumultuous events took place in this area of existence that affect your present-day Earth. To a large degree, Earth lost her sovereignty, and another force of rulership came in and claimed ownership to this prime hunk of real estate that you call home. These recently appointed godlike administrators have not always been the kindest and most benevolent sorts. Earth was established billions of years ago for a purpose. She was to be an intergalactic exchange center of information, part of a vast library system where data from many, many galaxies was stored—a Living Library, to be precise.

The creator gods, those who believed themselves to be the forces of creation, came together, pooled their knowledge, and created forms of life. They borrowed DNA and combinations of genetic material from many different worlds. They stored this material in Earth's library system, which was connected to a system of twelve cosmic libraries. You can see that the plan for Earth was a grand one.

The Original Planners of Earth were members of the Family of Light, beings who worked for and were associated with an aspect of consciousness called light. Light is information. Members of the Family of Light created the information center they had conceived; they designed a place where galaxies would contribute their information and would be able to participate and share their specific knowledge.

The project of the Living Library on Earth was eventually fought over. Skirmishes took place, and Earth became a place of conflict and duality. Certain creator gods who had the right to do whatever they wanted—because Earth is a free-will zone—came in and took over. These creator gods raided Earth approximately half-a-million years ago—the time period, historically speaking, that you would call the beginning of human civilization. This is merely the time period that you, in this present day, are taught was the beginning of civilization. In actuality, it was only the beginning of the latest phase of civilization, the phase of modern humanity. Variations of human life have existed for millions of years.

When these skirmishes occurred, a certain group of entities fought in space and won the territory of Earth. These new owners wanted the native Earth species to remain unevolved and uninformed so that the species would be easier to control. The original species of human creation experienced great destruction, and its DNA was scattered.

Imagine Earth as a principality of some grand empire far removed from you. Perhaps when parents in a ruling family had trouble with their children, they said, "Go down to Earth and play for awhile." By suggesting this, the gods did not realize that what they were setting into motion would gridlock them in the future. When the children of the gods began playing with gold and genetics—and with the blood, toying with the power of the female—they had no idea what they were creating.

What the gods now realize is that we are in a dilemma in the Pleiades. There is a tyranny that was let loose on Earth, and that tyranny has returned to us. Did you know that *we* made the tyranny, that *we* stripped you of your heritage of a fully functioning, twelve-stranded DNA? Do not be naive about Pleiadians, including us. Why do you think we are doing this healing work on your planet? Consider that perhaps we need you for our next phase of development. If we wish to grow, we must heal a past that we have been connected to.

Our ancestors have played havoc with your planet as well as assisted you through many, many changes. You have had both influences from the Pleiades. Records of influence indicate that the Pleiadian energies were very loved and honored on Earth, and that most cultures on your planet did not have negative feelings toward the Pleiades. However, we are the first to admit that, far in the distant past, Pleiadian energies manipulated the genetic line of human beings, and were connected to the reptiles. That is what we have come back to heal. That is the purpose of our visit.

In our search for why we are in such a big mess in the Pleiades, we were led into the future to show us that our system will go nowhere without you. In other words, we cannot evolve further as creators until we give all our abilities and all our rights to everything we have created. We cannot police and control what we create. This is our dilemma. This is why we wait for you to discover your own experience as a creator. When you do, you will give off a code of formulas. Perhaps, even if you become very highly evolved, you will never understand the formulas—not for a long, long time.

Others may access the formulas from you, and in exchange you will experience states of ecstasy, alterations of consciousness, or perhaps trips into other worlds. You may not realize you are emitting the formulas when you do this. Others who need the formulas will use them to replicate lives, or to reestablish systems that are being destroyed. When those codes of information or formulas are set out in existence, we will be free, because the codes of consciousness contain the songs of your own freedom, sung as frequency and broadcast from the cells of your body.

The further one goes with the mantle of power, manipulating and transcending realities, the further one can fall. To some extent, Earth has been turned into a magnetic vortex that attracts fallen energies. These energies have moved into the entire area around your solar system, not simply Earth. Do not think that every place else is fine while Earth is the blemish. In actuality, your entire solar system is going through some difficulties at this time. There are other solar systems, versions of your solar system, overlaid on this one. When specific thoughtforms begin to occur, they draw and entice others of the same nature. When you get into a negative kind of energy and cannot get out of it, what happens? More and more negative energy is drawn to you. For long periods of time, Earth has been pulling negative energies to herself. Beings associated with these energies have fallen from very idealized heights where they made decisions, perhaps the wrong or inappropriate decisions, and lost the power to construct uplifting realities. Yet, this was all part of the plan.

The falling-away of power and the manipulation that takes place stimulate life forms that are unevolved into finding something better. So there is a great benefit in this whole process, and nothing to be frightened of. Absolutely nothing. There is absolutely nothing to fear in these times that are coming. We want you to be very well aware that you are honored for who you are, and as you begin to honor yourself, you will draw to yourself opportunity beyond your conception.

One of the most exciting aspects about being on Earth right now is the retooling taking place in your DNA. Cosmic light-encoded rays, as photons, have been coming onto Earth, stimulating change and a reordering inside the human body. The scattered data that holds the history and awareness of the Living Library is now reorganizing. The Galactic Tidal Wave of Light, as expressed through the great Uranus/Neptune conjunctions of 1993, brought an infusion of cosmic rays onto the planet, creating a potential third strand of DNA in the masses. New helixes or strands of DNA are being formed as the light-encoded filaments are impulsed to rebundle themselves together. The scattered data is being pulled together in your body by electromagnetic energies from Prime Creator. We are here to watch this process in you, to assist you, and to evolve ourselves as well.

As this rebundling and reordering progresses, you will

create a more evolved nervous system that will facilitate new data to move itself into your consciousness. You will awaken many brain cells that have been lying dormant, and you will begin using your full physical body rather than the small percentage with which you have been functioning.

You have agreed to carry light and return light to this planet. As you begin to fill your body with light, your memory must be opened. You must evolve as the DNA evolves, into a multidimensional version of yourself, spanning many layers of reality. Picture yourself spiraled with twelve different strands of DNA. The double helix has two strands. Imagine twelve strands all hooked together. You can picture them as six pairs, although that is not necessarily how they combine. Play with this image making. Outside of your body, picture energy highways coming out of your twelve chakras. You live in a web of invisible energy. The twelve strands of DNA serve as links to this web through the twelve chakras that act as energetic doorways into your body, connecting you to the vital force of existence. It is through the opening and activation of these portals of energy that you can know yourself.

You are aspiring to develop full use of your brain, more than the mere 8 to 10 percent currently employed. The complete universal history of yourself is in light-encoded filaments that have been scattered inside your body by beings who did not want you to be very talented, because then they could not control you.

Learn to use the material of your own history to show yourself something. Without judgment, joyously move through life rather than create soap operas that keep you starring in the same reruns. As all twelve strands of DNA begin to form, whatever issues you have not dealt with and peacefully cleared in your personal history will form chaos in your body. Feelings and memories will emerge, offering you an opportunity to experience the fabric of your being, reveal-

ing who you are through events and beliefs intricately woven
into you.

We are reminding you of what you know inside yourself.
We have come onto this planet to trigger your memory
bank—to inspire the human race through light, so that you
will begin to remember who you are and create your own
reality. You will alter the frequency on the planet and claim
rightful ownership of yourself and this territory. You will rise
to the opportunity to master the situation as you trust in abilities that you did not think you had.

We have a very deep fondness for each and every one of
you because you have helped us—you have assisted us in
delivering something. Your planet is a most miraculous
place, and there are those who see your planet from a distance and realize many things. You do not see your planet
from a distance. You experience your planet firsthand. It was
just a number of years ago when pictures of Earth, viewed
from space, were shown to you for the first time, offering all
of you a visual image of yourselves as a whole. If someone
were to study you from space, you would all look alike if that
someone did not know how to read the vibrations you emit.

There is something that we are getting at here. These last
few years, you have been impulsed into diving more deeply
into personal exploration, the meaning of identity, and connecting with your cosmic overview of life itself. Perhaps at
first it seemed as if you were reaching far beyond what the
parameters of civilization supported. As you met in quiet
clusters everywhere, letting out your deepest yearnings and
knowings and secrets that you had your whole life, you
began to realize that perhaps you were not so far outside the
parameters of civilization. Perhaps civilization was moving
as *you* extended the boundaries.

Your dedication to reevaluating, reconsidering, and reorganizing your basic assumptions about life has expanded the
expressions of civilization itself. You humans have no other

choice than to reach out to the new territory that you lay forward as both charted and uncharted discoveries.

For the last half-million years, various civilizations on Earth have been seeded from different star systems that were part of the original library program. Each appeared at a different time period, penetrating a controlled force field that isolated Earth and kept it inaccessible as a library. These civilizations would flourish for 500 years, 5,000 years, 10,000 years; then the forces that owned the planet would somehow shoo them away or destroy them. These civilizations could not establish ownership here, so they left clues or steps to the ladder as part of the master plan.

When enough humans can read the clues seeded by these civilizations, Earth's keys for harmonious cosmic existence will be understood. Egyptians, Incas, Balinese, Greeks, Tibetans, Sumerians, Native Americans, Maya, Aboriginals, and many, many other indigenous peoples have contributed keys of understanding, all pointing to the heavens. If present-day humans could read the steps and clues left by these cultures, they could once again liberate and own Earth. Each culture, in some way, held the Library open and was able to infuse its civilization with life-charging stellar connections. Each was creatively unique, leaving a mysterious psychic footprint in your cellular memory as a piece of the puzzle.

Where did these civilizations come from? Do you think they sprang up out of the ground like daisies? They were created from thought. They were impulsed into being. All the cultures that achieved high ideals were conceived of by the Game Masters. In each world and each domain, the idea of freedom was completely different. On Earth, the idea that humans could be owned and treated without respect came onto the planet half-a-million years ago and was very pronounced in many areas of the world. Humans, or versions of humans, were used as slaves to dig in mines or to vibrate with certain emotional patterns.

Over time, an idealized form of civilization was transduced here on Earth to meet the greatest needs of the people. The greatest teaching brought to the planet was the ideal that all humans are created in equality and that life is to be honored in all forms. This idea was unable to filter down to every level of existence, although it was certainly anchored as a practice in numerous societies. There were those, of course, who were able to honor the rocks, trees, plants, animals, and humans. However, for many, the main issue of what to honor involved themselves, the ones who were here to operate with intelligence and figure out the magnificence of the planet.

In some way or another, the Game Masters had to find different ways to gain back Earth and reteach the value of life. So, over periods of time, the Game Masters conceptualized entire civilizations, imagining them down to the most minute detail. Then they seeded and implanted these civilizations on Earth by bringing the inhabitants from the stars. This was done after these beings were honed to fit the genetic line of humans.

Expand your concept of existence and imagine this. For an occupation, Game Masters orchestrate realities and then insert these realities as life forms onto different planets. Game Masters get together, like you would for a game of cards or racquetball, only their game involves creating civilizations. They alter and change worlds by allowing variations within civilizations to enter into the realizations they orchestrate. These civilizations act totally by impulse, yet all impulses are fed to them through blueprints. All blueprints are formulated ahead of time, just like you, as the Family of Light, are actually on assignment following a plan designed by yourselves.

Game Masters are brilliant. Not only do they conceive of

the game, and create the entire blueprint for the civilization to flourish in, down to the finest artisans and beggars, they seed *themselves* into the civilization as well. They know their civilization is complete when their own identities merge with the civilization, so that they are *in* the civilization and *creating it* at the same time.

The Maya, who lived at one time in Mexico and Central America, were masters at doing this. They were skilled at confounding realities and moving from system to system. Their world was in the Pleiades, and yet they certainly did not reside there; they had their own world. Today, the Maya are on assignment everywhere, confounding many worlds, taking Maya with them as if their civilization had never stopped but simply had transferred from one world to another.

The word *Maya* refers to the illusion of reality. The Maya were so advanced as Keepers of Time that they literally were able to create realities to steer future seekers toward or away from discovering their true identity. Much of the story that is told about the Maya is part of the Mayan trick, part of the illusion. Until you are able to go into other realities and travel these realms, you will not understand this. The Maya were as adept in their own way as the Egyptians. The Egyptians were able to conjure many thoughtforms of reality and travel into worlds in a different way. The Maya were able to orchestrate time to create time locks. Different cultures have different purposes, all of which are interlinked.

Why were these civilizations all here on Earth? Why did each civilization have its season? These are questions we want you to probe. Then ask yourself, "What is my part in this process?" These civilizations all had commerce with one another at different junctures in their flourishing. In their own seasons, they shared ideals. Some of these civilizations existed for thousands of years.

You see how richly layered civilizations are? Think of the

following example as a way for you to conceptualize this idea: A movie is made, and it is a success, like *Rocky*. Then, *Rocky 2*, *Rocky 3*, and *Rocky 4* are made. Imagine that someone shows you these movies back to back. It appears as if they run sequentially, when in actuality there were lags of time between the making of one movie and the next. There had to be in order to construct them. It is the same thing with civilizations. They are seeded, and then there is a time lag while the Game Masters make up the next installment—part 2 or part 3 or part 500—and install it in a similar area. We are suggesting that all over your globe there are civilizations layered one on top of the other, all connected. This concept gives you a few new ideas to feel out.

We, as Pleiadians, are a Game Master experiment. The Game Masters are formless, and yet they can overlay themselves and infuse themselves in many different shapes. The movies *2001* and *2010* revealed the idea of the Game Master, showing behind-the-scenes influences on certain life forms. That is a good analogy; however, don't hang your hat on it.

The Game Masters are unbounded, formless, shapeshifters. They can take any form they choose, for they move between and beyond sound and geometry. The Game Masters create in their minds the entire blueprints for cultures, and then they open portals to literally insert cultures into the Earth plane. Then they allow these cultures to develop and grow, to seed and influence other times. On Earth at this time, there are sacred sites and cultures that you think are lost and that you will never be in contact with again. During the great awakening and shift in consciousness, these cultures will come alive and will all operate simultaneously because their blueprints will be recalled and magnetized back onto this opening multidimensional plane.

The Game Masters come up with blueprints for civilizations. Now, here is the tricky part. When Game Masters create a particular blueprint for a civilization, it has many s of itself and is expressed on many worlds and in ـalities. Part of the Game Masters' task is to juggle all ــ ـ realities at once and to learn from every single version of that blueprint. It is like making capes. A tailor makes one cape and gets the idea to make hundreds of other variations of the cape to suit everyone's needs and to suit a necessary essence of the cape itself. That is how the Game Masters work. So, when Game Masters create a blueprint, a language, and a method to transduce it onto the planet, the blueprint is not simply anchored into one realm. It is anchored into many realms.

Sometimes these civilizations last for a much longer or shorter period than your archaeologists believe. They can simply appear as if they exist for many eons, when in actuality some of these expressions, called civilizations, can occur in an afternoon. That idea may be too vast or foreign for you to digest at this point in your expansion. However, one day we will push you to those limits so that you can begin to realize that reality is, indeed, quite flexible.

We *want* to push your boundaries of identity. We want to confound what you believe reality is, because then you will be able to feel information from your higher self penetrate. The entire purpose of our coming to Earth to speak with you is not to give you a whole new blueprint for existence and to say, "Here, put a nail here, two-by-four here, build it like this, this is how it goes." We are not here to redefine your world. We are here to help you dismantle the blueprint that you have been living within and to give you suggestions of very general laws around which you can build new structures. The umbrella idea behind this is that whatever you think, you can create. That's the essence of our purpose. By freeing you up to experience this grand concept, it is our intention that eventually you will come into your full brain capacity. Given this great free rein to unfold to who you completely are, you will eventually release the great codes of consciousness within you. These codes are literally valuable pieces of data that much of existence is seeking. You have treasure hunters on your planet that look for gold and ancient artifacts. We can be thought of as treasure hunters along the corridors of time, playing the game.

The codes and master numbers we seek are geometric formulas and combinations of intelligence stored within the human. The human, of course, is an integral part of the design for the Living Library. Each creation in the Living Library has its purpose and has a great amount of data stored in it. Inside the human body are formulas to replicate other forms of intelligence throughout your universe. Feel that out. Inside the evolved twelve-stranded human are formulas to create life for other forms of intelligence in this universe.

When they designed Earth, other forms of intelligence were able to grasp the reason for Earth's creation. They understood that perhaps their own civilizations might one day be annihilated, and they did not want to lose them entirely. So, libraries were built throughout existence, and each was filled with specific data. All forms of intelligence that made the libraries valued their identities and valued their civilizations. They understood how their civilizations were constructed. They valued life.

The master numbers are achieved when a critical mass of individuals is able to emit specific vibrational codes. The master numbers allow different time locks to be put on a given civilization, creating an immunity to any kind of disruptive energy. Yet, the disruptive energy is quite necessary to create the whole process in the first place. That makes it a game.

In this universe, duality and polarities are essential in activating free will to its greatest potential. The parts of a duality actually serve as an impetus to reflect themselves back to each other so that their polarization eventually becomes unified. Reality is multilayered and continuously birthing new versions of itself, so it is not the same from one moment to the next. The pulse of your universe is experiencing a massive change. There is a movement at this time to create healing and to restore and retune Earth to a certain vibrational frequency. With specific beings returning, occupying the lands and bringing their stellar consciousness, eventually Earth will be reestablished as a very different colony. There will be a sense of exaltation, a sense of harmony and cooperation and unity, creating greater opportunity for all.

The same thing is happening on a universal level. Earth is one of the essential libraries of this galaxy and universe, so this is why the drama is so big. As Earth goes through her transmutation, the combined psychic energy of Earth's inhabitants will send the message of her transformation process, which will eventually ripple out vibrationally and create a great shift in how all worlds participate in the sense of polarity in this universe.

It is our intention to convey to you a larger perspective of your Pleiadian and stellar heritage and to inspire you to be more responsible, courageous, daring, and fun-loving human beings. Your Pleiadian ancestry is much bigger, more complex, and more all-inclusive than you currently recognize. We want you to remember your ancestry and discover a very ancient truth.

We will go deeper into what the game, the codes, and the master numbers mean. All existence can be viewed as a game. Indeed, it is a game that can have endings if one does not play it properly. Endings only appear on certain levels, and on other levels there are no endings. However, the endings that appear on certain levels are awesome enough. Within the Pleiadian system, we are facing a crisis of ending. That crisis of ending has to do with our karma returned to ourselves. In order for us to grow any further in our evolution, and in our search for new forms of energy, meaning, and life, we must make certain that all forms of life that we have created and set into motion have as much freedom as we ourselves desire to have. The pain of the Pleiadian experiment has to do with finding a way to appease the Mother

Goddess, because it is the Mother Goddess with whom we are all connected.

Somehow the reptilian energies are sneaking out of the closet these days. There are many things going on: comets, meteors, asteroids coming from space, planets that move at will, all kinds of phenomena getting people to wonder what is happening to this world as the global grasp of reality is slipping away. We want you to understand that it is all in divine order.

The times are changing, and it is not for you to panic over what is coming. It is time for you to feel the exhilaration inside your being. The time you have been waiting for, your purpose, is on the cusp of being fulfilled. We remind you that you are the Family of Light, and millions of you are on assignment on Earth at this time. As members of the Family of Light, you each carry the ability to pull the light frequency into your body and disperse it onto the Earth plane. In this way Earth herself, a viable living creature, can move into her own transition and die to an old order. Some of you are petrified that Earth is dying. You want to build a big wall to stop the death of Earth and the deterioration of the environment. In actuality, all of the events that seemingly are distasteful, difficult, and heinous, create the impetus that is needed to move and activate Earth's six billion people into change.

You are a transducer of energy. Just as we transduce energy from one system of reality onto yours, and our teachers and others transduce to us, you must take what you know and very gently transduce it—playfully, without fear for Earth's inhabitants. Others will see that you are stable, grounded, and loving and that you work in the name of peace. Stay clear on that. Always adhere to the concept of peace as you reach for something, currently unknown, and make friends with energies whose looks could frighten others. You are doing very, very powerful work.

As a member of the Family of Light, you are bringing in the age of unified thought transmission, the Age of Light. As you are able to take in and hold these waves of light, you will understand that the transformation of this planet is based upon the power of your mind. This mind revolution is taking hold very quickly in all cultures. We are crossing cultural boundaries; you will cross galactic boundaries. It is our intention that those of you who know us and are familiar with our energies have a lighter step on the planet and are able to live the keys that we share with you. We give you keys straightforwardly and we trick you; we always trick you. It is wise that you be a little suspicious of us. If you are not, you are a fool. Learn to have skepticism with all things and learn that sometimes we have great reason for what we do, even though perhaps this is not apparent to you at the time.

We say to you in all honesty and sincerity that your greatest interest, your integrity, your safety, and your nurturance are our first concerns. We do not want to lose you. You are a key for us. Can you conceive of that? Can you feel that in the core of your being? If you can comprehend what we are communicating to you in this moment, it will make all the difference as to how your years unfold. If you can comprehend that we need you, and that we want you, and that you are valuable, and if you can lay your ego aside and open your heart and walk through these territories of the unknown, your days will be marked with splendor.

As you evolve the story of who you are, and as you experience more, we will assist you in understanding how the story relates on a cosmic level and who you are within it. We will give you many clues and remind you that it is always our intention to teach with the kind of energy that leads you to become your own teacher, your own source of knowledge. If we are successful in activating you as an intelligent being, then you qualify to trigger certain codes and master numbers within your being that will shift the entire spectrum of existence on this plane as you know it. You literally will establish an open library once again. And, by finding your own answers—by us assisting you with the clues, and you putting the pieces together—you will come to understand that you need only yourself. Not that you are to work alone, or without us. There is a harmony and cooperation between all species—a sharing of light, a sharing of knowledge that all are one.

All we do is create imagery from which you can evolve. Do not hang your hat on our story. Listen to the stories of everyone and then make your own synthesis. Figure it out for yourself. Every teacher on the Earth plane at this time is offering you a clue. We offer you one clue—we simply have our own snazzy way of doing it. We have our own personality, and our own agenda, and we know how to stimulate you—to get you to move and be uplifted. We know how to set you free, and that is what we are after. It is our intention to return the value of human existence to the forefront of creation.

Energy Exercise

Take a deep breath and allow yourself to relax and go inside. Intend to make maximum use of the energies that are presently flooding you. Stretch your consciousness out to the twelfth chakra, wherever that is for you. From your twelfth chakra, hear the sound of intent that resonates inside your body. Imagine waves and pulses of light from far in space moving your way. As these waves of light travel toward you, listen to the response throughout all of existing life. Imagine a fine spiderlike web that makes up your cosmos. As you pull energy through that web, it begins to buzz and sing and inform all parts of itself.

Let these waves of light come onto your planet and feel that you are a magnet for expanded consciousness. From this moment forward, intend to access the frequencies of consciousness that we, as the Pleiadians, make available for you, effortlessly and joyfully. Feel an abundance of creativity express itself through your being, and with great nonchalance and courage use this creative light as it moves through you and gifts the planet with new options.

As these waves of light come through your twelfth chakra, image Earth being impacted by gigantic light waves, thousands of miles in length and width, that are flooded with tiny geometric shapes. Each of you has the potential to reactivate the Living Library by using the gifts of your mind, impulses, and intentions. Feel Earth being flooded with waves of light. For a few moments, imagine that every particle of life knows it is never destroyed—that destruction is an illusion of the game of Prime Creator. You are indeed a Game Master. Find that treasure chest you have stored away. It holds your most valuable truth, which you hide even from yourself. As you dare to open the chest, what you see is yourself—a version of yourself that is Prime Creator, creating peace and freedom once again on this world.

Intend that the sum total of your intelligence be given freely to one another, and that the gifts, talents, and abilities each of you have be broadcast to the rest of the world in order for a healing to take place.

Intend that your body beams love. Create a spiral with this love and know that you are connected to a grand purpose. You are not alone, yet you must walk and act alone in order to discover yourself. Enclose yourself in that spiral of love and intend to remember who you are.

TWO

Redreaming the Living Library

As the concept of the Library immerses itself within you, you will begin to understand the value of feelings and how you are a key to the vast knowledge stored here.

We work with very ancient beings called the Keepers of Time, who steer your universe. Can you imagine this? Just as you steer a car to stay on the road, the Keepers of Time steer the universe on a course.

The Keepers of Time are the original instigators, the innovators of the Living Libraries. They are creations of the Game Masters. You must be, and we use your human terms here, "very highly evolved" in order to make contact with the Keepers of Time. Many know of their existence, but how do you find them and get them to communicate? Stories exist of highly evolved beings upon your planet. Yet, how do you meet them, and how do you get them to work with you? How do you get them to impart their secrets to you? It is simple: you must learn to match their frequency.

Like the yogis and shamans of your world, the Keepers of Time possess ambiguous personalities. They are enigmas. Although they are known and respected, none know where they dwell, how to contact them, or what they look like. It is our fortune to be able to work with the Keepers of Time. They are our teachers, as we are one set of your teachers.

The Keepers of Time have tricked us into discovering the Living Libraries. They have tricked us as well into figuring out how to activate these libraries, because the Keepers of Time do not want to lose their universe. The Keepers of Time will keep your universe separated until that point of existence when the whole universe understands that it is one. When this occurs, the universe will collapse in upon itself, so to speak, becoming one with Prime Creator, and understanding what it is.

The Keepers of Time do everything in their power not to lose this universe because if your universe destroys itself before it completes, it will not fulfill its purpose. In order to do this, they separate the universe by creating what you call "time." Time separates everything, allowing the universe to explore itself, discover that everything works together, and come to the eventual understanding that it is whole and that all is one.

The Keepers of Time are watching their universe be taken over. They see that it is headed toward destruction and separation—a separation that they, in fact, support. They keep your universe separated in order for it and each separate other world—to discover on their own the importance of every other world. The separation that the Keepers of Time are concerned with is the separation of existing life forms from their essence. It is through this method that reptilian and other energies are creating tyranny. There is a point, far into your future, where the Keepers of Time are very concerned about the direction this has moved into. We are using the best terms we can to create concepts for you.

We have learned that mastery in teaching often comes about with trickery. Trickery involves confounding a current belief structure in order to perceive another. We are students ourselves, figuring all of this out, just as you are, and we have our own teachers who trick us into doing certain things, one of which is working with your planet. We are on a quest, looking for our own ticket to ride, adventurers that we are, and there is a whole story around how we got involved with Earth. Our quest involved finding the Living Libraries, and your planet happened to be a key. We said, "Well, isn't this interesting. Our ancestors have been tiptoeing in and out of that place for eons, and here it is the key we are looking for and we don't even see it under our noses." It is interesting the way things are hidden in realities. We, too, employ similar strategies to entice you to go into realities, to meet other portions of yourselves so that you can bring about a change within your own lives and within the universe itself.

We come from the future and are searching through the corridors of time. This is our assignment. From the probable future that we are coming from as Pleiadians, we are intending to alter the past. Our intention is to change the probable future that we are operating with, because that probable future in one direction of your universe's new movement has turned out to be filled with tyranny. This is a free-will zone and a free-will universe, and that means all is allowed. In this particular experiment, all things are Prime Creator. We remind you that, in this world of duality, shadow defines light. Go take a walk on a sunny day and see what the shadows do. Begin to study your world literally and symbolically, and see that your world speaks to you all of the time.

Earth is an absolutely miraculous place in existence because it has been filled with the story of the universe, as has the human body. The human was designed in this fashion because of the Living Library.

When the universe is functioning in a harmonic, without tyranny, one civilization is free to exchange information with another. This facilitates great commerce and a great trade of ideas for single energies to come and explore. The Living Library is like a gigantic potluck dinner. A collective of civilizations working in harmony generously gave all their knowledge and energies to form it. They created locations in your universe where information was stored. This information would be available to facilitate the universe's development when the time became necessary for it. That time is now.

There are civilizations in space that are dying because they do not have access to the Living Library, in the same way masses of humans are dying because you do not understand and have access to your own bodies. You are integral keys. The courage and faith that you have in yourselves will determine the course of experience for all of existence. As Earth moves into a place of balance and synchronistic union, she will create a geometric lineup with the eleven other libraries that make up this library system. When this alignment takes place, the twelve libraries will create their own configuration of light that will reshape your universe, signaling connection—a certain victory, so to speak, for all of creation.

You are linked to the eleven other libraries, and your task is to unite all twelve, creating the spinning of the twelve. Just as you are spinning twelve chakras to open and connect information inside yourselves, you are going to spin twelve libraries back into existence. The spinning of these twelve systems—twelve chakras and twelve cosmic libraries—will draw energies that will intermingle and move throughout many information centers. This will trigger new versions and meanings to events that perhaps before seemed irrelevant and insignificant. As you piece together the larger picture, you will begin to understand the so-called gods in action, and how they employ your world.

As members of the Family of Light, you are quite a neutral source, like a compilation of pliable energy that easily mutates into a variety of forms. The flexibility that you demonstrate allows others to employ you, to merge with you, to become you, and to enter systems of reality that without you they could not experience. We want you to understand more of who you are, and how valuable the Family of Light is. You go into systems of consciousness and change them when the systems are stuck in their own evolution.

Often, it is very difficult for systems to bring about their own changes.

We want you to become sovereign to yourself in a greater capacity, and to worship no one. The principles that you are to honor above all else are your physical vehicle, Earth, and all of Earth's occupants. Honor your physical body as if you have been given an impeccable jewel, and act as if you own the most valuable creation in the universe. Honor Earth first and foremost. This is part of the assignment, and where your value lies.

We think that the concept of the Living Library is quite appropriate because you have a very basic understanding of a library. This analogy is easily understood, for what we speak of is very complex. We are making it more digestible, like baby food, in order for you to grasp the concept. We will tell you another story at another time, for as you change, we change the story. In the future, you will be able to reach for something other than what you can now conceive.

The twelve strands of DNA and the twelve chakras have many parallel twelves that move with them. The story of twelve is quite profoundly expressed all over your planet. It is deeply embedded within the mass psyche of human consciousness, and has been employed throughout time, in your terms, as a method to structure and convey information from one system to another. The story of twelve grounds the idea of meaningful existence into your world.

The earliest use of the ancient teaching of twelve was the concept of the zodiac, a narrow belt eighteen degrees wide on either side of the ecliptic, which is the apparent circular path of the sun around Earth. The zodiac was divided into twelve signs, with twelve houses, conveying knowledge about creation through the idea of interweaving and linking twelve significant parts. The zodiac was believed to be alive with memory, and it played an integral part in Sumerian, Hindu, Chinese, Egyptian, Chaldean, Greek, and Roman civilizations.

Human development is deeply linked to universal cycles distributing the twelve zodiacal energies through which new expressions came into being. Today you use clocks and calendars as reminders of the division of energy, for these also mark time through the significant use of twelve.

The Bible and other ancient texts refer to many relationships based on twelve—twelve gates, twelve tribes, twelve angels, twelve sons, twelve apostles/disciples, even twelve knights of the round table, and now, today, the twelfth planet. We use the idea of twelve chakras, twelve strands of DNA, and twelve libraries because you are keyed, so to speak, to respond and remember a grander vista of reality through this symbol.

Your twelve chakras are collections, or pockets of energy, where events can emerge. They hold memory and identity, and each corresponds to a strand of DNA. The seven main chakras are in your body, starting at the base of the spine and moving upward. There are five more outside your body, making a total of twelve vortex centers, or twelve suns, as we like to call them. Oxygenation, light, and conscious intention will activate these centers, and once they are switched on, your challenge is to translate all of the data that is carried through them to the DNA strands.

The chakras inside your body can release your body memory—your body experience from this lifetime, as well as from other incarnational journeys. The first chakra stores your core identity; it deals with who you are and how you survive. It opens you to journey into yourself and the foundation of your core beliefs. The second chakra relates to creativity and sexuality; it opens the records of your beliefs and experiences in these areas. These first two chakras correspond with your traditional knowledge of two strands of DNA. The issues affiliated with identity, survival, sexuality, and creativity have challenged you for millennia.

The third chakra relates to your solar plexus—your gut, so to speak. When open, it assists you to feel and intuit your way through life. In women, because of menstrual bleeding and childbirth, this area is often more active and regarded with great respect. Your will, power, and feelings lie here. The fourth chakra aligns with your heart, which when open connects you to all life. Compassion flows from this center, allowing you to understand the why and wherefore of what you perceive. The flow of compassion takes you beyond judgment, which acts as a trap to separate you.

The fifth chakra is found in your throat, opening the great gift of vocal expression through which you speak your truth. The sixth chakra activates your third eye, stimulating your ability to see beyond the confines of 3D. The seventh chakra is at the crown of your head. When open, it connects and circulates spiritual energies to your cranial area. Once stimulated, the pineal and pituitary glands, as well as the hypothalamus, play active roles in linking you up.

The eighth chakra is in close proximity to your physical body—anywhere from a few inches to a few feet above your head. It relates to the invisible realms outside your body. The ninth chakra is outside the Earth's atmosphere, perhaps as far away as your moon, connecting you as a steward and watcher of Earth. The tenth chakra reaches into your solar system, offering you access to all that is there. The eleventh is a galactic chakra that offers information about your local stellar influences. The twelfth chakra reaches outside your galaxy and gives you access to what is in the rest of the universe as you picture it. In general, you do not have access to information outside of your universe at this time because your body is not evolved enough to handle it. One day, you may evolve there. However, at this time you have agreed to take on conscious evolution here on Earth—to become a radio station, broadcasting a tone or frequency that everybody else can handle.

These twelve energy centers must be accessed from the inside, where you can feel the data corresponding with them and translate the experiences within the context of your mind. This is you, evolving into your multidimensional identity, remembering who your version of yourself is—out in the galaxy, and beyond.

Many of you have been taught that you evolve through reincarnating, and that you have a soul that has many versions of itself. This is only a small part of the picture. You understand your reincarnational selves in terms of the human form. However, your selves are not all human. They exist in a variety of shapes, sizes, and guises, showing that all is part of one.

Since you are human, it has been the safest practice these last few thousand years to believe that you evolved on the reincarnational cycle through which your soul's incarnations were always human. The human portion is only one creation, or one aspect of your identity. You exist in a form that is part human and part animal in many places. A portion of the drama that is now occurring has to do with other versions of yourself seeking their own evolution as the dimensions merge upon this planet. A meeting of your multidimensional selves is in the making, and your initiation and task is to incorporate all of this.

The creator gods can be thought of as combinations of all of the beings on your planet. They are represented in the insect family, the animal family, and all of the families of consciousness here on your Earth plane. Many of these beings that created you look like combinations of humans and animals.

When this planet was formulated, the combined wealth of intelligent species was pooled and distributed within the Living Library into every rock, plant, animal, insect, and other living thing. Since all things are alive and have consciousness, the Living Library is found even in grains of sand and bits of charcoal.

The human species, steward of Earth, can be thought of as the library card. As the concept of the library immerses itself within you, you will understand the value of feelings and how you are a key to the vast knowledge stored here. This discovery will unfold for you over time.

Energies that would like to meet you merge with other forms of the library, so it is quite possible for the animal family to have other energies looking out of their eyes to observe and gather information. The key to the Living Library is you humans, because you can unlock and access the entire library. It does not mean that others cannot come in through trees or other plants to merge, peek out, and understand your reality. When you make peace and surrender and do not go around violating life forms because they happen to overstep a boundary that has been falsely set, you allow yourself to have meetings with civilizations that are perhaps much grander than you conceive of.

The purpose of certain star energies in the last half-million years was to interact with various sentient civilizations on Earth, offering them a notable shift in understanding. These civilizations were tucked away—housed in very small geographic areas where they were left undisturbed. When the owners of the planet got wind of various experiments in which love was predominantly used, the civilizations were dispersed or destroyed.

Those who believe they own and operate your planet are enamored of power, and they hold onto power through creating the frequency of fear and chaos. It is simply the way that they operate and the way that they are learning about their own power of existence. We will remind you over and over again that all things are Prime Creator, so all forces that you meet are Prime Creator meeting itself and seeking to understand itself. Prime Creator seeks to harmonize and find the purpose that opposing forces of the same energy achieve. This is excellent to bear in mind. When you can keep in your conscious awareness the concept that all things are one, directed and chosen by the various aspects of self, and that all things are a result of thought seeking to understand and evolve itself, then you are out of the bleachers and into the game, playing ball. We want all people out on the field as valuable players, playing the game of life.

In order for Earth to serve a much grander purpose in the plan of the universe, it is becoming necessary for her to activate herself as a Living Library. This activation begins with yourself in your own backyard. You then spread this frequency around the planet. In less than twenty years, there will be some major changes.

The Living Library is not simply a historical record; it is an entire library of knowledge from which anything can be created. There are formulas and blueprints stored in the life forms on Earth for all kinds of realities to be developed. Other libraries located in various sectors of the universe store their knowledge in light forms or collections of molecules that you would not even recognize. For each of the twelve centers, the creator gods designed a unique storage method for the knowledge. The intent is to protect the integrity of the libraries, each alive in its own way. From a perspective of the future, the libraries have been lost, and the need for rediscovery and opening is now. Ideally, each of these twelve libraries creates an electromagnetic alliance which houses a stupendous shift in realization. The twelve together create the opportunity for a brand-new harmonic for all of existence, as you perceive it.

Here is a conceptualization for you: If the twelve libraries that you are a part of were all activated at full capacity, they would create a gigantic instrument in space that would connect itself through conscious beams of energy. This instrument could change the course of the corridors of time and completely alter the future universe by simply erasing its presence from where it began, without annihilating anything.

There are portions of yourself that are on this assignment from many, many different worlds and different points of view. Some of the contact that you are having now is from another part of yourself, a part of the self that is needing to meet the *your*-self version of you in order to make sense of all of this multidimensional experimentation, which is designed to provide a sense of unity for the future.

Once this energetic geometric relationship is set into motion, the Living Libraries are designed to send forms of wave particles through space, creating a new method for your universe to access itself. When these universal highways are connected as gridlines, information and energy will suddenly open a system of existence that was never there before. In your reality, you are constructing information superhighways that broadcast what is occurring on Earth, sending it out as an energy shift everywhere. Eventually you will realize this shift in your body as it truly becomes the superhighway to life.

There are multitudes of civilizations that want to get back into the Living Library so they can change the course of the universe. We come from the future—and there are many futures—where Earth and a multitude of worlds are overrun by a tyrannical force in this free-will zone. Many are excited and wait in great anticipation to be introduced to you so that they may work with you. They understand that their energies are completely and totally foreign to your concepts. Yet, they understand that, from a future point of view, you know them and you are them and you were sent back in time by them.

We are acting as gatekeepers, allowing in certain energies with great care, for we have a plan of intention to alter a distant future by altering a very distant past. You are simultaneously located in all of these places, playing your part. We have agreed to be a stimulator and energy facilitator for you in many of the different realities where you are located. Versions of you are also located in some of the eleven other libraries throughout this universe, and you are operating as systems busters there as well. Remember, as a member of the Family of Light you carry the vibration and intent of change wherever you go—altering the system you find yourself in. Feel this out, and be open to an infusion of knowing how vast you are, and how grand the plan.

Many members of the Family of Light will become library cards or tour guides to those who will match you frequency for frequency, and love for love. You will bring about a merging through love that will create a new ownership and direction of this place that you call Earth. Remember that Prime Creator is in all things, so part of the true purpose of the Living Library of Earth is to blend and merge consciousness so that you may experience and access the magnificent knowledge that is stored here. The key here is to love and value yourself and Earth.

When a world such as yours is in the process of spiritual evolution, there is an opportunity for any and all who have ever been involved with the library to make a cosmic leap. Therefore, many beings come from far and wide to participate, bringing their own agendas and creating plans within plans. There is much healing to take place, for many species who you would consider to be dark or negative are also drawn to your Earth at this time. They are here to wake you up and stimulate you with their own "badness" to remind you of something.

Remember, this is a world of polarities, and shadow defines light. These energies are here not to be bombed, killed, or destroyed, even though your governments may tell you that these visitors are evil. They are here to heal, to infuse themselves with the vibrations of light and love, and to come into a higher state of being in their own species because they have forgotten what those on Earth have forgotten—that you are all one. Those in fear will attract the unclear and unhealed portions of themselves as exterior beings. Misuse of life and power draws its mirror experience. You will come to understand that you *are* what you are afraid of.

You are beginning to realize at the close of this millennium that genetic engineering is no big deal. You, Earth's inhabitants, would go into immediate shock if you learned what is now possible by fusing genes together—if your so-called news sources were to do stories concerning goings-on in some of the laboratories around your planet. Creatures have been created and life forms have been unleashed on the Earth plane in many places.

If this power to create life is now available to evolving humans with two-stranded DNA, imagine what kind of genetic understanding is held by beings who have existed for hundreds of thousands of years. This is how worlds and species are created and are born. These so-called gods, like waves of energy, split off from Prime Creator and set out in this free-will zone. They take the energy of Prime Creator as the web of existence and experiment so that they can learn about power and energy. They have free will to do whatever they want, and if and when they get lost and forget and create things of darkness, it is all part of the same game. It is the same energy. It is all connected, and it all needs to be healed.

Once you transform Earth and move into the Golden Age, it will alter the rest of the universe. It will take one or two thousand years for you to know the change that will move over the whole universe. The change could happen simultaneously; it is just that you will not see it simultaneously. It will take you a thousand or two thousand years to experience the change from your point of view. Yet, when you change on this Earth plane, it will happen instantly everywhere.

Those who would deem themselves the owners or gods of your planet at this time will attempt to keep you from the loving, cooperative emotion that will facilitate your evolvement. They will do everything in their power to bring about unrest, chaos, war, and fear, which keep you from accessing the Living Library.

Those who took over your planet won it in a war. They knew Earth was valuable; however, they were far removed from the memory of what Earth's value was. They mined your planet for gold, came for water, raped your psyche, and robbed you of your essence, thinking they were reaping the abundance. Yet, once this planet was won, they overlooked the true riches because they didn't know how to recognize them.

These owners or gods know that humans can access something by operating out of love, and that is why the love frequency has been so scarce on your planet. The owners did not want the riches to be discovered by anyone else until they could discover the riches for themselves. They will not discover these riches until they operate in the love frequency. This they must learn, and you will teach them.

Even though these energies have been unable to activate the library and get what they wanted out of it, they have figured out another use for it. They have been intent all these years on increasing the population and gearing Earth up for as many humans as possible to emit an emotional frequency of chaos and fear on a regular basis. They've done a good job. It is time for the story to be told, and for all people to stop believing in this foolishness of religions and gods that limit them, calling them sinners and telling them that their lives are wrong. *What is wrong is all life not being valued.* The lives of grass, of humans, of animals, of flowers—all are valuable. That is universal truth. You have a right to your sexuality, to speak what you feel, and to follow your own truth and not obey someone's silly rules.

You must grow and change beyond your current ideas that offer only one version of existence. Understand that as humans you have been told many different stories so that you could grow into the comprehension of the universal spirit, the great web of consciousness of which you are a part.

Your religions serve a purpose; however, they are steeped in falsehoods.

Religions were created to give you as humans some way of comprehending your identity, which is a valuable thing to learn. However, the information disseminated to you through the various religions gives you a limited perspective of who you are and keeps you disempowered. Any religion is a perspective upon existence. The stories, the individuals, and the myths that make up religion are all used in different ways to affect the behavior of populations. Remember, as any group of people focuses their energy and intent, their collective thoughtforms produce an energetic mass that moves out into existence.

What was appropriate from a religious point of view a few hundred years ago is no longer significant today. Times are changing. Just as you go to school to learn, the soul graduates from lifetime to lifetime. Or sometimes the soul has to spend many lifetimes in one grade until the information, in the form of lessons, is learned. Then the soul moves on to the next level. The place that the human race is moving to involves an understanding that you can be equal to beings whom centuries and millennia ago you called gods. You could not have been equals five to ten thousand years ago because you did not comprehend the abilities of these gods. They came in technologically advanced craft, and your cultures had no words to describe their technology. If you go back twenty or thirty thousand years, there were technological advancements on your planet that were very interesting. However, these things have been misunderstood, covered over, or hidden away.

There are a number of corners on your planet where small clusters of civilizations hold part of the Living Library open by imbuing love into themselves and onto Earth. Earth then returns love to them, making life creative and sustaining. When the Living Library is activated and feeds information, cooperation, and love back into human stewards, things will become less of a struggle. As a matter of fact, when the Living Library is completely activated, you will be able to manifest, construct, and find out anything you want. The human nervous system and DNA structure are not evolved enough at this time to hold the exchange of information and frequency that would take place if the Living Library were to be completely activated. It would involve too drastic a change from how you are used to perceiving nature.

When the Living Library is in full bloom, intelligence will speak from all parts of existence, and we mean *speak*. You will spend an hour communing with one particular flower. During this time you will be entranced by the knowledge you discover in walking three feet. There will be a gradual adjustment within all living life forms so that each evolves and opens simultaneously, creating a matching and a meeting of vibration and consciousness. Remember, everything is alive.

Animals are brilliant and are much smarter than humans. Many are now moving to this world of light, which is why there are many so-called extinctions taking place. Animals are very clever. There are many distinctions between the animal species and yourselves. One of the greatest is that the animals know that they do not end when they die. They know that they go on. They don't buy funeral plots and they don't worry about where they are going to die and be buried. They trust that they will be taken care of. They have an innate wisdom and trust. They don't take out insurance policies and they don't watch TV. Many of these animals are very in tune with the quality of life; they know that the quality of life they desire cannot be found any more in your global sphere, and therefore they are departing.

The animals were given to you as companions upon this planet. It has been up to you whether you eat them or not. The animals do not object to being eaten if that adds to the quality of your life and to the quality of their lives. However, animals are not presently respected and honored for the quality of their lives. They are treated as if they are not alive, as if they do not feel, and as if they are slaves of the human species.

Animals were designed and created to be your companions, to occupy the space to teach, show, and share the way with you. The animals are a biogenetic creation based upon genes that were gathered from many different solar systems and planets. Their creation allows representatives from those systems to have a genetic link with Earth and therefore the ability to peer into and broadcast into this world. This facet of creation has never really been understood.

Animals have a certain intuitive sense that lets them understand their roles with each other. They come from a variety of extraterrestrial communities and look just like their ancestors, who are sentient beings upon other planets. If you knew how many millions and billions of planets there are in existence, this idea would not be so boggling to you. Those that created your planet asked for different seeds from different places. These seeds were biogenetically engineered to create companions for you and to seed Earth.

Some of the animals here are utilized as transmitters. Your cats are direct transmitters of information to a species of consciousness that uses the cats to monitor you. In ancient times upon your planet, it was in vogue in many cultures to have a lion or other large cat next to the ruling entity. These animals were always there. Look at ancient statues all over the planet and what do you see? Lions. The cat family represents a biogenetic tooling of a species that looks like you except that it has the visage of a cat. The cat people, or lion people, have come in shifts upon your planet and worked in South America, Mexico, Egypt, and in some island cultures. Statues have been built to honor them. When they taught the human race, or when they mixed their species and created the rulers here, especially in Egypt, they left cats to transmit information so the rulers had direct contact with the species from the stars. This is how many of these rulers made decisions. This is how they were guided. The cats gave them tele-pathic information. They were like transmitters or cosmic radios. In more current times, cats were owned by witches. Do you think witches were fools? The cats were links to other realms. When energy that is not so uplifted comes in, cats can intercept it and alter the vibration. Now many of you have little cats in your houses that transmit much informa-tion to you. However, in this time period, you are not gen-erally working with this kind of information. The cats are guardians and assistants for you, great companions of comfort.

If you are allergic to cats, it indicates many things. We have worked with many people on their allergies. One of the prime things that being allergic to cats indicates is that you have difficulty allowing closeness of love to come into your life. You cannot let love in. The kitty gives you a certain amount of loyalty and love, and when it gets close to you, you may be unable to accept this deep connection with another being. That is one symbolic representation of an allergy to a certain animal.

Each species serves a purpose for you. Cockroaches that are overrunning your life may have to do with issues you are not facing that are attempting to come to the surface. You don't look at cockroaches and say, "Oh, you beautiful little cockroaches. How nice to see you upon my kitchen sink this morning." Often you smash them or get out the bug spray. Yet, they are becoming stronger and stronger, are they not? They are quite a hardy species and have survived many a shift of energy, learning to transmute toxins over and over again. They are here to remind you to look at that which is not necessarily dressed in its own finery—that which is inside yourself that needs to come out. What is it inside you that is pestering you? And how can you become more hardy as a species?

It is quite easy to live in harmony with nature. All you need do is telepath exactly what you want to experience. Talk to Earth and to nature in your mind and out loud. If you find you are invaded by nature's creatures, then simply say, "How clever of me to teach myself in this capacity. I am understanding, little creatures, that you are attempting to show me something. Now I will gather my wits about myself and begin to look inside." You like to put up veils and screens and annihilate what is irritating you so that you don't have to face who you are. If you face who you are, you will need to change, and that change may involve too many things. Often, you hold onto that which keeps you unhappy rather than face the unknown alone. Please realize that you are never alone.

The creatures are here as companions for you. There is nothing that is here that is out to get you. You are trained to believe that things are out to get you, so you put out that vibration. Then, because you create your reality, you do your best to force reality to bend in a direction to harm yourself. It is not that easy to harm yourself, you know. You must put out a great amount of effort to create disease and harm.

It is well known in the scientific community that many things that are promoted are not in your best interest. However, economics and money are always involved, making a dollar on your fear. What do you think it will take to stop that process?

The animals are now mirroring for you the pain in which you find yourselves, psychologically and spiritually. The animals take on this pain and are going to take on disease as well. You are not connected to the way animals are raised for food, and there is tremendous discomfort in the many animal families at this time. Discomfort moves into diseasement. These animals are here to teach you. They will mirror to you what you need to see about yourselves. Your pets very often will take on things you cannot see to show you, out of great loyalty and love.

When you approach an animal, the animal knows if you are coming in peace or if you are going to lash out at it. When you allow forms of animal life to sit in equality to you, then you will be ready to sit in council on the higher planes of existence. You will be able to comprehend how the god force disguises itself in all of its various creations throughout existence. There is intelligence in all living things. It is quite erroneous for humankind to think of or label itself as the most evolved species. That is completely false. There cannot be a comparison because there is a life force, a consciousness within all things. The rocks and the mountains sometimes have a greater understanding of their purpose than the species of humankind has ever been able to achieve.

Plants grown in a toxic-free, loving environment, nurtured and spoken to, send out a response to that treatment. The plants and trees outside the house want the same thing. So do the plants in the field next door. They want the same love and may bend and move in the direction of love being expressed. The plant kingdom is very generous, as is the animal kingdom. They both freely give. The plants and animals that you energize share that energy with all they know. They give off hormone-like substances so that instantly what one plant knows and experiences is sent to all the other plants.

There are plants that, when ingested, connect you to other forms of self and other forms of consciousness. The whole concept of altering your consciousness through plants has been given an unfavorable name in your Western world, associated with what is called drugs. In many sacred ceremonies and rituals, it is understood that certain parts of the plants of the Living Library are ingested so that you may further understand the Living Library. So, if you would, open your mind to the idea that Earth grows things that allow you to understand her in greater detail. There are those who do not want you to gather more information and become free, so they say to you that something is bad. They turn something that is quite beautiful into something to be frightened of. In actuality, the purpose of being human is to alter your consciousness by intent, by will, and by the gifts of the planet in a fashion of ritual and honor—and to discover the magnificence of living.

Many of the substances that your Western world could benefit from exist within the plant kingdom. It is quite interesting that there is a program to destroy the parts of the world where people have made use of the Living Library through the plant pharmacopoeia. Plants offer you the opportunity to understand your planet and yourselves. There are those who are burning the rain forests and purposely destroying portions of the Living Library. Sometimes antennae of beetles and bark or roots from trees hold keys used to balance, heal, and bring the human body into a state of higher consciousness. All things are here for a purpose, and when they are explored by humans, they will give back and gift humans. In actuality, Earth has been waiting for humans to discover this living miracle. Now is the time for a movement on the planet—a courageous growing multitude that will rise to the call for the purpose of Earth. You will make new paths and roadways toward what is possible by working in harmony with Earth.

You have all known by intention, plan, and blueprint that your purpose is to evolve, to create a literal mutation of form inside the human body. You are to seek out those energy places on the planet that will accelerate from outside the internal process as it is developing. Love, which exists as a force you have not yet been able to comprehend, is the key. Therefore, the way you presently conceive of love will change. As you discover love from inside yourself, you will create a mirror outside yourself to reflect your inner beliefs as your thoughts take form in your life. Your exploration of love as a vital force of existence will affect the planet, and the planet will become that vibration as well, no matter what they say in the headlines of the newspapers.

Remember, love is a frequency, and light is a frequency. They both exist as electromagnetic broadcastings of energy. The whole planet is a Living Library that can be activated by adjusting the human genetic structure. This is so because you as humans are the keys to the Living Library, and emotions are what allow you to read the information. Those who own your planet, and would claim to be the gods in charge here, are learning about love. There has not been a civilization upon your planet that has held the love frequency open for any great epoch. Each had its day and its time, then was invaded and destroyed, from your point of view.

Throughout historical time periods, the love frequency was held by different civilizations. For periods of time, Native Americans held a love frequency, and the Living Library was open to certain degrees throughout numerous native and indigenous cultures. When their time of stewardship was complete, the frequency was transferred to other places. There have been many experiments from the Pleiadian system sent here to imbue the love frequency onto the planet and to keep it glimmering. Those from the Pleiades have been able to open portals and hold the love frequency, so that it could be activated when the time became necessary, which all of you know is now.

Our task, which seems impossible to many, is to set you free. In the ideal, you will establish yourselves as your own authorities. You will learn to look at yourselves as equal with all of creation, and not to worship any other creation. You will say, "Look at me. Who is it that I am in relationship to all of these things? I am a miraculous being in my own right. I am a source in my own right. I can find the answers. I can see the future. I can see into the past. I am sovereign."

Sometimes you may get annoyed with us and say, "Oh, those Pleiadians are too much. They are too pesky. When are they going to leave me alone? They are pushing all of my buttons." Yet, if you listen to the undertone and you come back to the center of our purpose, you will find that we do everything to turn you to yourselves. When we do not answer your questions, it is not that we are withholding information. It is that we are turning you to you. We intend to bring each of you into sovereignty, and empowerment, a place of peaceful acknowledgment within your own being. In this place, you can create life as you choose, no matter what is going on around you. This is our purpose. And in the times that are coming, these qualities will serve as your most valuable attributes.

We have had to qualify for the stewardship of our energy. We were not born with golden spoons in our mouths. We evolved, and we learned. We learn from you, and, in a manner of speaking, we learned so much about who you are that we are refashioning ourselves in our reality. We cultivated humor and joviality because they are completely necessary. If we took our work too seriously we would be finished, just as you would be. We would all miss the point.

There is a reciprocity that is taking place. On the Pleiades, there is a huge difference that is being made through all of the work that you do. We want you to comprehend that. This is an exchange, not a one-sided event. It is open ended. The changes that are evident in your lives have corresponding effects elsewhere as a result of your clear intent and investment of energy. It is our intention and deepest desire that you live to see and feel these effects—to know your multidimensional selves as spanning the worlds of both Earth and the Pleiades.

We are the intermediaries—those who open the gates, make introductions, and show the way. A gigantic force of intelligence awaits, stating, "We want to meet the humans. We want to work with them. We want to be involved with this project." And we have said, "Hold up! You cannot flood into their lives, because they are fragile. You must be patient until they get to the place where it will be easy for you to meet."

Understand that, to some extent, the Living Library and the story of twelve is a concept far beyond your grasp at this

52 Earth: Pleiadian Keys to the Living Library

time. It is going to become a process through which you as humans will activate yourselves during the next twenty-year period. Your imagination and your ability to dream fantastic concepts into being will create the library. We want to assist you in redreaming the Living Library, making it into a new place, with a new form of vitality. There are a few places where the Living Library is already activated. It is not just that the land itself is alive; it is necessary that human consciousness translate and work with the aliveness. That is what makes the Living Library, because it is through *you* that the Living Library is accessed. A Living Library without humans is incomplete. You are the essential component within the Living Library.

We would like each of you, as you walk on Earth, to speak to the blades of grass, the grains of sand, the petals of flowers, the butterflies, the insects, the ants, the birds, the bees, the ferns, the leaves, the drops of water, the dew—and to state your presence. State: "I am here. It is my intention for you to release to me what knowledge has been stored within you as a living form. I am now here to receive it, to translate it, to understand it, and then to transduce it out to the rest of the planet. I am desiring to activate the Living Library of this planet." We would like that to be your living meditation and intention. Allow the land, the Living Library that is alive with the love frequency, to move into your body.

As you redream the Living Library, imagine the value of Earth. As you hold this image of the library, all the people who support you and know you as a member of the Family of Light will feel what you are gaining, because you are all connected. You are recognized by your commitment to saying, "Yes, I am of the Family of Light." You impulse everyone everywhere with what you know in this moment, and those in the Family of Light can then reach out and touch others. It is a big dream.

We want you to glide through this time of worlds opening and realities shifting. There are patterns of energies in your bodies stored as cellular memories, and we must go gently to create an arena in which you can grow.

Energy Exercise

Open your imagination and journey within. Take a few deep breaths and relax. Imagine that you are standing in a circle of people. You are holding hands with this group of people. There is a brilliant fuchsia, gold, and white light coming down from above, creating a pillar of light. Now imagine Earth as a Living Library with incomparable vitality. Everything is radiating light, and you have never seen Earth this alive before. Maintain the image, holding hands in a circle, and at the same time, let a part of yourself break away. Step forward as an individual into the circle and the pillar of light. Access the pillar of light and follow our intent so that we can bring you to another home, the Pleiades. Let your imagination and your trust carry you upward. Feel a lightness, a joy, a deep sensation of connecting and longing.

Now, find yourself in your conception of the Pleiades. Observe and feel and acknowledge. Give something to the source that created you that would make a difference. The greatest thing that you can gift is your compassion, which is your ability to understand why things were done the way they were. This compassion opens your ability to see and feel the results of eons of time. Corridors are open to you to unlock the very truth that pulsates within every cell of your being. Give what you can and what you will to this place that is home, and find a rejoicing and a purpose within it. Intend that a change be made and that a prophecy be fulfilled. Intend that the creations themselves return to their creator to set the creator free.

Bring your attention to your breath, breathe easily, and send a vibration of playful upliftment, release, and understanding to this place that is your home and our home. Feel for a few moments what is returned to you.

Now imagine yourself in the palm of a huge hand. You are in a circle ringed together with other people in your group. A huge hand reaches from the Pleiades and gently places you back on Earth in your own garden, as if you are the most delicate and valuable of creatures. See yourself running and frolicking and playing as if you were a child. The vitality of Earth and of yourself is grander now than it was when you started. Put a smile on your face and allow the emotion and tears of recognition to do their work—to open your heart to all realms, in all worlds. What you have accomplished in this very moment of compassion is a hallmark of achievement.

THREE

Earth Speaks

Imagination is the most powerful force available to humankind.

Think about this: Earth is alive and holds the knowledge you seek, and your consciousness affects what Earth reveals. How do you access this knowledge? Where are the keys to unlock it and make it yours? The information is stored in stone and bone.

Times have changed. It used to be that each individual who evolved and studied the mysteries had one teacher, and knowledge was passed down from teacher to apprentice in a long line of tradition. Today this is no longer necessary because what you seek is being released from storage inside your body. Light openings and genetic mutations are bringing about unprecedented change within the human form. You become your own teacher by activating what is inside you, through *clear intent*, and by following the impulses and knowledge that accompany the process.

All people who penetrate and discover the realms of the unknown and the domains of the mystics have unique experiences and interpretations of reality. If a person comes from Tibet, it does not mean this person is more holy than someone who comes from the Bronx. The spiritually evolved can spring from any geographic location. You teach and learn from a unique stance designed to develop your beliefs and character as your individual consciousness moves through whatever experience you select at that moment. Honor those who have been your teachers and continue to recognize yourself and all that you create as a part of your growth process, without overinflating anything. It does not do to put teachers on pedestals; they only fall off.

Our teaching is designed to produce an accumulation of energy that will motivate the collective, impulsing multitudes to reach new plateaus of experience and creating a series of simultaneous global awakenings. For this reason, your own spiritual process is tempered by both the progress of global consciousness and the individual blueprint of your purpose. Even though you are sometimes frustrated because you would like to be further along than you are, be patient, for you are bringing yourself closer and closer to what you want. When you share what you know, it is broadcast around the world. Codings are fired, and masses of people evolve. As a species, you are time coded and interlinked to respond to patterns of awakening to your greater identity. You are triggered to move with the masses, waiting for a large group to gather on a certain plateau of consciousness before you can move along yourself.

Humankind is coded and, as you evolve, you follow a pattern. Your blueprint leads you into a concealed library of knowledge within you. The gods who formed Earth planted devices called chronometers that measure the evolution of human consciousness. When enough people awaken and trigger the chronometers, new data is opened on the planet. It is like the millionth person walking through a turnstile and winning a prize. Only instead of one person winning the prize, the mass consciousness is suddenly opened because enough people on the planet are able to follow their blueprints and respond.

The ancients who lived on this planet built libraries of a

very different nature than you build today. Prior to building temples, tribal wizards and leaders of certain cultures journeyed to places that were known to have a special stone. This stone was cleansed and prepared to hold data and information that would be transmitted telepathically from people's minds into the stone structures. A form such as a temple was designed, and the builders used the natural geomancy and energy flow of a location to store the total of what they knew into the very stone of the construction. Information was stored in stone and bone, with stone being the bones of Earth.

When you visit ancient sacred sites that you call power places, you experience electromagnetic formulas for higher consciousness. You often pick up what you left there thousands of years ago for you to reclaim. By journeying to these places, your body is exposed to these energies and accesses the blueprint along which you can evolve.

The ancients built temples and megalithic structures in particular places to utilize the accumulation of energy in vortices. Each of these sites had a specialty. The great stone circle of Avebury in England was used as a dimensional doorway for various star systems, particularly Sirius, the Pleiades, and Arcturus. The stones were placed in a specific configuration that used light as a key to draw these stellar energies to Earth. Thus, an exchange of information was possible through a human-Earth-stellar linkup. Such sites offered the energy of fertility, and couples would journey to make love at the sites in order to conceive, creating lives energized and characterized by the vortices. Other locations were designed as broadcasting stations, as calendars, or as oracles to read the future and expand reality.

Most civilizations have stored data in stone. Earth reads you as you live and breathe on her, and she knows the stage of your development and your ability to accept responsibility. Sacred sites, therefore, become activated by individuals who use their own keys of consciousness to unlock the sites, remembering and releasing the knowledge stored and experienced in them. When you enter sacred sites and intentionally imagine your chakras as doorways of energy opening to your personal memories, the sites become activated. *Imagination is the most powerful force available to humankind.* The ancients had the ability to feel the abundance of energy in these locales. They tapped into and used these enhanced places where lines of energy joined forces and there was a merging and meeting of dimensions and other worlds.

Every time you visit a site, you bring about a quickening and activation. At the same time, you assist in triggering events that will propel the people of the world to recognize and value themselves as spiritual beings, or face catastrophic annihilation. In these next few decades, the pace is going to quicken. You will think there is a frenzied drummer calling the beat of Earth. This is because you are within a cycle of evolution that is pressuring the spirit to be born and known in all humans. To recognize that you are a spiritual being is a key to the corridor of the future you seek.

If you never get to go to a sacred site, and you spend time only in your backyard, you are not going to miss out. The intent to open your memory banks and to activate collective memory, plus your exposure to the frequency of materials and artifacts from others who have been to these places, are all you need to experience your own awakening of the energies.

Stories were built into the stone structures that were tempered and fed with sound. Individuals capable of broadcasting specific frequencies implanted these frequencies into the stone structures. Today, the stones continue to hold the frequencies, not merely the written forms. There are countless sacred sites still below the surface of Earth, waiting for a dimensional merge to take place. In the region that is now the United States, there have been numerous ancient civilizations who left remnants of knowledge. These remnants were buried and covered over quite cleverly, often with great purpose. They will begin to break the surface during the next twenty years. Innumerable discoveries will be brought about, more than in any other time period of your recorded history. Earth is an exceptionally vital place, and she is revealing her very essence to you as you are able to perceive the keys and redefine yourself.

You have a great advantage because you are aware that a process of spiritual evolution is occurring. Reality is crumbling, and that is disturbing and upsetting to many. As visitors at sacred sites,you are opening the time locks with keys of consciousness and triggering the energy combinations that have been holding memories of events until you demonstrated that you were ready to receive them. When you infuse yourselves with energy and surrender and work with intention in sacred sites, you literally send bolts of great change around the globe.

All people have the opportunity to decide where their values lie. Unfortunately, very few select honoring the Earth Mother. Therefore, they will find their greatest challenges manifested before them. You have been given the great gift of being on Earth at this time—a gift which you have given to yourselves. Trust your inner guidance, for it will lead you along the various paths toward self-knowledge, revealing the purpose of life and the basic meaning of existence. In these days that are unfolding, you will find your inner guidance to be a most handy tool that you have created for yourselves. Use it. Benefit from it. Do not judge those who are not as impulsed as you. You are different, yet there are millions of you all over the globe quietly holding a new meaning and understanding of reality. You are in a world with a system of belief that is dying, just as you are symbolically going through the process of releasing what no longer suits your lives. Reconsider the very essence of what you learn and how and why you think. Challenge yourselves to seek communication and the sharing of knowledge with the Earth, for she offers many an untold mystery and has unique ways of speaking.

Since the early 1980s, crop circles have become conspicu-
ously abundant in and around the Wiltshire and Salisbury
Plain areas of Great Britain, where numerous stone megalithic structures remain to this day. Mysterious markings appear
as if by magic in the grain fields throughout the English
countryside. They are synchronistically aligned to the sacred
sites of Stonehenge, Avebury, and Silbury Hill—all widely
recognized as places of celestial attunement. The forms of
intelligence that make these geometric shapes do so in a very
playful way. Geometry involves more than a subject you take
in school; it is, in fact, a form of intelligence. You will discover that higher intelligence often has a wonderful sense of
humor. The crop circles are made with sound and have a definite purpose, for they silently speak to the mass consciousness. They impulse themselves onto Earth to alter dimensional possibilities and open doorways and portals for other energies to enter.

These crop-circle glyphs hold their own symbolism and
are encyclopedias of information. Your body holds a far
greater recognition of the message of the crop circles than
your rational mind can currently grasp. The crop-circles
speak of many things and truly make symphonies of preparation for Earth's people. They speak of what is coming and
of the great choice that you all must make—the choice of
which world you will choose to dwell in. The crop-circle
glyphs speed up the evolutionary process and the evolving
DNA, calling your spirit to awaken.

Part of the purpose of the glyphs is to pave the way for
the mass consciousness to grasp what is inconceivable at the
present time. You are not alone. The complexities of the
markings will become more pronounced as the glyphs accelerate your awareness of other life forms. Ancient prophecies
speak of signs upon Earth and signs in the sky. There is a
plan within a plan within a plan. There are friends in the sky
and beyond, orchestrating layers of influence over and above
what you can conceive of now. There are combinations of

forces within the crop circles, and you will see them as light geometry dancing around in the air. The glyphs create shifts that will bring data to you. Then your challenge is to comprehend this new knowledge and to have your feet on the ground and your head at the top of the universe all at the same time. Can you hold that imagery? You are vast, and you are capable of connecting with the deepest cosmos and grounding it into Earth.

If you look carefully into historical records and manuscripts, you will find that the crop-circle glyphs are not a phenomenon found only in this century. These glyphs of sound and light geometry frequently come and go from the Earth plane. They are one way that communication between life forms is gently being introduced. The glyphs do more than a ship landing with strange beings saying, "Hey, we are here. Let us give you the scoop." They confound your scientific community and make them look foolish, which is absolutely necessary—with humor, of course. Your scientists are in a rut, and it is time for humanity to question everything. In particular, it is time to question those who claim to have all the answers. Realities are merging, and Earth is hostess to many unusual events as the ancient sacred sites, the calendars, and the libraries in stone speak. The crop circles act as a herald and accelerator, announcing with intricate and elegant simplicity, "The paradigm shift is upon you."

Geometry and mathematics, coupled with planetary and star knowledge, are the basis for the construction of dimensional doorways. Knossos on the island of Crete, Stonehenge, the Great Pyramid, the Acropolis, Delphi, Machu Picchu, Tiahuanaco, and many others serve as doorways to other dimensions. These structures, built through the use of sacred geometry, totally confound present-day science.

Light can create certain distortions in realities, and in order to work with light one must bend geometry. What is missing in modern-day architecture is the combination of light and geometry. In other words, the influence of light on the third-dimensional form is not taken into consideration. Your buildings collapse because light is not factored in when they are built. After a while they erode or are destroyed, even if there is no war going on.

There is a mental distortion that prevents geometric structures from anchoring themselves more permanently on this plane of existence. Because your human capabilities are incomplete as linked through your DNA, you cannot mentally assist a structure in maintaining itself into being. All influences, both inner and outer, must be factored in. The elements of earth, air, fire, and water are as crucial to consider as the element of human thought.

Geometry conveys its own teaching as it manifests into physical form. It has an impact, and there is an instant transmission of energy from the forms of geometry into the physical body. This is a gift of the gods to the humans in order to create a higher ideal. The geometry of the gods is transduced into a geometry that exists in third-dimensional form. Shape and size radiate the essence of sacred geometry, creating knowledge transmitted from dimension to dimension.

Perhaps you do not realize that you yourselves have different physical shapes. For example, dolphins are another version of humans. Dolphins exist not only in water, but on land and in the air; they exist in many dimensions at once. A joyous nature is one of their most outstanding characteristics. It arises from a very highly evolved consciousness that knows it is never destroyed, a consciousness that has a deep bonding with its human counterpart who has forgotten and believes that it *is* destroyed. Dolphins and whales create specific sound vibrations to hold your planet together. Like you, these creatures are descendants of ancient beings from the stars, and they are here to transfer to you, the people, the ancient wisdom and truths for maintaining and loving your planet.

Dolphins and whales are members of the Family of Light, and for eons they have carried frequencies from some of your ancient civilizations. The dolphins of your Atlantean culture were coded before the demise of that civilization and were given much information to retain and pass on genetically and telepathically. They are presently transmitting that information to the human species. They are also giving you a message that is clear: Their quality of life is in question, and if *their* quality of life is in question, *so is yours.* They are a mirror for you at this time.

Dolphins are leaving your planet in great numbers. Not only do they beach themselves upon your shores, they also catch themselves purposely in the fishing nets. Dolphins are very smart creatures; they are not victims. They are leaving the planet to you because it is time for you to take stewardship. Animals trust themselves and know that they simply change form when they die. They know there is a new world forming, so many of the species that are becoming "extinct" are actually moving through dimensional frequencies and advancing onto a new Earth as the old Earth is dying.

Countless numbers of you seek to swim with the dolphins because you respond to an inner coding that creates a new vibrational frequency as a result of your contact with the dolphins. This frequency connects you with your heritage and your right to know who you are.

It has not always been easy for assistance to come to Earth. Yet, by hook or by crook, there have been energies from the stars who have seeded various cultures, offering teachings to the biogenetically rearranged humans and encoding them with light for the purpose of holding fragments of knowledge upon the planet for 500 or 5,000 or even 10,000 years. When each civilization was finished, its artifacts were passed on or submerged into Earth. Each civilization that held a vestige of light always, in some way, created arti-facts that told stories. These artifacts were sequestered for epochs of time, to emerge only when they could be properly interpreted.

Earth stores many remnants of civilizations, some of which spring from a point you would call the future. Your "now" can be seeded and influenced from many directions. Some of the so-called "foundation stones" of your current world beliefs are not remnants from the past. Distortions can be constructed in the future to plant in the now and appear as if they came from a point a long time gone. Planted arti-facts can purposely divert you from understanding the iden-tities of "invisible" rulers that you perhaps call gods.

If you can reach the point of understanding that the material realm is a symbolic representation and not get lost in hoarding, then there are many magnificent artifacts that can reappear. Your planet has numerous changes to go through over the next twenty years, and these ancient artifacts laden with coded knowledge will begin to reemerge. At the end of these times, in December 2012, as decreed by the Mayan cal-endar, there will be an anchoring of many dimensions. This will reveal the mystery behind existence, and it will be as if Earth suddenly blossoms overnight, even after some portions are seemingly destroyed.

You may have visions of these happenings. People will be drawn to specific places and will see forms appear. Perhaps no one else will see the artifacts because a particular aware-ness is necessary to pull them into this dimension. In order to be completely anchored in third-dimensional reality, there will have to be an agreement by the mass consciousness to call this kind of energy into existence once again—to wel-come it back by showing that you have respect for Earth. As you learn to value your home, her mysteries will continue to unfold and fill you with awe.

Various cultures have left their imprints all over the world, permeating and peddling their vibrations through language and sound, as well as by artifacts of stone and gold. In the United States, there is an influence from Greek civilizations, particularly on the eastern seaboard. The state of Rhode Island, for example, is a land unto itself that parallels the history of Rhodes. Syracuse, Ithaca, and Utica are ancient Grecian names, and there are many Spartas and Athenses. Names carry an imprint of influence that will come alive and convey more meaning as your inner and outer knowledge unfolds.

There were codes of conduct by which people lived in ancient times. In Delphi, to "know thyself" was considered a key to living. Knowing thyself embodied the concept of going within and exploring versions of the multidimensional self, discovering questions and answers and access to other worlds. The codes of conduct concluded that you were to take nothing in excess, and that you were to always show respect and properly value what was around you. Today, you are pushed to consider codes of conduct and communication in order to reestablish a world in which all things are significant. Your uniqueness lies in your diversity and the innumerable ways in which you, as humans, have sought to experience and interpret reality.

Tibetans understand many of Earth's cosmic keys. There is a portal in Tibet, a huge energetic opening. When visitors wish to come to your house, they can come through the window; however, it really is easier for them to enter through the door. Planets also have doors through which you enter. Portals are composed of corridors of time. So, when you enter a planet, how do you know which era you will end up in when all time is simultaneous? The ability to locate events in time takes great mastery of self within the moment, and it is no easy task to perform. The Tibetans, basically up until the 1950s, diligently maintained an energy doorway. Over hundreds of years, they have acted as guardians and emissaries for those who ventured through.

The Tibetans have been working with extraterrestrials for

eons. At one time, the region known as the Himalayas was at sea level. Under the mountains of Tibet there are huge veins of gold and caves filled with crystals. There are artifacts stored there that indicate the ancientness of civilization. Included are many physical bodies that have been preserved. The Tibetans had a predilection for preservation just as the Egyptians did, only they had a different method involving gold. The Egyptians employed the mummification process, which involved memory from Atlantean times when people were rejuvenated and restored if their DNA was intact. This possibility is currently being rediscovered and applied today.

The ancient Tibetans did something different. They were not looking to rejuvenate the body so much as preserve and maintain the frequency of consciousness that the body had achieved in a given lifetime. They would mummify—we use that term loosely—the body in gold, outside and inside. It was a complex process that took many months to complete. If a person achieved a rare state of consciousness and maintained this frequency throughout life, then, when that lifetime was completing, a summons appeared, requesting the person's retreat deep into the formidable mountains. Called by the masters, the person sat and awaited the time of death in a certain position. When death came and the spirit evacuated the body, couriers immediately began a procedure to preserve the body, layering it with gold to stabilize and hold the rare frequencies of consciousness that were prized above all things. Hundreds of these "statues" exist underneath the mountains of Tibet. Today, those privy to this information understand that they can blend with these preserved vibrations and access particular frequencies of consciousness.

One of the greatest Mayan secrets was their hidden gold caches and their understanding of how gold functioned. The Maya were not foolish and did not flaunt their gold. They made it seem as if they did not need gold.

Gold is part of what allows dimensional doorways to be opened. It anchors portals and brings about transmutation, and is reserved for more than costumes, crowns, masks, and jewelry. It holds the highest vibration and is a premier conductor of electrical current. When gold is stored or created in great abundance, light portals can be opened and access to other dimensions unfolds.

The gold caches around the globe are not made to be spent or hoarded. They contain great secrets that are utilized to open doorways and anchor energy. There are huge veins and rivers of gold conducting frequencies throughout Earth that are an essential part of life. The ancient Egyptians believed that the veins of the gods were made of gold. Throughout medieval Europe, the pursuit of alchemical gold intrigued many a man and woman. Within Earth, gold is most often accompanied by quartz crystals, which are modern-day founding stones in all your communication devices. It is important to understand that gold is a cornerstone for civilizations. They are brought into being through the influence of this substance. Remember, in the ancient records of your race from Sumeria, stories are recorded of the gods who, tens and hundreds of thousands of years earlier, ventured here in search of gold.

The Maya had many secrets. The clues they left for the outside world were clues to lead you, deceive you, and trick you—to have the archaeologists see one thing and the spirit eyes see another. The true essence of many cultures is just beginning to be discovered. There are groups of government and university people who decipher codes and come up with new pieces of the past. They do not always pass their new views on to archaeologists because they may not want the public to know about the latest discoveries. An area closed down and off limits is often indicative of something going on. Remember, the codes of value and intent broadcast in your being will determine what will be discovered, deciphered, and understood.

Understanding the communication process, both inner and outer, is a key to a peaceful Earth. The inner you communicates continuously with a you that can be called your higher self, or your inner teacher. It is a version of you, invisible to your current perceptions, that nonetheless has a powerful influence. Your higher self is connected with a vista of reality in which there is a purpose to all you select to experience. Ideally, your higher self communicates this grander view to you by way of impulse, synchronicity, and emotion. It is up to *you* to translate your own messages and realize that, as you decree, reality conforms. This is shown to you by your higher self over and over again. In addition, you have your own thoughts, as feelings and beliefs, that are constantly broadcast in your field by the very essence and presence of you. As your psychic awareness increases, it becomes easier to know what someone is about because it is energized by their being. You are able to read energy as your communication skills expand to consider new ways in which to translate meaning.

A form of communication that can free you from the traditional interpretations is toning, the process of allowing sound to move through you, playing you like an instrument. Toning is a key to releasing stored knowledge. It unlocks a doorway and allows information to flood into your body.

We recommend that you have toning ceremonies for your crops and gardens. The plants feel what you do for them. If you walk in the garden and touch a tomato plant, it gives off a communique as its plant hormones fill the air waves and say to the life in the garden, "The tomato plant has been touched. Humans are here." All the plants know before you get to them that you are coming. Animals do the same thing. When you dedicate your toning to animals, plants, and Earth, you are reciprocated with phenomenal responses, reenergizing and realigning your connection to Earth as an intelligent being.

If you listen to Tibetan toning, you find that each person simultaneously makes a number of tones. The toners are able to carry a variety of tones and notes in one sound. These overtones tend to open and unlock energy doorways, changing your perceptions. Basically, this is what toning does—in a very subtle way, it changes your perceptions.

At a power site or energy vortex, you can tone with the intention of releasing energy that has been stored or trapped there, and you can tone to merge yourself with the site. When you tone, you create various vibratory rates. At sacred sites of stone, the sounds that you feel trigger data stored in the stones and in your bones. The stones work very well with your bones—the stones feed the bones and the bones feed the stones, sharing data.

In this age of information, you are steered away from the natural sources of gathering knowledge for yourself. You have been sold the idea that television is a great source of information. This so-called tool has been touted as one of the greatest inventions of this century. However, your media is owned and controlled by those who wish to keep you entertained and unaware. They peddle chosen versions of reality and completely ignore others. Television slows down your evolutionary process and limits you, especially as a young child. When you are young, early impressions and imagination play a key role in how your life unfolds. Television keeps you in a very narrow band of emotional expression—basically chaos and fear. Today, more than ever before, there exists a great campaign to sell televisions, to have free cable television, and to entice people to stay glued to the latest version of scandal and violence, as if what is broadcast is *the* most important issue at hand. Learn to observe how you feel if you watch television. It is a form of frequency control. This control is being tremendously accelerated as fear is rapidly being promoted all over the planet through television.

The large majority of people on Earth are being hypnotized by television right this moment. Our campaign encourages you to experience life *firsthand*—not only through the image making and ideas of others. You damage your own consciousness and the potential that your consciousness has when you give over your time to television. You suppress your imagination and do not use one of the greatest gifts you possess. It will be understood centuries from now how in the latter half of the twentieth century people were induced into dazed states and made to behave, to be asleep, and to be sick through television.

You are wasting your time with any kind of television watching. It keeps you from life and acts as a substitute for experience, which, dear friends, is the primary way you learn. Some of you may say, "Well, there are some good programs on, and I only watch educational shows." We ask you: What is being beamed over or under the "good programs" that you do not consciously see? If you insist on having a television in your home, keep it unplugged. Frequency waves are transmitted through your television even when you do not have it on. Have we made our point? Reconsider what you've learned about life and choose to listen to nature's broadcast—the voice of Earth as she speaks.

You are on assignment throughout all your days. It is what you have agreed to do as a part of your essence. You know you can expect things to get challenging, for this is how you learn, and no one said it was going to be easy or guaranteed that things would always be effortless. Perhaps you are beginning to understand the degree of commitment that is needed to transcend the boundaries of realities. As you approach those boundaries, you can feel what it is like to have your foot in one world, your finger in another, and your nose and toe in yet another. It is quite an unusual feeling to have the energies from many worlds meet in your physical body.

Joy, safety, harmony, and clarity are very fine words. Sometimes, in order to really understand a concept, you must go into its polarity, for in this world of light and dark, shadow defines light. So it is that we explore polarities with you. Remember, you always have choices, and the more you understand the various opinions and influences on Earth, the greater your choices become.

When you are on the journey to know yourself, there are many paradigms from which you will break free. These paradigms are like boundaries and fences that you had not realized surrounded you. Ask for a grand enhancement of your identity and learn what it is to feel expanded—to experience yourself on many levels of perception. Most of all, learn what it is to *trust the process*. Communicate your intent for being alive at this time and let Earth feel it. If, by chance, you are uncertain, then it is most definitely a priority to create a purpose and to believe in yourself. We cannot do this for you. Only you have the ultimate effect on Earth, your life, and your version of the illusion.

There are not too many manuals written about what you are doing. Many people feel as though they are tiptoeing through the land of strangeness. Well, there is a certain strangeness, along with an exhilaration and joy within the eccentricity. There is also a charisma that you carry and with which you vibrate.

You all know you are here for a reason, which is growing as you discover each other's talents. The puzzle pieces and threads are weaving a tapestry of meaning together. The story that is unfolding for yourselves is a story ahead of its time in many ways. You each desire to live a life of significance, to claim a territory of consciousness, to become adept within it, and to go where no one has been before. We would say you are on that course. Often, when you first begin a trek, you do not always understand all of the implications involved. On the trail to higher consciousness, you are in the midst of a deep undertaking, and you cannot yet see the path in totality.

The training that you are receiving is from your inner teacher. You have a blueprint inside you that leads to a different pathway. You learn by following what is awakening from within. You are here to create a new blueprint of possibility for the entire race. You will gain the greatest amount of knowledge through personal experience—through doing this on your own and not hanging your hat only in one place. We encourage you to seek many mirrors, to look under the rocks, to speak with insects. Acknowledge that there is something for you to learn in every event you encounter in your life. Every person, book, and piece of paper that you find in front of you, and every crumbled, dusty leaf at your fingertips, offers you some speck of knowledge that makes up the whole.

Keep yourself open. Intend with clarity that you are available to evolve into an arena that is brand new for the human species—an Earth that encompasses joy, safety, and harmony—and you will be taken there. Think new concepts of self, and of the importance of continuously intending, using your mind to bring about the experience of life.

We remind you that there will not be *one world*. There will not be a world in which everyone agrees on what is taking place. This is the time of the vast shift in consciousness, so each one of you will find yourself in a world of your own creation. When you hear stories of takeover, understand that for some people, yes, they may experience this. They will draw to themselves what they need to learn from. Just as you move down a buffet table and pick and choose what you want, know that you do the same in life. You always have a choice. *You* make all the difference in what you experience.

Let us say this: In your wildest dreaming, you cannot currently imagine where Earth is headed. The masses are entranced by a world of facts, encyclopedias, television, and newspapers, and the multidimensional anomalies have not yet penetrated your plane of existence too deeply. When they do, things beyond what you can conceive will begin to occur.

Energy Exercise

Relax your body and clear your mind. Imagine a pillar of light flowing through your body and sending light fibers into Earth. Picture these fibers being pulled down into Earth, moving through dirt and worms and other creatures, and passing through layers of soil, rock, water, minerals, crystals, and gold. Your fibers are going down very far. They are looking for a vein of gold, so continue to send them down until you feel that the taproot of your fibers has touched a vein of gold deep, deep in Earth—an ancient vein. Notice what it feels like. Gold transmits a certain frequency. It is very deeply connected with the force and vibration you describe as love, the connective energy that supports all things. The gold and crystals inside Earth move this consciousness through Earth like your veins move blood through your body. Many creatures know about these veins and use them.

Do a very low, deep toning into the fibers of light that extend into Earth. Rumble and stabilize the light, sending energy along the vein of gold so that it travels around a core layer of Earth. Know that your sound is going to stabilize something deep within the core of Earth. Even in her heart, Earth will always recognize you and know who you are.

Once you have stabilized the taproot, create a higher pitched toning to extend a dome of light above where you are. This dome is an umbrella of energy under which you are currently being inspired. Picture a violet-blue twilight tone inside the dome, which is being showered with white moonlight on the outside.

Everything that you think, you energize into form. So please, dear friend, free yourself from burdens and reimagine Earth as a splendid place within existence. See yourself dwelling in harmony amidst the splendor.

FOUR

Earth is Your Home

Understanding Earth and the secrets that lie within her involves mastering the riddles inside yourself, especially the portions that are hidden in the roots of your subconscious self.

As your journey continues, you will discover the roots of your human identity here on Earth, your chosen home. Soon you will realize that you share this home with a myriad of curious life forms aside from those you currently recognize and agree upon. Opportunity for enriched growth and personal enhancement will be found by exploring both your human roots and your stellar ancestry as they are stored, recorded, and *felt* here on Earth. At this point in time, we speak to you as a dweller on Earth whose genetic lineage is rich, vital, and intimately connected with many other realities. We remind you that there is far more to this home of yours than you have been taught. Be open to the story of your lineage—as collectives of race and culture, you have far more in common than you suppose.

As a journeying entity, you were called and impulsed to explore Earth as a place within this solar system that serves to stage life and is a home for ancestral codes. We have referred to Earth as the Living Library, a biogenetic center where vast quantities of data are stored as incomparable translations and tools for the creation of life. This data exists in patterns beyond what you can fathom at this time. Earth is a birth house where life is created and experienced. Traditionally, parenting on your planet has to do with a biological process in which two people of opposite gender come together to create life. However, you are now experimenting with making life in laboratories, so you are challenged to expand and consider that perhaps there are different ways to parent and create life.

Recollect for a moment the idea that the Game Masters are parents of civilizations by means of conceptualization. They create and hold thoughtforms and then proceed to distribute untold plans to draw meaningful life onto their creation. They experience the web of existence as a force and field of unlimited awareness that is intelligent and responding. You may perhaps conceive of this as Prime Creator. Remember, we do our best to create stories from which you can evolve. We offer concepts for releasing yourself from invisible root assumptions, inherited as beliefs and manifested as unqueried facts. Please expand your concept of Earth. Earth is unique in existence because life can be manufactured here, which is one reason it is attractive. Perhaps you are aware of those who watch over your home and experience it as a place to visit and play with reality. This is your recognition of yourself. You are becoming aware of yourself as a Game Master, experiencing Earth as a native within your own creation. Recollect the concept of the Game Masters creating civilizations, then becoming immersed within their construct of reality—only to awaken to this knowledge.

Earth, in terms of time, is quite ancient, and there are stories concerning her that have long been buried and hidden away. The ancestral lineage currently revealing itself involves trigger points and events from approximately half-a-million years ago that proceeded to punctuate themselves throughout various experiences in time. Sumerian records hold numerous keys for expanding an understanding of your ancestral lineage. The records maintain that for eons a cast of celestial characters, with multiple agendas, graced the stage of Earth. These ancient records recall a time hundreds of thousands of years ago when two ruling brothers, Enki and Enlil, were in charge of the project Earth.

These visitors, called the Anunnaki, came to Earth from the heavens and played god. They created what they wanted on Earth, based on their own intentions. Among other things, they came in search of gold. Please understand there are many things here on Earth that can be taken and enhanced in the homes of others. Earth is home to many keys in the galaxies, and it is more than simply *your* home. You are the care-takers—those who dwell on Earth.

The visiting gods from above, the Anunnaki, came to Earth and began to take products from this home to their home. Their purpose was to experiment with life and create humans to dwell on Earth. These gods are your ancient parents, having seeded a version of Earth's genetic line with their influence. When you choose to dwell on Earth, you know that part of the program is to discover sovereignty and free will within a biogenetic cosmic experiment.

Numerous anthropological discoveries offer clues to your past through old skeletal forms. The forms depict a human album of change throughout the last few million years. These archaeological discoveries portray what your scientists call stages of human development or evolution, assuming that human life was the same everywhere. In actuality, gods created various experiments employing the genetic material stored here in the library. A prime characteristic of this particular area of existence is the exploration of what is possible. Most crucial for you to consider is the concept of the gods as parents. Consider who they are as well as who you are in relationship to the stellar energies that are asking to be recognized.

Understanding Earth and the secrets that lie within her involves mastering the riddles inside yourself, especially the portions that are hidden in the roots of your subconscious self. Objects of import can be hidden in the ground of Earth, as well as deep within layers of energy inside your being. Feel Earth as your home and act on making it a better place. Acknowledge that you, as a biological being, have the emotions, feelings, and intuitional knowledge that connect you to Earth. Your biology establishes roots that keep you connected with who you are. As you learn to tune into Earth, you will feel the changes transpiring. Earth is providing you with an opportunity to extend the knowledge of your roots and to connect to the very essence of life.

Where have you come from? Who are your creator parents? Who conceived of you, then made you? The Sumerians understood the visitors from the stars, who for hundreds of thousands of years influenced and played with experiments of life on each continent. Purposeful interaction and commerce between representative experiments was often limited. The gods changed their names and created new sounds as they moved from one continent to another, altering the biogenetics of life to see what could be done. The gods watched and participated with their creations on Earth, accruing their own lessons through the laws of cause and effect.

The Sumerian culture, considered by most experts to be the cradle of civilization, flourished about six thousand years ago in an area called Mesopotamia, located between the ancient waters of the Tigris and Euphrates rivers, in modern-day Iraq and Kuwait. This civilization was rediscovered in the last century. The area where it thrived is a political hot spot in late twentieth-century Earth, where war and many disruptions of power and value of life persist. The Sumerian culture was directed by those who came from the stars—the stellar reptilian ancestors. They were establishing a civilization once again, creating one more experiment to look at what could be done with the biological forces of Earth.

Ancient myths and legends hundreds of thousands of years old tell of the serpents, dragons, and reptilian visitors from the skies. For eons these creation stories were conveyed orally through the generations. Momentous events were recalled through the spoken word and passed down to groups of people gathered to hear or see dramatizations of the ancestors. Much later, the special moments were captured by the Sumerians on their famous cylinder seals, devices that recorded selected aspects of reality in pictorial form. Today, these seals furnish clues to significant symbols. The symbols are depicted as artifacts on cylinder seals, though actually they are keys in form, revealing another language of intent.

Cultures all over the planet carried inner truths that are not spread to the masses. This was done to gain power over others. The gods kept themselves in power by authorizing a few, rather than empowering all. This created a hierarchy of separation, which is part of the great misunderstanding that continues to plague you today.

People all over your planet—including Aborigines, Maya, Incas, natives of North and South America, groups on the European continent and throughout Africa and Asia—all embrace the idea of dragons or serpents as the creators of life. Dragons could breathe fire, and though some were feared, others were credited with bringing power, prosperity, and life. Over time, myths and stories were changed and rewritten according to who was in charge and what purpose was desired. You can understand the nature of these mythical beings by looking at these tales to see whether they conveyed a sense of power to the people or implied that the few had power over the many.

Imagine yourself living in a vastness of time in which years in your terms are mere moments. What would you do to occupy yourself? What kind of virtual realities would you create to peek into now and again? If you had the ability to access the keys of genetics and to make life, what would you, as a human, do with that much freedom, spare time, and knowledge?

The reptilian race, or Lizzies as we affectionately call

them, are an integral part of your ancestral line. They are an awesome, ferocious, and gracious collection of consciousness, for they are many things combined into one. These reptilians are important for you to understand as aspects of existence that connect you to the deep taproot of your own heritage, your past. In order to grow further into understanding yourself as a blossoming entity on the wheel of life unfolding into the story of twelve, it is essential that you understand your home, your roots, and your genes.

Understand that the reptilian energies are creator gods. They are master geneticists who assisted the Original Planners in designing the Living Library. They are an ancient race and are very advanced in creating sentient biological forms. They were some of the prime instigators in putting together the human species on this planet. They learned their craft from the ancient ones. As master geneticists, Lizzies know their trade; they are highly skilled in genetic organization and manipulation. They far surpass many brilliant beings in their ability to genetically adjust life. So, in the vastness of existence, the reptilian families are known to be creators and are responsible for organizing the genetic structure of life forms.

These ideas offer you something to feel, dear friends. As you contemplate this subject, search out the branches of your ancestral tree. Consider the journey through the reptilian family as a key to take you deeper into your roots. Reptilian influence lies at the core of your biological structuring, and today these creatures are returning to your conscious awareness. They appear as toys and characters in movies and on television, as stylish depictions in advertisements, lending their name to all who dare remember. They spring forth from the subconscious as a part of the self that needs to be expressed and understood, loved, healed, integrated, and accepted. Your spiritual and biological selves hold the key to this process.

At one time, far back in its own history, the reptilian family was a very benevolent and uplifting race. Members of this family came to Earth and were deeply involved with creating the Living Library. However, they eventually created civil war among themselves and amongst other representatives of the creator god collection. The wars were all based on separation from each other to gain power. Remember, part of your journey as evolving humans is to understand that you are separate, unique, classic human creatures with free will. You are discovering other separate, uniquely classic creatures with free will and realizing that you are all one. It is time to acknowledge the vast uniqueness of intelligence, as untold creatures reveal themselves to your world, stripping away the barriers to inner truths.

The ancient reptilian ancestors, once they are recognized and acknowledged as beings in existence, can be freed by you from the role they have been playing. You are multidimensional creatures, and one version of yourselves is this one on Earth as human beings. Simultaneously, in another version of reality, you can also be these very beings that have influenced you. You can move into and experience an identity where you are these creatures and feel their dilemma, their restriction within their own paradigm. As your beliefs about yourselves and your own home are altered, leading to a new sovereignty, you affect your roots in all directions—past, present, and future. You are intimately linked to the vast web of existence, and as you change, the significance of your thoughts sends new impulses through the web as possibilities to all aspects of existence.

As Pleiadians, we hold a broader view of reality than you currently do, and we are here to share it with you. We have an open ticket—a gold card into a Renaissance Fair taking place throughout the cosmos. We can tell you what we see. You often think that what we convey is the whole fair, when what we share are simply the quirks and corners of an immense event, emphasizing particularly curious and significant areas. You do not understand that this is one big "now."

Chaos and free will may seem to rule, and yet through this very process energies are scrambled and then reconnected to experience the innate value and inevitable cooperation of life.

Remember, we do not intend to overdefine your reality. We intend to convey key vista points where you can stop and take in good views. Looking at the biological aspect of existence will help you comprehend the scenery ahead. On your inner tour of your family tree, the reptilian consciousness as a branch of your ancestral line is well worth acknowledging. Without it, a loop of experience as a stage of development is missing in assisting you to understand your roots, where you are going, and what you have come from. For some of you, the idea of a reptilian heritage carries quite a charge of fear. This fear has actually been put upon you so you would not discover where you have sprung from. For ages, your reptilian ancestral line has had a need to keep itself from your conscious mind. There has been many a detour in thought and reality seeding by the so-called invisible influences that share your world. Today, reptilian memories surface from your subconscious self as dreams, vague ideas, symbols, and past-life scenarios—all essential links to patterns of human behavior.

Memories are buried in your cells, and you are not quite sure what's there. *Feel* your body and imagine your spinal column, chakras, and twelve strands of DNA as a tree of life growing upward. At the bottom of the tree there is a serpent, like a taproot connecting you to Earth. Imagery will help you get in touch with your reptilian ancestry so you can have a neutral look without labeling anything. Visualize the serpent energy climbing your tree, rising up your body, electrifying you. As a member of the reptilian family, serpent images trigger cellular memories of the gods who made you, showing you that you sprang from the serpent and that the serpent brings you life.

Clues and indications of reptilian ancestry abound. Carved and formed in stone, they can been seen as symbols at numerous sacred sites and at places along the great ley lines of Earth. Serpent, dragon, and reptilian myths and legends lie at the core of the intimate understandings and principal teachings of almost every indigenous culture. The serpent, reptile, and dragon portray powerful influences as totems. Often misunderstood, they are revered nonetheless as ritual symbols that acknowledge power and where people have come from. In the modern world, your medical profession uses the caduceus, an ancient symbol depicting intertwining serpents around a staff as an indication of the roots of its heritage.

Sometimes the ancient reptiles that your myths call dragons hoarded crystals. Crystals are senders and receivers of information. Many of the highest civilizations were anchored by reptilian energies who had access to the human blueprint and carried this human blueprint from another system into this one. The reptiles did this by bringing a tremendous amount of crystalline energy and hoarding, collecting, and storing it inside lairs or caves as underground bases of operation. Then they sent versions of themselves to the outside world as their representatives, very often in the form of snakes. It was the only way they could enter the outside world without being harmed. If they had come out in their dragon nature, the consciousness of the existing humans at the time could not have withstood the encounter.

Today you are exploring wider points of view and grander belief systems. As you consider reality, it begins to bend in your direction. The vitality of Earth is waiting to be discovered by you. She can provide you with a greater abundance in life if you can understand who she is. She can be thought of as the Mother Goddess—as an aspect of existence that provides, nurtures, feeds, and nestles you. She is your home and your mother, the source from which you have come.

Imagine yourself unbounded, with an opportunity at every turn, and this is what you will create. Set up limitations, and you will find them. Remember, you effortlessly attract the energies that support your version of life. Every moment that you believe in yourself creates momentum through which you will continuously blossom light and brilliant alternatives of living. This process involves growing into the recognition of yourself as an equal to your stellar family.

Many people would like to abandon Earth at this time, as if she is no longer a worthy place to live. Angry voices don't like the conditions of the cities or the water, as if the Earth herself created these conditions. We would say to you: What better place would you find? Your home is what you make of it.

Without the cooperation of Earth, there are many things you cannot have. Unpredictable weather patterns have become the norm; flash floods and surprising events appear out of nowhere. Reality can no longer be charted as reliable and consistent. As a human, a reoccurring theme throughout the events in your life is your sense of irresponsibility and victimhood. You repeatedly return to the core assumption of human powerlessness. You have accepted beliefs of victimhood and powerlessness for far too long.

Make a commitment to Earth to open your heart and transform your home. It is crucial to shift your consciousness into the domain of responsible living. You scurry over Earth's surface, waiting for what is owed you next in the form of monies, goods, and services, forgetting that the cooperation of Earth as a stable, reliable place to live is essential. Your challenge within the global blueprint of intent is to realize that Earth is alive and that you must take care of her and get along as a family.

The reenactment of lessons for responsible living will accelerate in the theaters of human drama, returning with an encore of what you have set into motion. If you do not like where you dwell, then reevaluate and speak to Earth with all your heart. Speak with the cells of your being, pull light through you, and say to Earth, "It is my intention and my pleasure to experience you to the fullest of my capacity in this lifetime. I am asking you, great Earth, to help and assist me in locating a place of comfort, joy, safety, and adventure— a place where I can come to know myself and to know you as home." Earth knows who you are. Therefore, it is a good idea to speak to her and acknowledge her.

Many of you are very disturbed by the masses of people that continue to choose to kill and go to war. We remind you that those who believe in this experience will create it and seek it out. You can exist in a parallel reality simultaneously with this and not attract it to yourself. There is a great cleansing that is occurring, and you cannot stop it. The energy of Earth is being sped up so that those energies with which you vibrate in the core of your being, and those truths you discover from your ancestral line, you will manifest forward. It is a traumatic time because it seems as if the systems that represent family and civilization are falling apart. Those systems that do not work are indeed falling apart, and you will be rattled to the core of your being to find something that *will* work and that values Earth. If you cannot take care of your home then perhaps you do not deserve one.

You have in your world numerous systems that support taking care of others. Caretaking is a noble process indeed. Often, though, if you continue to catch fish for others, they become dependent on your fishing. It is best to teach others how to fish for themselves and how to garden and grow food. Often those who continue to take care of others get caught up in the role of providing, and mistake this for their identity and purpose. The gods, your ancestors, to a certain degree got trapped in this. They became empowered in their own game as their creations adored and existed for them. But the gods eventually found that they were trapped, that they could go no further. It is best to give away what you discover—to enhance the environment of Earth and the family of humankind.

We refer to Earth as a home, a place that you need to commit to. Remember, it is a home for many beings. You share your reality with forms of life that you have yet to meet. This is part of Earth's revelation to you: How many parallel dimensions exist within the same space as you? Who are the energies or entities that can move through these dimensions? Many of the myths and legends that are dismissed because there is no validation for them are the true stories of your home.

Earth is a priceless jewel, and you are considered by many to be the integral key to this gem. Yet, in your own misguided sense of purpose, you have sought to exalt the self without honoring the stage from which you can explore life. Conflicts exist within the mass consciousness as to what the priority is today. Many people will lose and/or give up their homes in the next few years, bringing you closer together so that you may experience humanity as one big family. When you unite, perhaps through challenging situations, you also will understand those who have been outside your family. These other forms of life, who are waiting to be integrated as the dimensions open up, will reveal the immense creativity and variety of reality.

The teaching of Earth is ready to unfold to you because you are now at the pivotal stage of understanding it. You are redefining your home, and this is sensed by Earth. She releases her codes and stories, knowing, "Ah, there are humans who are seeking what I have." Think about what you want. Earth reads you. She is a living, biological entity. She is alive.

Earth needs you in the same way that you need the billions of bacteria that live inside your body, performing functions that operate without your conscious directive. One isolated microorganism could be quite toxic. However, together they know what to do. They don't poison you; they eat everything so that you do not die. If they were not inside you, the food you eat would not pass through you. You tolerate these so-called toxic beings that live in you and, actually, you can't live without them. In the same fashion, Earth cannot live without you and all of life.

It is here on Earth where life is made. In this solar system, Earth is the home of life, the grand laboratory where life is created. Please understand the purpose of loving Earth, for her response will be to release to you everything that you need to be at home here.

Imagine Earth restored to her regal beauty. Stately trees seem to brush the deep blue sky, and clouds billow to form majestic peaks. The songs of the birds fill the air, creating symphony upon symphony, each one orchestrated for the moment.

Learn to feel alive. Discover meaning to your life as you explore the aspect that is stored away as your subconscious self. Send your taproot like a serpent into Earth's records and call back to your mind a majestic Earth as a home for you, the rightful dweller in this place.

Energy Exercise

Take a deep breath and send a wave of vitality and relaxation through your body, creating space. Use the breath to create a vehicle on which you can travel into your imagination. Find the place that you enter inside yourself that is imagination. Picture your world suspended in space, a beautiful jewel, reflecting and radiating light. Feel your connection to space from your heart, from the very essence of your being. Feel that this place is home. If you were traveling across the parsecs of space, you would get excited as you recognized that you were in your neighborhood.

From your heart, send out a great beam of radiated love that has light. Send it out to Earth. Then let yourself be drawn to Earth as if you are skydiving from the depths of space, drifting closer and closer to Earth. As she grows in stature and size, feel her magnitude and feel that she is alive—that she has a vitality and a power that is unnameable, yet her gentleness and vastness are open to all.

As you feel yourself being pulled toward Earth, allow her vibration to draw you from space. Imagine yourself landing like a feather, gently gliding down to the most ideal spot. On a gentle glide, like a feather, land in the softness of Earth's vibration.

Look around you now, to see where on Earth you landed. What does Earth show you about where she calls you to be? In this imagining, feel yourself grateful and excited that Earth speaks to you and offers you an adventure. Take a deep breath, look around, and feel inspired by what you have found. Send a message to Earth that you are available for a peaceful life, and that your intent at this time is to restore the integrity of Earth and to live close and honor her in all the days that you dwell here. See yourself living, loving, and trusting, walking the surface of Earth in great peace with all of the elements of existence in accordance with your intention of harmony. Now begin walking very slowly, surveying Earth, taking a deep breath and feeling what it is to truly be alive and love your home. Feel this gratitude, for it will sustain you. Trust yourself. Earth is your home.

FIVE

Galvanization of the Goddess

*Embracing the Goddess will open the Living Library to you
and teach you the secrets held deep within the bosom of Mother
Earth, for who is the Earth Mother if not the Goddess herself?*

When you think of Prime Creator, what or whom do you
picture? In your society, you have been taught that the god
energy represents the source and that the feminine energy
represents the use or activity of it. We would say it is the
other way around—the feminine represents the source and
the masculine represents how the source is used.

It is true that Prime Creator is a female vibration. The
Source, as we know it, is a feminine vibration. The consorts
of this feminine principle, the male vibration, in competition
for love of the Goddess, began splintering off in a misuse of
energy millions of years ago. You are one fragmented part of
that misuse of energy. Two Pleiadian sons of a mediocre god
took over Earth, had a battle between themselves, and created the present-day dilemma. In the larger picture, it was a
minor family squabble. The divine Mother Goddess fragmented and made herself into many forms to be the consort
of numerous gods. They wanted to appease and love and be
in this vibration of the mother, because this is where all of the
creative vital forces came from.

The Goddess is of such consciousness that she allows all things. She is the source that holds things together, the glue of creation. It is a difficult concept for some to absorb, let alone consider. It is a difficult concept for women to think of an empowered entity that courses through their own blood in a likeness to themselves. It is shocking for men to think that perhaps a female vibration could be the source behind all things.

Feel in the deepest core of your identity the nurturing, the gift, and the mystery of the mother. There will be a return and an awakening to Mother Goddess energy. You will find in this decade that all of your religions are based on a false ideal. They are all based on a controlling, cold-hearted, patriarchal movement, when in actuality it is the Mother Goddess who is behind all things. We in the Pleiades have discovered the root cause of our misuse of energy: We have not honored the mother. We have done things to gain the attention of the mother, yet we have not valued the mother's creation, the mother's gift.

Your planet must learn who the Goddess is as a creator. You must. Understanding the dark side of the Goddess is part of exploring her energy, because the Goddess did something to lose her power. It is in the cells of your being because all of you, man and woman alike, have the Goddess within you.

The Goddess is going to be birthed through you, whether you are male or female. There was a decline and fall of the Goddess for very important reasons. The Goddess energy always acknowledged the rights of fertility. The Goddess energy was not like your Western world; to her, sex was not shameful. The Goddess loved sex. Sex, of course, is your natural heritage. However, like all things, there was a misuse of sexual energy.

There came a time within the Goddess realm when there was a tremendous abuse of the male vibration. Women, influenced by outside sources, lost their honoring and partnership with men, and their sense of unity between man and woman. After a while, within the realm of the Goddess, men became nothing more than a stud service. Women got so lost in the Goddess power that the men were not considered equal. Men were considered to be objects to bring about the rights of fertility. Many men were killed after one-time fertility rituals with representatives of the local Goddess. Castration and other sacrifices were performed. It is true. Women misused the sexual energy of men, creating the current backlash. This is all changing, and you will find the Goddess, with compassion, entering the lives of those willing to feel.

The Goddess energy was infused at one time with a tremendous negative force and became distorted in its purpose. This was in pre-Christian times. Then, the pendulum swung the other way, so that when the male vibrations began to play their role, they acted out with vehemence in response to what some of the females had done. Your memories are stored in your cells and blood, and you determined your experience by the choices you made.

You have been overlaid with a negative, controlling Godlike energy, and it is time for the Goddess to be acknowledged. There is a balance that is needed, with no worship of one vibration over the other. Men, in honoring the Goddess, will learn to honor life. Women will learn to redefine how they bring life into being. Life can come in with one heck of an orgasm at childbirth. This is an area in which you are going to restructure your beliefs and experience.

When you explore the Goddess, you begin to value life. When you value life, you don't overpopulate Earth, and you don't kill. What must come to the forefront of the world's paradigm is an understanding of what life is, what death is, what all species are, and the fact that everything is interconnected—that everything is connected to the same source.

The patriarchal movement changed your history, banishing the Goddess to the whisperings of myth and legend. Where is the Goddess in your Bible, your Koran, your Torah?

The battle between the Goddess and the patriarchy has been ongoing, and today you are so removed from the energy of the Goddess that you do not even have an image or role model before you as to who the Goddess can be. What Western society do you know that honors the Goddess? Yet, the very gateway to the East Coast of the United States is represented by a gallant woman holding a light.

The Goddess is very generous. She has remained behind the scenes in this battle of the patriarchy because she knows she is the creative force in all things and that all things must eventually find her. In her generosity, she allows. What does it mean to give birth, to love what you have created, and to allow that creation its process of evolution without interference? Is love protective or is love allowing? If a divine force was protective of its creations, it would control what it learns from its creations and therefore could only learn so much—based on what that allows. A force that allows all things has the opportunity to learn in unlimited ways because it has this ability to say, "Show me. Teach me. I am you. You are me." This is a state of consciousness.

We would like each of you to get to know the Goddess. Make it your quest to call the Goddess to yourself in some way. Invite the Goddess to teach you about life. She will begin working with you in ways that are quite profound. Many of you have called us, the Pleiadians, into your life. We play with you, and you know our vibration, our humor, our tricks—even we work with the Goddess.

Things must change. The Goddess is indeed orchestrating events as part of the solution. Goddess energy works with your heart to keep it open. We ask you to keep your heart open, not only for yourself, but for those whose paths cross yours at this time of great lessons. If you honor the feminine principle within yourself and on the planet, this recognition will serve as the new foundation for your communities and civilizations.

We want you to look for that life force. Look beyond what you have been taught. Find that portion of the Goddess, the feminine energy that is in man and woman alike, that is waiting to be birthed. Playfully observe how you can affect others and how they will talk about the things you are discovering. Everything you are learning will be magnified and telepathed quite loudly to those who are sharing this journey with you.

The Mother Goddess represents the love principle. We have mentioned the frequency of light—light being information—and the frequency of love, enlisting creation. The deepest underside of Pleiadian information is its sensuality and sexuality—its creation through the love vibration with the Goddess. Working with the Goddess energy requires a deeper exploration of the feminine principle.

It is time for women's knowledge to be spoken, shown, and shared in a magical, mystical way. It is time for women to discover more about their own mysteries—their processes of menstruation and birth and the cycles of their emotions. It is time to share this with men. Many women say, "What can I share? I don't understand it myself." Well, it is time for you to go within to say, "What are these feelings I have? If I had to explain to someone else what it is to be a woman, what would I explain? What can I do to become more of a goddess in a woman's body—more of a magic maker?" The Goddess within is the one who knows—who takes information from one system into another.

As the decade progresses, there will be a marked increase in female teachers and leaders, for the Goddess embodies through her kind. This is not to say that the Goddess does not work with male vibrations, for men will also learn how to embody the Goddess. There is no discrimination with the Goddess, and there is no anger. The Goddess is a very allowing entity. She has allowed much to happen over the eons so that everyone could learn. Now the Goddess is calling for an honoring of what she allows to be created through the core mystery of the blood—through the very gift from her own womb.

The blood and its mysteries are key to understanding yourselves, your genetic line, and the Living Library itself. You are a part of all of your blood's journeying—backward and forward in time, so to speak. Your ancestors and predecessors can be accessed, felt, experienced, and affected with conscious attention placed on blood. As humans, you grow and nourish yourselves into being with the blood of your mothers. Through females, this rich and vital substance appears, as if by magic. To male and female alike, the bleeding of women has been acknowledged as both an act of power and a curse of shame and ridicule.

The blood is a living symbol, demonstrating cyclic evidence of your connection to the ancestors and the codes of consciousness stored within all beings. You are a genetic library, and catalogued in your essence of spirit are the archives of personal, planetary, and celestial experiences. These experiences avail themselves to you, in your third-dimensional form, through your blood.

Your blood is rich with stories. It is filled with patterns and designs of a geometric nature that reorganize themselves according to your state of consciousness and intent. In order to awaken to a new view of life, you must be willing to reconsider and make changes. Your thoughts are recorded by your blood. They are imprinted with a distinct font according to your feelings and then radiated outward for all worlds to read. You are the sum total of yourself in physical form because of your blood.

Within the bone caverns that serve as your skeletal structure, blood is produced. It is enriched or deprived according to your blueprint of intent, and is combined with your ability to decode life as a series of self-created lessons. Your blood can easily be enriched and restructured.

The way your blood can be altered and enriched is by

intention. Inside your brain are tiny particles like magnets that are affected by the rays of the sun. Great waves of energy and telepathic codes for civilizations are sent on cosmic highways from the Pleiades to your sun. Your sun transfers the energy to you and to the moon. The energies go into your cranium and are held through an electromagnetic process by these small magnets in your brain.

Bodywork can change the structure of your blood. As you align your consciousness to become more whole, your blood becomes more purified. It becomes something very, very sacred. Information is stored in stone and bone. The red blood cells are manufactured in the bone marrow. When you realign the bone, it starts to change what the bone does to the rest of the body. The realigned bone purifies the blood, creating a more accessible blood line, and sorting out the inner secrets of identity.

Often, women have been in disdain of their menstrual blood, rather than understanding it as the source of their power. The blood carries the genetic code, and because the Mother Goddess is the source of all things, this is where the code comes from. It is where the story is hidden. Menstrual blood can be used to nurture plant life, to mark Earth, and to let Earth know that the Goddess lives again. In general, women don't bleed into Earth anymore. Doing so is a direct transference of the energy of the Goddess. When women put their blood onto Earth, she is nurtured. Women have been told for eons that their blood is a curse, and they have become afraid of their own blood. They do not understand that it is their source and their power. As you let go of old taboos and work with menstrual blood, you will find that you have a different effect on the animals and plants of the Living Library.

Women, if you are still bleeding, become wise in honoring your body and your blood. Your blood is one of the highest sources of fertilization and territorial marking that you can call upon. Understanding the blood mysteries is key to connecting to the source of your power and deep inner knowledge.

You can mark the land where you live with your menstrual blood. You might start out with the cardinal points: north, south, east, and west. Then, over time, you can continue to imprint Earth, like a painter laying strokes on a canvas. You can dilute the blood with water, thereby increasing the amount. You can bless it, and use crystals to hold the vibration. This process is considered to be marking the Goddess territory. It will draw plants and animals that have a new vitality and that feel they are one with the Goddess.

In a number of your ancient stories, blood was used to ward off evil or make a statement of intent. Perhaps a door was marked with menstrual blood. No one would dare touch that door or those living behind it, because it was understood that the Goddess reigned there. In those ancient times the Goddess was still respected. It was understood that if you fooled with or disobeyed the Goddess, your work was not divine.

As you build and develop new communities, we suggest that women of all ages gather together and intend to understand the bleeding time and to share their power and knowledge as keys with men. Explore the blood mysteries as a natural process of community life. Your body, and its cycles, create the image of life. Power is a very important thing for you to comprehend. Think about the dynamics involved with a woman having a baby. She maintains a life force that creates movement and desires to be born. There is a mysterious power in that. So much power that the male vibration came to fear the process and the magic of birth. Because the male forgot how to bring birth onto the planet through his body, he became threatened by the power of the female. Men need to get used to the bleeding of women and support it. There will come a time when you will want to know about your lineage and the responsibility of appropriate and timely childbearing, because life is going to become very valuable.

The bleeding of women will become a very important part of community. As women gain understanding through this power, the Goddess is galvanized and returns to all of you.

If you want to have a fertile garden, the best garden in town, use your blood diluted with water. Your garden will flourish. You will find that your blood can accelerate the growth of food. It will accelerate many, many things. It is not a mistake that women bleed. It is one of the grandest gifts. It is the elixir of the gods.

Aboriginal women save their menstrual blood in pouches and use it to heal wounds. There are many things that women can do with their blood. Some of you don't like the idea that you are women. When your bleeding occurs, you find it an unpleasant, uncomfortable, painful, inconvenient time and experience. Men often have no idea what goes on, so it is an awkward time for them as well. In the days ahead, contact the Goddess, open your heart, and discover where the bleeding can take you and teach you, for within the bleeding process lie many of the keys to bringing the Goddess back onto the planet. There is a need to return to the sharing of power through partnership.

There are many more mysteries to unveil, unfold, and reinterpret. Some of you may be wondering why we are covering this subject. *It is very important.* If you are not interested in the Goddess energy and the mysteries of the blood, we will say to you that you will miss an integral part of life and will not understand what is occurring on the planet. If it turns you off, or if you think it is irrelevant, you are completely missing the point. This is one of the most powerful teachings that we can give you at this time to assist you in understanding what is coming. What you need to do completely and totally, as men and women, is honor the Goddess vibration that comes through your hearts and helps your hearts open.

Menstrual blood is highly oxygenated, the purest of

blood, and it carries decoded DNA. It is the oxygen that decodes those strands and allows the restructuring of the data. Your scientists are now playing with a third strand of DNA. They are learning how to build strands of DNA based on photon lights—fibers in the body that we call the light-encoded filaments.

The mystery of the blood has been subverted in your modern religions. Do you ever wonder about Christian communion? You are told to eat the body and drink the blood of Christ. What is the significance of that? If you were raised Christian, these are words that you heard over and over again: "This is my body. This is my blood." This ritual is a distortion. Taking the body and blood invites a sense of cannibalism and is based on an ancient and unhealed reptilian infusion.

A pathos of the planet is the tendency of the multitudes to be willing advocates for a cause without knowing what the cause is truly about. The era of ignorance is ending. You are coming into an era of blissful knowing. We strike a few key phrases, using sound, that mean something to your minds. Yet on another level, there is a language being spoken that is decoded by your bodies, just like the crop circles.

We want to add something else to the pot here. The moon influences the rhythms of Earth. Who is to say that it is not designed? The moon reigns over the flow of energy in the body in the same way that it governs the tides on your planet. It is a very powerful electromagnetic computer. If the moon affects the tides, it also affects the tides in your own bodies, the blood in your own bodies, and the hormones within the blood.

There have been different cycles on your planet, accompanied by swings of the pendulum. There was a long reign of the matriarchal energy on Earth. Then the patriarchal energy came into rulership and eradicated any indication of feminine leadership and knowledge. Feminine knowledge was only passed on in myth and legend, where the feminine was recognized as a participant and perceiver of life. She felt connected to the web of existence through the birthing process.

At one time there were forces of extraterrestrial intelligence that worked to activate feminine principles. This was done because of the feminine ability to bring life and to feel. That is where the female association with the moon came from. There was an influence from the moon, which transmitted a feminine energy program. The moon is like a big computer, so different beings and forms of intelligence can own the moon or have the ability to program the moon. There were beings who programmed the moon into a feminine cycle. That is remembered because it involved a loving, benevolent time. Then, of course, things changed.

The energy from the moon has been beaming electromagnetic frequencies onto Earth for eons now to maintain the two-stranded DNA. Don't get mad at the moon for doing this. There is nothing wrong with the moon. It is only broadcasting programs. The moon establishes a breeding program within females. This reproductive cycle creates the possibility of producing children much more often than the solar cycle.

Understand that the moon outlines your breeding program. However, as a species you can move into a new cycle for procreation. This will help stabilize the overpopulation running rampant on the planet. There are fears today of doubling the population of the United States in a very short period of time. You are already bursting at the seams. Over the next fifty years, there will be a different influence on the moon, and the moon's cycles will change the Earth cycles. Everything is going to change drastically. You have been available to breed every month. It involves a very different experiment if you are available to breed only once a year. The changes will alter the whole female cycle so that the rate of pregnancy changes. The current system does not work; you would destroy yourselves overproducing. At this stage of exploding world population, it does not serve you to be available for conception every lunar cycle.

For many centuries the midwife was considered to be the greatest enemy to the Christian religion because she could alleviate pain, she could tell other women about the mysteries of their bodies, and she understood herbs, a sacred part of the Living Library. The Christian religion became very patriarchal and afraid of the Goddess and women. They feared that female power took authority away from the church, and away from men.

The abortion issue has nothing to do with whether you can have an abortion or not. It is designed to keep people separated and confused over female energy. It is a plan against the Goddess to disempower women and have them think they have no choice; or, when choice is available, to have them think the choice is abortion. There are plans to confuse women about their bodies to a very large degree. This is fine. There is no problem, because each of you chooses the lessons you need to learn. You can open your hearts and send healing energy to people, inviting them into a state of expanded consciousness; however, you cannot make them change.

The energy of the Goddess is moving rapidly, ready to work with those of you who are willing to remember her call. Her instructions are to honor your bodies and Earth and your sexuality, because it is through this process that you are all created. We know that some of these ideas make you uncomfortable, and that is why we bring them up. Embrace the fullness of your bodies and of what needs to be done, and get on with it. Work together, play together.

Women, wake up and read the owner's manual of your bodies and discover that you own something valuable. Men, you own something of value as well, and this something called a body has cycles, rhythms, and patterns. It can do miraculous things.

It is a grand distortion of your identity to think that sex is only for procreation. It is a travesty that this has been taught. No one ever has to have a baby if she or he does not want to. Begin to think and feel in terms of influencing all of your body's functions, including conception. You can say, "I know that my thoughts and feelings control the functions of my body. I influence it, and when I'm ready to have a baby I will energize that. Otherwise, I am not available." This is a very freeing concept to consider.

If every woman on the planet really knew how much power she had, what do you think the patriarchy would do? Eons ago a version of the patriarchy became threatened by the power of the female. So women, in order to hide their power, doubted themselves so that men could take a stance and say, "Let us have a chance to run the world and see what it is like." The feminine force took a back seat. Women agreed to believe that they had the curse within their bodies and that bleeding was bad. Women doubted the very life force within themselves, and whether they had any influence over it.

It is not only women who are affected and controlled by the moon. Men are as well. You are birthed through the cycle of the woman, and your sexual cycles are imprinted by this process. Also, because the moon controls the tides, and the human body is some 90 percent water, the moon affects the tides within your bodies as well. Men can also feel and work with the fluctuations of their hormones as their bodies go through their cycles; they can learn to recognize the subtlety to male rhythms. Because of relentless pressure and control around men, these cycles are not as noticeable as those of women, which are marked outwardly with symbols like the blood. The male vibration is out of tune with spontaneity, and very much in alignment with obeying. Obeying what? Obeying ideas they embrace, without *feeling* the appropriateness of the beliefs or ideas.

We suggest more men question authority and say, "I'm not doing that. To heck with that. I'm doing this instead." The male vibration is currently impulsed to seek the same emotional freedom as women. Without your emotions, you cannot discover who you are. In order to understand the deeper mysteries, men must make peace with themselves and understand that their emotions are the feminine portion of themselves.

The blood is more mysterious to the male vibration because all of a man's blood is inside him. It is not something he can see and feel each month like a woman can. War is one of the distortions brought about by the patriarchy in an attempt to give males the power of blood. Yet, this blood is not the same. It is brought about by violence, by destroying life, by maiming and killing, with emotions or feelings stifled and suppressed. There is only one appropriate way for a man to take into himself the power of blood—and that is for a woman to gift him with her blood, to share her own elixir. There are many ways this can be done. For a man to eat fruits and vegetables grown with menstrual blood is one obvious way. Also, a man may be marked on the back of his neck or the soles of his feet with menstrual blood. His body will absorb the knowledge contained within it.

Men are going to need women's blood, and women are going to remember the Goddess inside themselves and embody the Goddess principle. This principle will teach you how to create a balance on the planet. It is our intention that each and every woman understand the mysteries of her body and share those mysteries with the appropriate male vibration, with no secrets. Sometimes men are afraid of women's blood. Often, a man is hesitant to engage in the act of sex with a woman when she is bleeding. For a woman, anxiety can exist over whether or not a man finds the presence of blood unpleasant. If you enjoy sex during bleeding, whether you are a man or a woman, congratulations, for you have overcome a deep imprint. You are sharing with another on a profound level of cellular connection.

Having sex during menses, in a bonded relationship, is a very powerful way of sharing blood. This is a very ancient ritual, and we do not advise any random sexual exploits to share menses blood. It is a sacred and powerful act. Why do you think there has been such a taboo? Why were you steered away from the blood mysteries for eons? Perhaps because it would open doors of knowledge that the gods did not wish you to have. Blood contains the archives of personal, planetary, and celestial experience. When blood is experienced in a sexual union, you are flooded with waves of knowledge, much of it beyond your present ability to understand and integrate. It may take years for the profound knowledge decoded in your body through blood to unfold.

The male counterpart of menses blood is, of course, sperm. Sperm, like computer chips, carries the code of intelligence for the evolution of consciousness. This is presently being measured by the degree to which the male vibration can remember and embrace the Goddess. It is the sperm that decides whether a child will be a male or female. The egg remains the same; the sperm makes these decisions. Sperm is the Mother's story encoded in the male vibration, and contains the interpretation of how the male remembers that story.

Can you conceive that sperm has a telepathic link with its owner? When a man has sex with a woman in her menses, his sperm can act as an explorer and telepath back to him the power and knowledge of the woman. During a woman's menses, a man can access the woman's full identity. Women, if you are going to have sex during menses, you must be ready to share the deepest secrets of who you are with your partner. You need to be ready to have your partner take on and share your power. It is the oldest mystery. In the Sumerian stories, the gods Enlil and Enki disputed with each other over the treatment and conditions of the subjects, the humans. The ruler Enki championed the humans and, through the female, gifted the race with sexual knowledge. The ruler Enlil strictly forbade sexual knowledge to the humans, for fear it would make them equal to the gods.

These concepts and invisible, cellular root assumptions refer to a modern-day version of the creation story—Adam and Eve, the serpent, and the Garden of Eden. Sexual knowledge was Enki's gift, while Enlil wanted to manipulate and separate the humans, to keep them from knowing the acts of the gods.

In women, blood is the vibration of the color red. In men, sperm is the vibration of the color white. Mixed together, blood and sperm are another elixir. It has been the worst heresy to even think that men would touch women who were menstruating, let alone have sex with them, let alone mix semen with their blood, let alone taste it. Yet, far back in ancient times, when the Goddess energy was understood, and when women were revered, this mixture was considered the drink of immortality for men. Men understood that when they drank menstrual blood, or mixed their sperm with it, they became enlivened and invigorated. It was one of the keys to immortality.

These gods (we call them gods loosely, and perhaps godlings and godlets would be better terms) became so enamored of the energy of the Goddess that they wanted to ingest the power in the combination of semen and the woman's blood. Remember that semen fertilizing an egg still uses blood. It uses it in many different ways. You all have this imprinting inside you. We bring it up because we want you to address this issue. We want you to remember the powerful nature of your bodies and to take your bodies beyond things that you have been ashamed of. Realize that many versions of authority have taken you completely away from understanding your greatest gifts—the vital forces of the white sperm and the red blood.

In the myth of the Garden of Eden, the female vibration was given the name Eve. She was not the first female, of course. It is the Goddess who makes life. Later the story was changed to make it appear that the male vibration had the ability to make life. In this version of creation, woman sprang from the rib of a man. This is not so. It is always the Goddess who knows the scoop on making life, because it is the Goddess who carries the blood.

The Bible relates the story of the Tree of Life and the Tree of Knowledge. The Tree of Knowledge allows you to be informed. Sexual ability and practice equate to the Tree of Knowledge, the tree that humans were forbidden to eat from. They were forbidden to participate as well with the Tree of Life.

What is the Tree of Life? Many think that the Tree of Life is something that grows a fruit. It is rumored that through ingesting this fruit of the Tree of Life you can gain immortality. In ancient times it was understood that this fruit was the blood of the Goddess. That was the fruit of the Tree of Life. Think of your body and your nervous system as a tree. The stories are not talking about fruits on trees, but to the fruits of the body—the secretions and substances that are indeed gifts of the gods. For eons, the gods have been steering you away from this knowledge.

To have sex with a woman when she is on her blood time is one of the highest vibrations because you go through doorways into other realms. To share the blood is to take on the higher consciousness. At one time these things were very "in" and were respected because people understood what was taking place. Remember, at one time the greatest enemy of the Christians was the midwife, because she could keep women in touch with their bodies and assist with the birthing process. When midwives were outlawed and abolished, women had to go to male doctors, who were not permitted for centuries to alleviate a woman's pain in childbirth. Do you know why? Because the ancient religious laws said that women must be punished for pursuing sexual freedom. This law was actually taken into the medical field. It is only in the last hundred years or so that women have been permitted to receive assistance of some kind during childbirth, and this assistance is patriarchal, not in most cases based on their own innate knowledge.

There was a tradition of fear around the misunderstanding of women's power. The fear about this mystery that women carry needs to be dissolved. This is the time of partnership; it is the time of relationship.

We wish to speak of menopause. Many women are saddened by the fact that, just as they are beginning to understand the power of their menses, they are no longer bleeders. However, menopause is also a time of great power for women. In ancient times, the crone was revered for her wisdom and magic, and this respect is returning. Menopause involves a deep infusion of energy, marking the time when a woman is able to hold her own wisdom—the connection with the ancestors.

When a woman goes through menopause, she experiences a pause. If she is able to hold onto that pause, something transforms inside and she comes into a place of wisdom. Throughout most of recent history, when a woman stopped her menses it was believed that she was to be feared, because she could now hold the blood and keep all its power.

Most women around age forty, and some women in their thirties, begin to decree their death by energizing the aging process. Women are steered away from their own natural cycles, and through their thoughts, hates, and cursings of their own bodies, they throw their bodies off balance. There is a complete misunderstanding of menopause that is similar to the misunderstanding that bleeding is a curse; everyone tends to adopt these misunderstandings. There is a great gift in menopause, and there is nothing that is lost at this time of life. It is a time of tremendous gain and flowering, the very opposite of what you have been told.

Often, men who have vasectomies fear their own sexual power and believe they have no control over their bodies.

The symbolic representation of vasectomies states their sense of powerlessness—that their sperm and penises do not do what they want. The fear of sperm creates a fear of the body. Those who have vasectomies also speed up difficulties with their prostates, for shutting off the flow of sperm creates difficulties in the body. We do not recommend vasectomy. We recommend that you learn how to use your bodies rather than condemning your bodies' functions and creating detours. Be open to a sense of wonder as you reconsider your sexual beliefs.

The Goddess has the ability to put her secrets into blood, because it is blood that creates. This is why women bleed, and why women have been steered away from honoring their bleeding. These are all pivotal things.

We want you as people to develop an intimate relationship with Mother Earth. How do you do this? The primary work of the Goddess involves relationship. This is how you grow. You do not always grow by being alone. You can think, "Oh, I have more peace and quiet when I'm alone. I have more time to study. I have more time to work with my self and to do the things I choose." Yes, and you have all the time in the world to avoid the growing that takes place when you are in relationship. It is important for all of you to develop relationships with one another. You need to be involved with people—in love and sexual partnership, through business and community, and with family, if not your blood family, then the Family of Light. You all carry codes inside your bodies, and you all need one another.

The Goddess energy is not necessarily something that you draw in like the pillar of light. When you imagine bringing light into your body and chakras, you are literally opening these areas. You are taking a stance on how you view yourself as a solid, dense being versus a being filled with space and light. The Goddess is a force beyond all of this. You do not have to pull the Goddess in through your fingers into your eyes and into Earth—the Goddess just *is*. Become aware of her vitality in the very nurturing of all systems, for the Goddess is the bringer of and maker of life.

To be alive is to know the Goddess. Look for this force in yourself, and in everything around you. Say, "Show me, Goddess, who you are. I want to meet you." When most of you thought of Prime Creator as a male personification, you had no problem. Now, to switch to female, some of you can't conceive of it. Life comes from the female vibration. Eve did not come out of the rib of Adam. That tale served to empower the male vibration, which desperately needed to have some kind of identity during the fighting of the Goddess culture.

We are seeking a balance. If you look around, you are male *and* female, and all stories of your identity and creation thread the truth of both forces together for you. When you seek balance inside yourself with male and female, *in the ideal* you will draw to yourself a partner who is balanced in the same way. Inner balance means that you are your own source and that your next step is to pool your source with another in order to feel and become a bigger source. Not that you necessarily need a mate. However, your natural process is to build something together—to put your keys together, as male and female aspects. These aspects correspond to physiological aspects that convey you into the spiritual and emotional realms.

Androgyny represents a divine aspect of the integrated male and female. Each of you have stored in you the vital force called kundalini, which is an expression of the energy of creation. A large majority of people on the planet, however, do not even understand that there is a force within them.

The ideal in all of this is to have the male and female balanced. As men and women, you have this vital kundalini force within you. It has its own natural cycle, with great peaks of activity. You must make room for this vital force within all of your bodies in order to meet the Goddess energy and create a healing, a transformation, and a realization. This energy is likened to the serpent and is stored at the base of your spine—as it climbs the tree of your spinal column, its energy is dispersed throughout your body.

We can't move, because you can't move. You can't move because we prevented you from evolving by genetically rearranging you. We did that so you would not have the abilities that we have and use them to usurp us. Now, half-a-million years later, we are in the big crunch. We know we made one heck of a big mistake, if there are mistakes to be made.

Shortly, you will discover your ability to create life and your ability to be gods. For forty years, your scientists have been pretending that they are gods as they have created life in underground laboratories as a reinactment of an Atlantian drama lesson. In the ideal, the infusion of the Goddess will reestablish moral value and the value of life, because the Goddess loves her children, including the reptiles, the insects, the cat people, and all forms of life. Then we will watch you and we will see if, as you create life, you limit it. Will you be afraid that the life you create will be greater than you? Will you want to forbid the life that you create to interact with the Tree of Knowledge and the Tree of Life? Or will you encourage the lives you create, which are your children—the future race of blue children—to grow, seek, and change, endowing them with everything that you know? If you do, they will teach you everything in return.

We did not realize in creating you that you had anything to teach us. You were slaves; you were diggers for gold. Some gods are still trapped in illusion. However, some of us are evolving, and this is thanks to those of you who are seeded here on Earth to help us with this momentous task.

Now you must transfer your remembering into the deepest of Earth's density to those who don't want to remember, those who have been trapped here seemingly forever through genetic alteration. All must understand and forgive the drama of the story. The galvanization of the Goddess will anchor in a tremendous sense of healing.

The Goddess, in her compassion, allows. Embracing the Goddess energy within yourselves will bring all of you to a new understanding and valuing of life and a new and deeper love for all of creation. Embracing the Goddess will open the Living Library to you and teach you the secrets held deep within the bosom of Mother Earth, for who is the Earth Mother if not the Goddess herself?

Energy Exercise

Take a few deep breaths, consciously following your breath in and out of your body. As you breathe in, imagine your lungs being filled with highly charged oxygen, swirling and twirling as molecules of light. Imagine your lungs absorbing these light particles and sending a wave of light into your bloodstream, energizing your entire body. Locate yourself in your mind's eye at the base of your spine. Picture this area and your entire skeletal form filled with light. See yourself microscopic in size, observing from within.

Now picture an opening to a dark and mysterious cave at the base of your spine. With courage, step forward and feel yourself walking deeper and deeper into the cave, knowing as you proceed that it is the home of a grand serpent. Feel yourself walking further in, step by step. It is completely dark, and you can feel the hairs on your body stand on end. You tingle as you are pulled into your cave of power.

Visualize a huge serpent giving off a steady hiss, its eyes glowing like green embers in the dark. Picture the jaws of the serpent opening. You walk as a glowing figure of light into the mouth of this reptile. As you walk deeper into the mouth of the serpent, which is another cave of yourself, feel what it is like to go to the very core of your own creative energy.

Now go into the belly of this serpent. This serpent is the

Mother Goddess. Go beyond her belly into the reproductive area and become an egg yourself, like a ball of light. Using your intention and will, thrust the serpent that has its lair of power in your first chakra out of the dark cave. Feel it begin to coil and release its power. Feel the shimmer and sliding of the scales, the coiling effect as the serpent unwinds itself and bursts upward from the base of your spine.

Now feel it climb upward. Feel this energy rise. Feel your kundalini on the rise and feel it moving up your body and out of your head. Feel this energy lift you upward, connecting you to the web of existence. Seek to call this energy and imagine it flowing up your spine—this serpent is your kundalini, your passion for life that is your version of the vital force of existence—the force through which you can feel connected and can create. Claim your inheritance and be uplifted.

SIX

Landing of the Light Body

You think you are flesh and bone when in actuality you are a combination of intelligent electromagnetic signals.

The evolution that you are now going through involves the process of building and integrating a light body. Your light body must be tempered, exercised, and stretched to gently bring it into its own awareness. Clarity concerning who you intend to be in your reality is one of the prime keys in building your light body.

Your light body knows that it creates through thought, and links you to the fabric of creation. Through your light body, timelines open, accessing multilayered dramas, and your challenges gather force as you face a seemingly uncharted, yet familiar territory. You are connected to all of existence, and your evolutionary leap is to make sense of this new awareness and put it to use in your now.

Rest assured, dear friends, that a higher order and purpose exists. Your task is to translate your purpose into your body and onto Earth. This purpose activates a reordering on many layers of existence—all sharing the same now. Pivotal to exploring various aspects of reality is the essential component of you taking a deeper look at your vehicle—your physical body.

Your light body holds the essence of your multidimensional identity, which is accessible to you through your desire to unite with the greater identity you sense you have. Your light body will be able to juggle realities through the shifting of your conscious intent from one view to another, like turning the channels of a television. Your light body holds encoded data. It translates body communications from worlds and realities through your physical body to you. Your task is to notice the subtleties and synchronicities that signal you. To understand yourself, envision a multilayered being, each part having a distinct body that breathes and is connected to the others. You are a physical, mental, emotional, spiritual being, connected by a body of light that radiates energy and links you to an infinite progression of light beings.

Matter is simply light that is trapped. As you build your light body, a reorganization of your molecular structure occurs, loosening your grip upon materialism in order that a spiritual understanding may guide your day-to-day life. It is only through spirit that you can gain any understanding of what is happening to your world. The building of your light body allows less trapped matter to combine as light and become you. This offers you freer expression and allows you to seek your source.

You will literally see changes in your body. It will become more vital, more beautiful, stronger, and more capable of performing events. It will become the processor of multitudes of information.

You must be able to operate with a higher electrical current inside your body. This will eventually bring about solutions to all of the mounting challenges you face. Increased energy inside yourself will activate hidden talents and trigger a renaissance of psychic abilities: clairvoyance, clairaudience, telepathy, and perceptual awareness that involves "knowing" far beyond what you can currently consider. When the electrical current is fused with your body, a bypass is created around the traditional structures that mold you to communicate and exchange data only within limited patterns. You are going to climb a ladder and experience a different view from which to interpret reality.

In the next number of years, everyone, including children, babies, and elderly people, will be affected by this electrical current. One of the benefits of this is that it can bring about a rejuvenation of your physical body by assisting you to heal any separations you continue to carry. The more you grasp and live the concept of creating life through thought, the freer you become, for the stress of powerless living is eliminated. Hold your vision and allow your light body to add a meaningful purpose to all that you do.

To prepare for this energy, sit quietly, close your eyes, picture your body filled with light, and imagine the light flashing and cleaning your cells. Then ask all parts of your body to work together in their idealized forms. If your body works together inside yourself, then it is much easier for you, as an individual, to work with others outside yourself. Those who are sick inside often don't work very well outside. Attend to the inner mechanisms of your body, visualizing what you want.

Your physical body exists as a frequency device. You think you are flesh and bone when in actuality you are a combination of intelligent electromagnetic signals. You translate these signals as meaningful life through a physical body by eating, experiencing, using your senses, having sex—all those kinds of things. This is how you interpret the meaning of your electromagnetic signals, which are actually experienced by you as impulses. From outside your system, you can be viewed in numerous ways. Some beings interpret you solely as a frequency, a collection of intelligence emitting data and certain frequencies based on emotions. Others use the psychic/emotional frequencies you emit for many things. Much as the frequency of gold is used to transform your consciousness, and that of water to wash yourself or quench your thirst, the frequency of humans has untold purposes, as you are now discovering.

As previously mentioned, within your body lies a force of power called kundalini, a serpentlike energy that dwells at the base of your spine. Acknowledging and calling this force forward facilitates the merging and bundling of your light body. This force also helps maintain your stability and groundedness with the increased electromagnetic shifts. Traditionally, kundalini uncoils itself and electrifies your body at around forty years of age. By this time you are considered mature enough to house this kind of power. For most people, the power is so profound that they go downhill from there and begin to age, rather than rejuvenate and put the great creative electrical force to use.

When you have a kundalini experience, it may feel like an intense concentration of energy in the sacrum area at the base of your spine. Sometimes, when people experience kundalini, they feel as if they want to have sex because they don't know what to do with all of the rising energy. The whole planet is locked into using its kundalini to reproduce. People fornicate like mad without ever understanding that kundalini can move *through* the body and up into and around the head. If you allow it to do this, it will provide a new interpretation of yourself. You will understand that all of your creations, healings, manifestations—everything—come from the natural Goddess source inside yourself.

Humankind has a resistance to changing, growing, and finding new data. Much of that resistance, of course, is not natural. It has been programmed in to make you afraid to consider something new, to reach out and disobey the gods, or to become their equals. When humankind seeks knowledge, humankind becomes informed and comes closer to what would be called the Goddess.

You keep recreating the past by recalling it in nostalgic detail and anchoring it in the present. The cells of your body are quite free to come and go; they replicate themselves continuously. Where do they get their instructions from? They are provided by your blueprint and belief system, and by the energy patterns that you carry about reality. As you change those patterns by expanding your concepts, your molecular structure will follow. Each of you has the potential to have the body you want. You can regenerate the cells of your being by remapping them—sending them a different plan or alternative route. As you do this, your body and experience will follow suit.

Each of you has a natural vitality in your body. You have been influenced by people whom you respect, and whom you believe are legitimate, into accepting fearful and negative ideas. Perhaps one individual had a bad experience, and they interpret it and create image making for all others.

It used to be that you would have to learn many disciplines and prepare your body for years before you could successfully experience kundalini energy. It was indeed the rare individual who was able to access kundalini, for a number of reasons. Earth was surrounded by a fence of frequency control. As kundalini rises in the body, it meets the cosmic forces that come from outside the body, and the body becomes alive and energized. It is just like pulling a pillar of light into the body. Those who would keep you from knowledge have had their boundaries penetrated, and the frequency-control fence around the planet is like Swiss cheese. In other words, there are holes and other forms of light can now come in.

As cosmic energy comes onto the Earth plane, there are millions of you who are now increasing the opportunities to reinterpret what kundalini can do. It is the force of your lives, and you pulse with it. Used accordingly, it is going to bring a tremendous number of solutions. This energy connects you to a cosmic source and unifies you with a greater purpose and understanding of what you can do with it.

This energy may be utilized to heal, for when it builds up in your hands, you have the hands of a healer. Many of you would be very surprised if you peeked a few years into your own futures and saw the so-called unexpected, including what you will be able to do with the energy coming out of your hands. There are individuals now who are able to hold their hands together and make a piece of paper catch on fire. This energy in the hands is going to amplify in each of your lives. You may use it to purify food, heal, clean the oceans, and depollute the rivers and land. You will be able to transmute the toxic pollution that is everywhere around your planet.

The ability to do these things will be had by those who are willing to believe. As you believe and practice and search, you will be rewarded. Then you will show others. These are gifts that will make a difference in the shift toward mass cooperation on a planetary scale. Therefore, you are going to work on these abilities as a collective. The unhealed and the sick can also learn to activate this energy in themselves and direct it in their own bodies. The essence of what everyone must manufacture is the value of self: "Hey, if my body manifested sickness, it can manifest wellness as well. Whose limitation and whose decree of illness am I going to accept?"

You have stored within you an abundance of magnificent knowledge. You are the key to the Living Library, and you are what everyone is after, to some extent. It is a very interesting process that humans are involved with. Using your imagination, you can send a message to your brain and intend that the neurons connected to the area of imagination become more finely united. However, your toes have the same ability to carry the signal of imaging as your brain, because every cell in your body is composed of exactly the same substances, no matter where it is located. Each cell has the same potential to produce knowledge, and your cells are waiting for you to direct them. When you allow society, family, and education to direct your beliefs, and you let guilt and "shoulds" permeate your field, these are the programs to which your body responds.

Your planet is going to survive its transmutation process as you recognize the power of imagination, which is tied very closely to memory. Imagination acts as a movie screen in your mind that holds images and creates blueprints of consciousness. Your body is filled with memories of different worlds, as well as different time frames from the now you perceive. As Earth evolves, you will become capable of pulling up these concepts and blueprints and finding the teachings in their purpose, as well as their significance to your now, based on what you know. Bringing memories of other times and places into your current reality unifies the significance of your life. It creates a healing by helping you understand the purpose of self-inflicted wounds.

One of the most important keys we can give you is this: Love yourself, honor the vehicle that you occupy, and act as if you are priceless. Act as if you lucked out and received the best thing possible—*your body*. Honor Earth as well with love and respect, for it is here, on Earth, that you *stage* your fanciful dramas. Love yourself and Earth on your ride through the universe, and your journey will be lighter.

Your body is going to demonstrate absolutely miraculous abilities. Your sensitivities will develop to such a degree that smells and scents will have greater impact on your moods, emotions, and general sense of well-being. You will say, "I found that when I sprinkle this herb on my food, or when I have this smell in my house, I have more energy. And when I use this one, I am quieter." Learn how to use the plants around you that are gifts from the Living Library.

A tremendous and radical change is taking place within your physical body, and we cannot emphasize this enough. You are each guided, so to avoid burnout, *listen* to what's inside you. Too much new information too quickly, without your taking the time to slow down and integrate it, can lead to overload for your adjusting psyche. When you drive a car, you don't always drive it fast. You speed up, you put the brakes on, you stop at lights, you turn—you move at different paces. It is the same thing with energy. There are points of acceleration and points of slow down. This way, the body builds slowly.

Imagine you were a hairdryer and you spent a large majority of your time with your cord wrapped up in a little bag on the shelf. Then came the peak experience in your life: you were plugged in and used every day. If you were the hairdryer, you would feel you were no longer alone. You would say, "Something has happened to my identity here! Wow! I'm on!" As a human being, you are similar. You get plugged in, and suddenly something happens, so you must incorporate what happens. We liken the energy that runs through you to the electrical current that runs through the hairdryer, making it more than simply an object—making it a *useful* object. This is a very simple example, and it gives you an image of yourself. You can be switched on so that the current of life takes you to your purpose.

It is essential that you understand your body and that you are not ashamed of what your body does. What you do with your body is another story, however. There is a grand dignity to the physical form. Be generous in your body grace. If you are uncomfortable with what we are saying, then examine how much you love yourself and where dislike and shame of your physical body comes from. There is nothing wrong with the body. The modern concept of the Barbie Doll, as a perfected female form, contributes to hatred of the female body if the body does not conform to that mold. All images, from the simplest toys to the most complex computers, affect your perceptions about yourself. Often women who conform to the Barbie Doll mold have to force and restrict themselves to duplicate the desired and approved shape, reducing their freedom of choice. The human body has all shapes and sizes, and all kinds of expression. You can tell that variety is important on the planet by looking at the variety of faces. If you were all meant to be molded into one kind, there would only be a limited number of faces that would be available as model types.

For eons, you as a human being forgot who you were. You took on shame about your body and your body's functions. There has been little encouragement for you to acknowledge the very functions of your body. We often compare your use of your body to having a car, about which someone says, "Don't ever use the trunk. It is a really bad place. Don't open that trunk, don't use it, don't put anything in it. It is there, but don't touch it." Do you see the analogy? It is ridiculous.

Sex in 3D can provide the energy through which you can emerge to higher consciousness. It can lead to an essential part of your multidimensional development. Sometimes, it is difficult to hear about sex because you hold onto judgment of traumatic events that you are ashamed of or that you feel bad about surrounding your sexuality. Everyone has something stored away concerning the sexual part of themselves. To a large degree, there has been a plan to influence you to feel shame about sexuality and your body; this has kept you from discovering your power, purpose, bliss, and freedom.

As your body takes on and integrates the new energy, memory will be awakened in you. Cosmic memories, as well as memories of this lifetime, offer an unfolding of who you have been in galactic history. It is important for you to have room to remember. Some of you think, "Oh, well, I'll put some music on in the car and I'll drive some place and practice remembering." Leave a space for memory to come into. Utilizing nature is one of the best ways to get in touch with remembering: sitting out in nature, watching nature, being in idleness, being in the now and letting the now expand into the ongoing, spontaneous, synchronistic moment—the ever-expanding now.

Nature teaches you through the calling of birds, the beat of butterfly wings, the symphony of crickets and frogs, the camel's bray, and the smell of desert dust and fresh spring rain. All of these things trigger memories if you take the time to let the sounds and smells penetrate your physical being.

Activating memory involves disengaging yourself from all the "shoulds" you have piled up for yourself. Are you busy running nowhere? Do you truly lead the most meaningful life that you can? Do you await the approval of others, forever a shadow of the power of radiating your truth. Please, do not hide from yourself or others. Live!

Why are we telling you all this? We are intending to activate cellular memory inside of you. Before you come into the body, certain memories are made available and stored genetically within you. One day you will figure out how this is done and understand that you are worked on when you sleep. Often you feel these rushes—or zoomings—of electrical pulsation through your body. These are memory inserts being put in you to prepare you for your next adventure.

Please understand that there is little difference between a memory-insert experience and an actual life experience, because reality is very constructible. Reality is not designed to be gone. Realities and cultures can be re-created over and over again. If you are a newly born soul and feel that you have missed out on all the juicy happenings in the universe, you can have memory inserts. You can create places for yourself within cultures without overpopulating them. For example, everyone wants to have been Egyptian or Maya, and there was only room for so many. Yet, you all can have memories constructed of those cultures. You can become a part of them because, with the memory constructed for you, you can build another Mayan culture on top of the other one. This concept gives you a clue about the flexibility of your reality.

Memory is like a pool or a mirror inside your body, and it needs to be replenished and refreshed with the reflecting ability of water. *Water* is what enhances memory in the physical body. Kundalini fires the codes, activating the light-encoded filaments and bringing them into light. These tiny fibers are filled with information, and kundalini moving through your body gives you the opportunity to own your memories.

Many of you are experiencing deep memories of manipulation, perhaps painful recollections of being eaten by reptiles, or mating with reptiles, or of genetic experimentation. Even if you did not experience a specific thing, in your blood you have filaments that carry the entire history of all things. How to get those filaments to hook up to give you a viable movie is another story. You know what movie film looks like? It is made up of little squares or frames. You are like a big movie, cut and separated frame by frame, so that each part of you is disconnected from all the others. As we work with you, the energy that we bring to you reorganizes those tiny clips of film. This brings a story together inside of you that is personal, planetary, and galactic.

All of you are here to look into the dark, because in the dark you will find both the light and the reason the light is returning. You cannot simply go toward the light and say, "Hey, darkness is bad. It is negative. I don't want to see." Be open to what you do not want to see. Keep your heart open, and trust that the pain you may experience needs to be explored so that it can be released after being processed on a memory level. You are at the time when memories are floating to the surface, coming from deep recesses. These memories can bring emotional responses. Whatever you see needs to be looked at. It is you. Accept it and say, "Aha! Based on what I know, and on the preparation of my consciousness, I can look at this and see that it was a misuse of energy. That is all right. I will transmute it. I will turn it into something of joy."

Do you know how many people are willing to look at the negative and the dark? Not too many. Do you know how many people are living in the dark? Do not run from the shadow of life, for there is much healing to be completed once the pain of the darker side of life is felt, realized, and understood.

Emotions are the sum total of your wealth as a human being. Emotions trigger the inner pharmacopoeia, your body's personal drugstore. In the drugstore of your body, you are the pharmacist. You write the prescription according to your emotional response or reaction to events. Your emotions create a corresponding chemical release inside your physical form. The endocrine system, which is responsible for the chemical responses to your emotional choices, will evolve. New chemicals will be produced inside your body that will help you change. Choosing a different way of receiving or translating reality will trigger inner doorways to open and produce substances that will take you into the higher realms.

You are being reorganized on a subatomic level. Within your body, the light-encoded filaments—fine, threadlike fibers—are subtle forms of energy that connect everything together. These gossamer threads are reorganized in your body through stimulation by rays and photons that come to the planet bringing cosmic energy. They are reorganized to rejuvenate your body when you drink pure, clean water. They are particularly activated through the process of oxygenation and deep breathing. There are also ways of oxygenating yourself by ingesting herbs known as blood purifiers. When you purify your blood, it is able to carry a greater amount of oxygen. The reorganization of fibers on a cellular level builds and grows, and the fibers invigorate your body in a variety of ways. All this involves activating your brain. You have the keys and the codes to open up the rest of that dormant area.

The plan of intention is for human beings, based on the increase of light, to evolve into multitalented beings. Some people are operating on 6 to 8 percent of their brain capacity. Someone who is using more of their brain, an Einstein for example, is using at best 15 to 20 percent. Ask yourself these questions: What is the other 80 percent of my brain doing? Why is it dormant? What is not hooked up?

The endocrine system will evolve as DNA evolves, producing chemical substances that are combinations of intelligent geometric shapes. These shapes will exist all over the body and will not be localized simply in the brain. Everything will happen simultaneously.

The endocrine system can secrete psychedelic-like chemical substances that catapult you into new forms of intelligence. You have a conflict in your society about how you view drugs. Anything having to do with mind expansion has been promoted as very bad and fearful. Yet, at the same time, a good portion of the world is addicted to prescription drugs that keep people sedated. In your society, prescribed drugs that suppress the natural chemical process are fine, while drugs that activate the mind and open other realities are bad. Major control is in effect concerning your ideas about what you can and cannot take into your body. Take a look at this.

Your endocrine system is going to go through a massive upheaval. It is in the early stages of this at this time. Think of a small grocery store, one that is old and decrepit and has had the same brands of food on the shelves for twenty years; the store is outdated and is not suiting modern habits, tastes, and desires. Someone comes in and says, "This supermarket's too old. I am going to soup it up to meet the needs of society. I am going to change the products that this supermarket carries." Supermarkets serve certain needs, and as the needs and tastes of human beings change, the food on the shelves of the supermarket must meet the new taste qualities and requirements.

Your endocrine system is doing the same thing. What is making the endocrine system decide to serve new food? *You* are—you loving yourself, pulling the pillar of light into your body and reorganizing the basic genetic structure of who you are. As the strands of DNA begin to discover their identities and come alive, they will change the endocrine system. Your decision to be in the moment, to love yourself, and to work with love on the planet with yourself and all people will completely change what happens inside you. This is a key to rejuvenation, most definitely. Be willing to experience yourself, your life, and your body, as your own creations.

The accelerated energy will create havoc on your planet, leading to a great deal of confusion coupled with radical, revolutionary, overnight change. Never in your recorded history has there been as much energy on the planet and has there been the kind of consciousness that there is now, so you have nothing to prepare you for what is coming—nothing. The radical change that these movements will bring about is beyond your conception.

Focus on the best that you can be, knowing that you will affect many probabilities around you. Know that for yourself this will be the opportunity to activate a major change. Your pineal gland is being activated through the infusion of light energies, releasing a new vision of possibilities in which peace and freedom are felt and recognized from inside.

Your thymus gland is pivotal in sending the signal to your body to hold the pattern of rejuvenation. Your thymus gland shrinks the older you get; it shrivels up. It is like the gatekeeper at the base of your neck that regulates what comes from above and what comes from below. Your upper glands, the pituitary and pineal, as cranial temples are inactivated; they are basically dormant. Your thymus gland does not continuously remind your body of its idealized blueprint because it is not getting the messages to do so from the temples in your head. This is because your temples have been disconnected from the full strands of DNA. Your thymus gland will return to its own vitality when it receives the message that your body has done its preparation and that your consciousness is ready. If you think in terms of life expansion, some of you have barely begun your work. Others have had training that is going to implode you into the next shift; your work is a gift to the planet, a gift to civilization.

If you are beating up on yourself or feeding yourself negative ideas, then you need to examine your dual loyalties. To be here in this moment says to us that you have an interest, an excitement, and a loyalty to transcend the ideas that the human species has been fed. If you are fighting this—looking in the mirror and saying, "Oh, look how I look. Bad news"— then you have a duality, a doubt, a conflict. If you have such a conflict, then the more the energy builds, the more you will feel like a rubber band being pulled out and snapped back, over and over again. So, if you are feeling like a rubber band being snapped, then the corresponding avenue to look in would be the inconsistency of your beliefs as you are expressing them, silently or out loud.

Your hypothalamus regulates the temperature and water in your body. You are water, you understand—electrified water. The elements and balance of ocean water match the blood in your human body. Humans were made from the ocean. This is one of the greatest secrets of creation. The Pleiadian gods came and used the energy of the hydrogen and oxygen molecules. It is from this that you sprang. This is the basic key. The firmament was created, and from the firmament came life. This is one of the principles through which you were constructed. We want you to understand that there are many ways to construct humans. You have heard stories that you are made up of dust and clay. Some of these stories are not true; they are told to keep you away from the truth. It makes more sense to you that you are closer to the solid elements than those of water. Remember, we said that very often things are switched around so that you do not discover the truth of your identity.

Your hypothalamus can be thought of as the gatekeeper between your physical body and your outer chakras. Its time has not yet come. In your present stage of evolution, you cannot comprehend its function. Yes, it does regulate body temperature and the flow of water, and water is the essence of your life. We always encourage you to be around water, to be in water, and to use water because water enhances the function of your hypothalamus gland. It keeps it lukewarm for when it needs to get heated up. The time will come to further explore the hypothalamus.

There are ways through cranio-sacral adjustment to stimulate the hypothalamus. These will be discovered and shared when people have raised their consciousness to the degree that they are prepared for the great sunburst of energy that will come from this gland. Until that time, the information would be dangerous. People sometimes cannot moderate themselves, and they think they must drink the elixir of all experience without making the necessary preparations of consciousness.

You will never be the same once your hypothalamus secretions start. Have you ever ingested a psychedelic? How would you like to live, balancing that reality, twenty-four hours a day? It wouldn't work; it would be entirely too confusing. It is fine for what is called a trip. It is fine for a journey into learning—into the shamanic, mysterious, Living Library realms. However, it certainly is not something you want to have for breakfast every day. The rest of the nervous system is not in sync with that awareness. When you take what is called a trip, it is exactly that—like going to the country or to the shore for the weekend. You go, you experience it, and then you come back and contemplate it.

Your hypothalamus is going to move you to a new shoreline of your being, a new domain that will be chemically induced. This is what the endocrine system does. It introduces various chemicals into your body without you taking anything—without you ingesting any substances at all. The chemicals will simply begin to secrete themselves and influence the very way that you perceive and interpret reality.

Your restored hypothalamus will take you on a journey,

and you will change everything so that you will be happy to dwell there. You will not want to dwell in the old place. It will be as if you move to a new land, or as if you move to a new planet without leaving Earth. It will be a splitting of your world. Earth and Earth's reality in the Living Library will change before your eyes because the chemicals that will be secreted from the hypothalamus will give you a new interpretation of reality.

This you are not prepared for yet, not anywhere near it. First, you must convince yourself that you are loved and that you are the source of your love. You must maintain a consistent feeling of this before you can begin the subtle changes in your endocrine system that will prepare you for the awakening of your hypothalamus. If all things take place collectively, when can the Family of Light look forward to the awakening of the hypothalamus? We suggest that this will happen in increments between 1999 and 2009, a ten-year period.

With all the fuss about a health-care system in your United States, we remind you that *health is free*. The true cost of health care is a few moments of your time to develop the right attitude about your body. *You* create your health or your dis-ease, and you don't need anyone to tell you whether you are healthy. First of all, when you are *in touch with your body*—when you take a shower or wash, you can feel and know your level of well-being—you *know* if you are in a state of health or not. You may *choose to worry* and distrust your body. If you worry about your health, then you will create something. Your body follows the images you instigate.

If you invest in worry about what you might catch, or how cancer might be growing, or whether you have AIDS, or diphtheria, or tuberculosis, or whatever you wish to worry about, the probabilities are that if you don't already have something, you will create it and go from there. If you know you are healthy, you are. It is quite simple.

Fear is the killer. We remind you that your power ends where your fear begins. If you fear something, it is as if you put a sign up over your head and say, "Welcome. I am wait-

ing for you." The purpose of fear is to save your life, to catapult you into the now in order to take action. Often it serves
to direct you away from that which is dangerous and toward
the very essence of your vital being. However, when you
hold onto fear as a lifestyle, and when you broadcast fear of
life, you shut down your body and kill your vital life force.
This creates stress, ill health, and aging. *Your thoughts create
your reality.* Part of the initiation of consciousness is to move
through toxicity, and your physical body needs to go through
more preparation and purification of what would be called
intent and courage. When you dwell in fear, you dispel all.
You dispel your own power. So, in order to meet something
that is very unfamiliar to your logical mind, you must maintain clarity of intent and a tremendous sense of courage, safety, and nonchalance. Everything that keeps you from achiev-
ing something is simply an idea. Over the next twenty
years—the period everyone is buying the big tickets for, front
row seats here in Earth's amphitheater—many changes will
take place.

Do you remember going to a carnival when you were a
child and going on those big rides for the first time? Did you
beg your mother and father or your big brother or sister to
take you on the rides that seemed adventurous and so gigantic? Earth is going to seem like a huge carnival. You are all
going to get on some big rides that you cannot conceive of, so
you have some clearing and intending to do. The large majority of you will do just fine. You will emote your way through
it. Watch your whining—it is a waste of energy. Accept all
that you create and know that there is opportunity in all
things.

From our point of view, it completely boggles us that you
would invest in fear around that which is opportunity. On
some level, we know who you are and what you went
through to get here. We know why you are here on Earth and
that you were not sent here to flounder alone. The forces that
work with you have a capacity to influence and affect your

reality that is beyond your comprehension, even though you are not aware of the existence of these forces. You do not understand how their fingers move to nudge this person or that person: "Go here. Do this. Oh, don't do that." Events are being set up.

Understand that there is a deep seeding of cancerous ideas and thoughts on the planet, just as there is a deep seeding and encouragement of the idea of AIDS. People find these things and are attached to them. Right now people are afraid of the sun. They are afraid to go outside, as if there is a mistake in nature. The people who buy into this will find that their fear will act far more quickly than any rays of the sun would do in damaging them.

Fear is the killer. It is an idea that takes hold, like Paul Revere crying out and riding through the streets of early America. When fear runs through your body, it reminds the chemicals that go with it to come out and fill your body. They activate a downward spiral and an idea of death. It is basically that simple.

You have heard of AIDS and that it is caused by the HIV virus. However, now there is AIDS when there is no HIV present. AIDS is now being spread electromagnetically, in the same way that many disturbances can be spread electromagnetically. Remember, electromagnetism involves the great currents of electricity that are all around you, generated by humanity and other sources. Magnetism, of course, is the force that holds things together. You have magnetic particles inside your brain as well.

You can use this idea to help other people open their hearts. AIDS is spread electromagnetically, drawing itself from one carrier to another with a similar pattern or vibration: "I think like you do. Send your thoughts to me." Do you follow this? "I have those same fear beliefs. I am confused about who I think I am. I am not worth it. I have no power over my body." That kind of thinking is so magnified it is as if you carry around signs, posters, and bumper stickers over your auric field proclaiming who you think you are. Viruses can spread electromagnetically so that eventually you may have entire metropolitan areas infused. Why? You are drawn to live in a certain town or place because of the karma and vibration of the rest of the people. It is why many of you are being impulsed to relocate and move.

The same principle holds true for the heart. If AIDS can be spread electromagnetically, so can the opening of the heart and the Goddess. We want you to understand that there are always many, many plans in motion. People say, "Why do bad, negative, lower vibrational plans have to be in motion?" Because people wait for them. People don't sit around waiting for something exciting and good to happen to them. They sit around rocking in their chairs, smoking cigarettes, wondering when a car is going to come through the living room. Why? Because they watch television. Your main imprinting comes through this mind-control machine, which imprints you basically with fear. Chronic fear is going to be the killer. It will draw to you those things that you dread and that you are certain are going to happen to you. Of all the possibilities in the world, why do you choose what you do?

The more compassion you have for others, the quicker mass consciousness will change. We are asking all of you to play this heart game much more often than just when you have spare time. Make a commitment to have your heart open, and see that it stays open and that you use the heart energy of the Mother Goddess. This will make all the difference, because it is not just your heart that is involved—it is the heart of the Goddess. However, the Goddess needs your heart open to have her energy move through you.

Today, there are very few geographical locations on your planet that broadcast the love frequency. That is about to change, of course. Earth, as you well know, is going through some challenges—to put it mildly. However, if you think this is intense, hold on. You are in for a grand ride. In a very short period of time, there will be a catapulting of energies on a global scale that will take you further and further toward what will look like the destruction of your planet. We want you to know this. We want you to understand that sometimes, when energy evolves, even when you yourself go through evolutionary processes, there is a disorientation, a chaos, a confusion, and a lack of identity. Toxicity may come out of your body that makes you sick. You may have dancing of the bowels or an upset stomach or a closing down of the bowels. Many different things indicate changes at hand.

You can liken Earth to a gigantic mirror for what is transpiring inside human beings. Earth at this time is reeking in toxicity. She held it off for so long. For many, many years Earth was filled with toxicity not only from radioactive wastes and all kinds of garbage, but also from the collective dumping of human anger. Humans are creatures of energy, and your emotions create a collective force that is broadcast. You not only broadcast chaos and fear, which is basically what your collective lives have been about for a long time, but you also broadcast anger. The anger is about what you know you are being denied deep down inside.

There are almost six billion of you—on the verge of doubling—dumping your anger onto the planet. What do you imagine that does? It creates a stirring and mirroring of the planet's own anger from the lack of care and the lack of love. All of this is being spewed forward now, so in the long run you are going through a clearing. You are all coming to a new realization. You are being pushed, as a people and as a planet, to your limits. You are going to be forced to define new boundaries about what you will and will not stand for. No one is going to sit home like a couch potato and miss this one. You all must participate; if you don't, more than likely you will vanish in one form or another.

We remind you that you create your own reality and that the collective anger you feel has to do with the discrediting of your imagination. Feel that for a few moments. Imagination is the key to brilliance, to unifying conceptualizations, and to bringing ideas into manifestation. When was the last time you were encouraged on a regular basis to invest in your own imagination? You rob yourselves of the inherent qualities through which you can save yourselves, change yourselves, and redefine freedom. Imagination is, indeed, a ticket to ride on the mercurial carnival of Earth.

Earth is inhabited by a multitude of intelligent forces, not by humans alone at this time. There are dimensional locks that keep various life forms separated and segregated. With the collapse of time, humans are being impulsed to activate Earth's grid. When you are infused with cosmic light energy, it alters your nervous system, which is like a highway for energy impulses to travel to your brain. Like road construction, your nervous system is being rebuilt, widened, and strengthened to accommodate an increase of data, like traffic moving through your body. When you face an experience that is out of the norm, that does not fit into the category of the known, your nervous system tends to shut down. Your body goes into shock, unable to process the out-of-ordinary reality.

As energy increases on the planet, blocks in your physical, mental, emotional, and spiritual bodies are magnified. Unexpressed feelings and ideas create obstacles to the flow of energy, whose purpose it is to connect you. You must help the process by being responsible for who you are. Wherever you have a prejudice or difficulty—"I don't want to know that. I hate this about myself. I don't like that."—you can trust that the magnifying glass will be put over it. You will squeal and squirm until you get it right. And if you don't, you will manifest the block in the form of a difficult challenge. Everything is intensifying in order to teach people about responsibility and maintaining a clarity of purpose and intent. Utilizing different modalities of bodywork in this day and age is key to your survival. Pursuing avenues of discovery through bodywork facilitates and quickens the recognition of your identity.

As more of who you are unfolds, the dramas that have trapped you can be more deeply understood. The dramas are released from cellular holding patterns that faithfully steer you into the very situations that are left unresolved and unforgiven. Actually, *you* invite all the players in your life, and you, as director, cast the parts and run the show. If you are now finally tired of your script, remember, *you* write it! Blame and victimhood are the ultimate traps to insure a state of disempowerment. Remember, you have dramas that are ancient god dramas that influence you now. All of reality is connected and is seeking a healing of union.

There is great humor in highly evolved energies, especially those who work with the love frequency. It can be recognized as a trademark. With energies you encounter, make certain there is an expansive sense of humor, for laughter is a key to freedom. There is plenty of room for joy in all of existence, and this is a concept you are seeking to grasp.

We encourage you to operate out of your feeling center— your solar plexus or gut. You have the same capacity and activity inside your stomach lining as you do in your brain cells. Reconsider yourself. You can instantly see that you alter your experience when you believe in and find opportunity in every event you create. We remind you that opportunity is often disguised as loss.

The solar plexus area is where you hold power in your body and where you extend your power out to the world. It is also where you perceive the world. This is the *feeling center*. This is where you get your threads of data, for through the solar plexus you *feel* your way through events that may make no sense to your logical mind. Step back and take a look. Reroute your decision-making process, taking a detour into your body. Notice how you feel and acknowledge your body's innate wisdom speaking to you as a loving adviser, if only you would listen! Your body wants to work with you— often it is you and your thoughts that work against your body. Your logical mind, remember, has been trained by those who want you to perform in a very limited paradigm and in a certain limited frequency.

We want you to accept the idea that you are very significant. There is great value in who you are, in what you intend, and in what you allow yourself to experience. We would like you to feel a tremendous upliftment and sense of personal value for your ability to weave multiple realities of consciousness together and leap into territory that many would not support. We give you a gold star for daring to be foolhardy, because you are playfully freeing the bondage of human perception as you explore the seasons of yourself. There are many teachers who will show you in which slices of time you have flourished and developed, and where you have affected an interconnected reality, and what those times and places have to do with now. One day, you will understand that those other times are now. Everything occurs in the now. This very moment of existence—where you are—is truly the ongoing, spontaneous, significant moment. It is, over and over again, where you can find yourself.

Be aware of receiving simultaneous information from other civilizations. Notice it and find out what you can synchronistically tie together. Often you are impulsed with a knowing. Yet, even though this commonly occurs, it takes you a while to convince yourself that you do, indeed, know something. There are adjustment periods. Be patient and you can go anywhere you choose. Be clear on what you intend and then let it go.

The dolphins do not keep secrets from one another. They willingly share the accumulation of knowledge they have. You can tell the evolution of individuals by how willing they are to share what they know. The more you share what you know, the more you are filled. The more you hold onto and grip the wisdom you have been given, the more quickly it will run through your hands and you will lose it. Open your hands and your wisdom will fly off like a butterfly; then new butterflies will land.

All life has chakra systems. A town has roads, cars driving through it, and refueling places that store energy. It is the same with the chakra systems. They are energetic storehouses around and inside of life forms. The chakras connect the internal workings—the physiological third-dimensional operations—with the multidimensional, etheric-layered goings-on. They bring energy from the nonphysical realms into the physical, if utilized properly.

All forms of life have these energy portals as doorways and places where they can be refueled. What each form of life does with its refueling is within the blueprint or the DNA of the form of life itself. As your DNA is being reordered into a new expression of itself, the frequency or identity that you carry is speaking something on a nonphysical level. Every place you go, you carry the mutating energy that announces itself. Your consciousness announces itself to all life forms. Maybe those who are next to you in a shopping mall or restaurant are not quite aware on a conscious level of who you are. However, when you take a walk in the woods and fields, or go into the oceans, you will see other life forms around you that are much more aware of who you are. They change their response, and their DNA changes because yours is changing. Through you, all of nature becomes more available as the Living Library.

From your perspective, there are very few people who have lived thousands of years, yet the creator gods are able to extend the longevity of the cellular body. Life extension and the rejuvenation of cellular life are coming back into fashion. This is part of building the light body, a body that is not so dense, so that it does not self-destruct—a body that self-generates and self-replenishes. That is what you are striving for. You would be there and you would feel it if your logical mind were not so worried about whether it is possible. We cannot emphasize to you enough that you must stop listening to society and to official versions of reality. This involves choice, not disrespect. This is going to be the hardest task for you, and the biggest break to make—to cross the bridge between your societal self and your spiritual self. Which one is going to become sacred? Which one is going to be your source of authority? The sooner you make that leap, the more you will enjoy yourself. Allow your intuitive self to be the standard bearer of your experience—an experience that no one else is going to validate, and an experience that springs from the assignment that you are knowing, and not necessarily remembering, you are on.

Energy Exercise

Put yourself in comfort, and become very still. Send a message to your body to relax, release, and let go. Take a deep, deep breath. Once you have exhaled, feel a wave of serenity moving over your body. Continue to consciously breathe, finding your own rhythm. Feel your chest expand and open. Feel your heart area get warmer. Relax your throat. Let your mind be clear and your vision centered. Track your breathing for a few moments. Imagine a pillar of light touching the top of your head, then entering your body. Breathe deeply in and out, following your breath, making yourself as light, calm, and peaceful as you can.

Once you are in this serene place, focus your energy on your third eye, and picture your world, Earth. Whatever you imagine is fine. As you hold the picture of the globe in your mind's eye, feel the existence of an individual blueprint and purpose for all of Earth's inhabitants. You may see these blueprints as sparks of light and geometric shapes.

Feel the uniqueness and multitude of lessons that are neces-

sary for consciousness to evolve. Not only is the consciousness of each individual being stretched, the collective consciousness of the globe is connecting in a unique way. Feel the contribution that each individual makes to the global plan, and from your now, send out a wave of intent, inspiring love and trust of the human form.

Now, as if your consciousness were a magnet drawing to itself all like consciousness, feel yourself rising out of your own blueprint, like a golden ball of light. Let your blueprint begin to rotate around the grid of Earth, looking for the other blueprints that are keyed to work with yours, whose ultimate plan is to activate a new global blueprint for humankind. Feel this global search. Let yourself as the golden sphere of light rotate around and around the planet, going from one place to another. Let it grow in size as it attracts like consciousness to it, forming a blanket of light and triggering an intertwining energy grid designed to be awakened by intersecting consciousness. Feel your golden ball of light being drawn to different locations around the globe. See yourself there, and see your presence altering, opening, and expanding wherever you are.

Imagine six billion people connected to that global blueprint from inside their bodies. They know that the coming change is an opportunity to live more joyous and expanded lives in which they have the freedom to look at life from a very different perspective.

Bring your consciousness back to your physical body. Visualize light running through you, infusing you, connecting you. Watch the energy flow at a rapid rate and let your body begin to pulse. Feel stronger and filled with new information, health, and vitality. Feel the pillar of light continuously with you, filling you and connecting you with your source. Keep that pillar of light always coming into your physical body. The pillar of light is your calling card into the higher realms.

Thought is. You are evolving toward learning to use your

thought in productive ways so that you can alter your world and create a brand new paradigm of reality. Trust yourself and listen well to what it is that you are discovering. The road that appears before you may be very interesting. Remember that you always create it, and if you do not like the scenery, you can simply take a new road. Pleasant journeys.

SEVEN

The Dimensions Dance

We remind you that Prime Creator makes up all the teams, and if you are in Prime Creator's universe, then you are on all the teams as well.

You, as human beings, are the library cards, the keys to the Living Library. All the information stored in Earth's library is accessible through you. You were designed to be merged with, influenced, and emerged through. You have come here to master the human version of the spiritual evolutionary process—to live with it, to merge with many different realities, and to allow realities to emerge through you. Eventually, you will become tuned into the consciousness of the creator gods from whom you have sprung. It will be like turning a radio dial to pick up a variety of frequencies. Allow yourselves to understand that the particular physical bodies you now occupy are sending and receiving centers, broadcast units that exist in many realities. All creation is designed to be influenced—to be puzzle pieces that lock and fit with other pieces of the puzzle. As humans, you have been kept ignorant of how many appendages you have that lock you into other realities. You have no idea of the intelligent sources in other realities that tune into you and affect you.

Nothing exists that is not part of the whole, and the

whole as designed is a free-will zone that creates an open-endedness of exchange and influence. Your task and responsibility is to make alliances and choices. Your parents may have said, "Play with good kids. Don't play with kids that hit, spit, bite, kick, or swear. You want to have good friends." They taught you how to pick your friends. Part of the parenting process was to teach you what to look for in people. Yet, no one ever taught you how to make friends and alliances with the invisible worlds around you.

As humans, your job is to own and take care of the Living Library. In the past, those who wanted to experience the Living Library would, with permission, look out of the eyes of human beings. As they looked, the humans would become the gods and goddesses in charge, the tour guides of this reality, so to speak. At one time, humans on Earth held very honorable and highly evolved positions. You had glorious, vibrant forms, emanating energy and light. Just as chefs have specialties in food preparation, humans had specialized ways of experiencing the Living Library and accessing information. Those who desired knowledge came to experience and discover the library of Earth. They merged with humans, who served as library cards into Earth and all her majesty. Becoming one with other energies and allowing them to look out of your eyes in order to experience more was a divine purpose. Humans made themselves available for this process.

Energies from faraway star systems that contributed to the library said, "We want to access the library to study some things and get some information." They needed to get permission and embody the love frequency in order to merge with humans. The humans knew they were having a merging of another sort, a meeting of the love frequency. The other energies used the bodies, eyes, senses, and entire beings of humans to check out the Living Library. Different humans had, of course, predilections for various aspects of the Living Library, and visiting gods and goddesses, if you wish to call them that, had certain data that they were after. So, it was quite an interesting job to be stewards of the Living Library because you didn't know what gods or goddesses were going to visit and go after what information. It was like being tour guides, and those who came in directed you to access the information they desired. The relationship was symbiotic and its success was based on the love frequency.

There is glorious information that is desperately needed in existence, and it is stored here, on Earth. As the reorganization of light takes place on Earth, there will be a mass merging of beings who are very benevolent, very uplifting, and very loving. They will come through and operate out of your bodies. You will still maintain your own integrity and your own identity; however, they will blend with you as we blend with our vehicle. They will be able to access the codes and master numbers that you house inside your bodies.

As Earth is catapulted into a frequency that will allow the Living Library to come back into full function, necessary experiences will be shared by all. In order to once again become valuable assets as the keys who access the Living Library from many cosmic points of view, you will have twelve-stranded DNA and full brain capacity. And, in order for you to be in partnership as library cards, you must understand that you are more than human. Throughout existence, where you are multidimensional in your truest form, you have many different guises. You are collections of sentient energies that are seeded all over this universal system. You make up one pool of consciousness that collects with other consciousness that has intents and purposes and that discovers things.

Earth is on a course that is taking a radical change in direction. She is experiencing an accelerated thrust in the ongoing evolutionary process. A cycle is coming to completion and a new age or new theme is about to take precedence upon Earth. You are assisting this new age into being in society. Currently, humans barely understand that they live many times as humans, let alone that there are many more identities to the self.

The self is a composition of many different life forms all making up a central soul. As Earth is being catapulted in a new direction, the occupants may perish because they do not meet the new speed at which Earth will vibrate. Or, they will begin the changes that will prepare them for the ability to blink on and off into the various personalities that make up the collection of the soul. You are forerunners in this and are meeting the portions of yourselves that are the most imperative for you to understand. There are many of these selves to meet.

Remember, you are part of a grander collective of intelligence that seeks to express itself in many realities. In order to further comprehend all the versions of reality, your central soul has many different personalities, tentacles, and outreaches. So, do not think that you are "goodies" in all versions of reality. As a matter of fact, when you are "baddies," sometimes you gain more information than when you are "goodies." When you are good people, sometimes you are so naive you have no idea what is happening. Your discoveries need not impact you with difficulty. Intend that they offer you interest, give you more knowledge, and do something very beneficial for you.

You hide your own cleverness from yourselves. You must learn to monitor how you create your reality, how many dimensions of thought you are in, and how you pretend that you are just hanging around waiting for something. The thoughts come racing through your heads second after second, bringing all this information, and you don't realize that you are creating your reality all of the time. You hide your beliefs from yourselves. You hide your power from yourselves. Remember, you have been programmed as a species to believe in your own disempowerment through your televisions and educational systems.

Do not fall into the trap of thinking you only create your

reality some of the time, while at other times and in certain situations you have no power. You must remember the vastness of your experience. You must remember that you make certain agreements to participate in things that seem to be difficult or bad. In actuality, uplifting events are very often behind experiences that you term difficult. Remember, there is opportunity in *all things* that you create.

You are Game Masters yourselves, those who orchestrated the reestablishing of Earth's freedom and the seeding of civilizations. These civilizations became alive and activated, and now you are living in one of the most exciting places and times of existence. There are many who support you and wish to merge with you, operate through you, and give you a hand with the job in front of you. You do not have to read a lot of text and balance a lot of computer sheets to carry this job out. All you need is to trust yourselves and design your reality according to your own wits by intending what you, as humans, want to accomplish. Whatever you intend to make as your signature—your mark on this world—it shall be. So, dream big.

Human beings, as library cards, access unique information that is very different from the information experienced through the insect, plant, or animal kingdoms. The Living Library was designed to be merged with, and by actually emerging through its life forms, other beings can experience a version of Earth's reality and gather information. The intent of what is sought results in the choice of the merging that is made.

Humans are coded to give full accessibility to the Living Library. When other energies merge with humans, formulas and blueprints can be found that they will not find merging with frogs, for example. Humans have been used as library cards by energies that do not operate with full understanding of the human vehicle, and this has caused imbalance and insanity in humans. Though certain entities intend harm to humans, many cause harm only by their ignorance.

Preparation of your bodies to receive the energy of merging, setting your standards for what you are available for, and discernment are essential. Remember, you have the assistance of the higher self, the version of you that navigates your experience through the universal laws of cause and effect. The higher self also acts as a gatekeeper and social secretary, regulating the appointments you set into motion based on your actions and beliefs in 3D, as reality is continuously translated from one domain to another.

The conjunctions of Uranus and Neptune in 1993, as a Galactic Tidal Wave of Light, sent a bolt of electrical current onto your planet and activated the potential for the third helix in humans. It triggered the light-encoded filaments to draw together and bundle that third helix. This bridged the electrical current inside your bodies that will access the self you know to the multidimensional self.

You are in for vastly accelerated times. You are, each of you, a personal energy vortex. As you play this twelve-chakra game with us, you open your chakras and create doorways through which all of your unlimited number of multidimensional personalities operate. These personalities can then blend and become one harmonious unit. There are versions of yourself that feel out of sync with you, and when they come in, your challenge is to learn how to teach them to be in sync in order to create this harmonious unit. You must know in the deepest core of your being who you are and what your standard is as a third-dimensional personality becoming multidimensional. As you set that standard, your experience and all the beings who wish to merge with you align with that choice.

When you're experiencing a multidimensional merge, it is a good practice to say, "Hey, listen. I am working for the improvement of the human race, since I am one of them. I am looking to evolve myself, to have greater abilities, and to have greater ease. I intend to use these abilities in a way that benefits myself, all of the people I am in contact with, which is the whole human race, and this planet, Mother Earth, which gives us a place to evolve." If another energy doesn't fit with that agenda, it will depart, or at best, be ready to change and reconsider. Often, an energy has come to be healed, to seek love, and to learn what it doesn't know. You are like a candle flame, and versions of yourself are drawn to you like insects. They fly into the fire and you transmute them, and they are reborn.

You can say, "It is my intention to have a greater understanding of how to utilize these multidimensional experiences. It is my intention to find out much more about how I can benefit myself and how I can have more fun with this." This sets the tone of the experience through intention. Intention is a conscious statement of what you want to manifest into reality. Therefore, if you want anything, intend it first, for this is how you bring about your reality.

You are living in a time when reality is being redefined, and you are the one redefining it. Follow yourself into an adventure of exploration by decreeing what you want and then asking for information and assistance to interpret what you experience.

What does it mean to be a library card? It means that you are on your first step toward certification—toward understanding, bonding, blending, and merging with other energies and allowing them to emerge through you into the Living Library. When you reach certain states of consciousness, you emit an electromagnetic pulse, like a radio program, that others can tune into. You then become very valuable because you can be merged with and others can access the codes. The codes contain formulas for replicating life. Many safeguards were designed so that the most important data, stored in humans, exists and is accessed only through a certain state of consciousness. Without that, the formulas do not even present themselves into being. The formulas exist through a preservation of a high level of consciousness within humans. If quality of life and existence is tampered with, humans are not able to produce the formulas.

We are asking all of you to *feel* the energy of these beings who wish to merge with you. Ask them to give you a sign. Say, "My work is for my own upliftment and that of the planet. If you are in alignment with this, welcome. If you are not, don't even come around. I am not available for that kind of nonsense." You need to state this.

You can also say, "Energy wishing to work through me, I am willing to be one of your life manifestations on the planet. I want to learn who you are and understand you. I intend to be energized by your presence. If you have abilities to access energy that I do not have, and I am willing to make room for this energy in my body, share these abilities with me please."

If the energies appearing don't appeal to you, don't be afraid to say, "The doors are closed. You are not my cup of tea. I'm going to find someone else." You will find someone else, because your standard will create your experience. Once you are comfortable with establishing friendships with the so-called invisibles, you may further understand and explore the "not-my-cup-of-tea types." All, indeed, are part of the whole relationship.

Be more in charge. There are many things that are necessary to prepare your body to accommodate awareness of multidimensional energy. Yoga, stretching, breathing, and algae and herbs to supplement your body create room for energy to operate. A body is needed that accommodates the vibration of multidimensional intelligence, so perhaps some of your work involves this preparation.

Question the energies that want to work with you. On Earth, it is considered rude to question a god or goddess, just as it may have been rude to question an adult when you were a child. "Children are meant to be seen, not heard." As children of the gods, you apply the same invisibility and unquestionable seniority principle. We are suggesting you question everything—including whatever we say—for not only do you have the *right* to question, you have the responsibility. This is key to being sovereign, owning your own body, and commanding your reality into being.

Learn to create spirals that come out of your solar plexus and reach into the visions of your various selves. You will find that the spirals will connect you with your purpose. Do not judge the selves that you see from your third-dimensional point of view, for judgments create traps and loops of reality that repeat the same theme in different costumes throughout time. One of the agreements that many of you made was to move beyond judgment on this journey, and it is essential to maintain that stance.

Your multidimensional selves can harass you into evolution. You are your own light and you are your own shadow. Of course, you play the game that you are separate. You play the game now that you are a member of the Family of Light and you are a good guy. We say that there are teams—light T-shirt teams and dark T-shirt teams—and you may like to think that you are only a white T-shirt. We remind you that Prime Creator makes up all of the teams, and if you are in Prime Creator's universe, then you are on all of the teams as well.

Your natural state of being, and what you are evolving toward, is a multidimensional character who will be able to make peace on this planet and take that peace into other worlds as well. Remember, peace involves a decision that is a standard chosen for your life. Someday there will be many parallel memories to integrate and ideas that suddenly emerge. You will realize that there are layers and layers of yourself *experiencing*, while a portion of you is so certain nothing is going on. These layers of reality are beginning to split and fragment, and you are moving into new aspects of your abilities and expression. Now the trick is to catch these things—to spend more time pursuing what you have been inspired to discover over the years.

You have come here to change the probabilities of Earth. You do things out of your body much more than you are aware. The day will come when you are suddenly aware of where you visit when you take a nap, daze off, or go to sleep. Eons ago, it took great training to develop these skills. Today, you are being flooded with light continuously, and the more light you have in your body, the more the reorganization of your greater identity is stimulated. Throughout this process, maintain a strong sense of self—the being that you are now. Hold a sense of love and well-being for the vehicle you have created.

Do you think that Earth is going through this change with no benefit to anyone? There are millions who are waiting patiently for Earth to become light so that they can, with love, come in and access what is here and change the course of events. In order for you to reach that place of valuableness, the knowledge of who you are must be realized and felt by all. Energy is being sent to Earth to create a stirring and a change from deep within. This is part of the design of the times, and as it comes together, you start to know, to remember, and to feel. Suddenly nothing is the same anymore.

This memory that is being stirred up inside of you can create bodily reactions because it dwells in the cells of your physical, mental, emotional, and spiritual bodies, and it needs to be understood. You are growing into something new, and you are building the framework. We encourage you to have your body adjusted through whatever modality of experience suits your fancy. You could use Shiatsu, massage, Rolfing, rebirthing, or some method through which you are able to access all your bodies—mental, physical, spiritual, and emotional. Use these methods to move energy beyond any place it may have become stuck.

We recommend that you drink great amounts of water, spend time breathing and oxygenating, do toning, and practice allowing unlabeled sound to express itself through your body. Keep your body active and alive. Spend time communicating, meditating with peace, and listening to whatever is speaking to you from the inside. Weave your discoveries into the structure of your life, and intend along the way what it is that you want.

You can play like a child with these games, and have a good time doing so, yet understand that on a deeper level you are exploring and practicing the art of shamanism—the ability to understand and affect many worlds. The shaman does not live in one world. As you learn how to evoke the assistance of other worlds and creatively exchange energy through harmony and cooperation, you change. Always return to your home station—the you of Earth, as a strong singular identity who is discovering the unfolding relationship to all that is.

You are being tested to see how consistent, reliable, and stable you are, for during the next twenty years you will be shocked by the anomalies appearing from other dimensions. Various dimensional doorways are wide open and are leaking, moving, and shifting things that were kept separate. So you may discover objects, creatures, creations, and events that have no business being where they are. You may find creatures considered extinct returning, animals suddenly disappearing without a trace, and different varieties of vegetation appearing all over the planet. Personal effects—things that you own—may just disappear one day, slipping through a crack. These are a few of the anomalies that will occur as you reconsider who and what you are in relationship to all that is.

It is much easier for you to be influenced by negative thoughtforms now than ever before. Why? Because people are creating more negativity than ever before. Do your newspapers encourage you to go into joy or negativity? The higher frequency of energy coming to the planet is causing the shattering of the astral realm, which is so overloaded with thoughtforms of fear that it cannot accommodate itself any longer.

The crash of the astral realm in its own population explosion is definitely intensifying the planet. People are more frightened and feel as if there is a heavier burden. Thoughtforms seek to attach to negativity, meaning that you often have woe rather than joy, and worry rather than upliftment, trust, and divine nonchalance. However, this is a matter of choice. What do you want to choose? What is your focus going to be?

Clarity is the name of the game here. If you make yourself available without clarity, it is very easy to attract energies that will not accommodate your vibration. This does not mean that those energies are bad; it simply means that they resonate out of sync with your vibrational intent, which may, of course, be unclear to you. When you are not firm in the stance of yourself, confusion occurs, because the energies are not integrating. Your emotions create the quality of your experience as the thoughtforms hanging out with you. Acting happy and perfect all the time is not the solution. Allow yourself to move through emotional experiences and learn from them. Dark moods and energies that you hold onto become habits or patterns that can create extreme difficulties. You can become what we call a cosmic hooker, an open doorway to any and all unqualified energies. Knowing that the Prime Creator is in all things, this indeed can create a dilemma.

Be aware that you are unfolding into the process of self-discovery in relationship to all that is. As reality and ideas emerge through you, you will be able, through love, compassion, and understanding, to experience more of the great duality and polarization that characterizes an aspect of existence. The key is to enjoy the journey of discovery and find the jewel within it.

Think of yourself as a doorway and your emotions as guardians that determine the kind of energy that is allowed onto the Earth plane at this time, because you are the gatekeeper for other dimensions. You must love yourself, for it is from yourself, in this reality, that you operate. The physical body you occupy represents your home station. The entire history of your physical body has brought you to this precise point of awareness, where you realize that you are significant. Your body is your vehicle of conveyance, your Mercedes, and there is no trading it in, at least not on this round. You are the one who defines your boundaries, the one who says, "This feels good and this does not. This is okay and this is not." Learn to operate without guilt by loving yourself and trusting that whatever you have created holds an opportunity for your spiritual growth.

Every single thought that you think comes into life and form, as if you are a baker, kneading dough and shaping cookies. Every time you think of something, a thoughtform is released into being. This thoughtform works with you and gains vitality throughout the ethers of mass thoughtforms. What you set into motion is what you will experience, for good or ill. You are the creator. Now perhaps you realize the depth of what you set into motion through your basic thoughts and beliefs. It does not pay to be jealous, nor to energize hate, revenge, or any of these things, because when you give them life, they come back to haunt you in order for you to personally experience your creative force.

When you love your body and yourself, you come to certain conclusions about what you are available for. You learn to call the shots concerning what your own molecules are available for as your intention is shouted from the cells of your being.

We are teaching you the rules of ownership. You must become sovereign in order to be strong enough to house a meeting of your multidimensional self. If your vibration of intention is clear and powerful, something that will not match this cannot even be magnetized to you. Remember, you each create your own reality in your own version of beliefs.

Energies live off your vital force—the kundalini energy

that nestles at the base of your spine and rises upward, ideally throughout your entire physical body. Often, the closest people get to understanding kundalini is the passion of sexual desire. Remember, this force that is called sexual desire can create life. In its own way, your passion impregnates you and makes you bring life forward. This force, even though you are unaware of its vitality and life-creating properties, can be sucked away or siphoned off in many different ways. Your responsibility is to raise your kundalini through all your chakras, first through your body and then out, and to use this force to create. This vitality inside you gives you the courage, grace, and confidence to use your gardening skills to plant with your mind.

Often, people who are possessed are experiencing their own thoughtforms returning to them. Psychic attack involves people intentionally sending something at others to disturb them; both parties are involved in creating the process. The sum total of any evolutionary journey is the integration of all things you have done and the acceptance of shadow and light. You must take responsibility for what you are creating—and how else can you take responsibility unless you know?

Sometimes an energy that is wanting to let you know it is present will do something so that you recognize you are not in your normal state of being. In order to have you understand that a presence is there, it will exaggerate something to see if it can capture your attention. You can say, "Hey, all right, I know you're here. I got it. I feel your presence. You do not need to go to that extreme anymore." The energy will learn how to modify itself as it merges with you. You must keep your lines of communication open. Do not think that because the energy does not come before you in 3D that it does not understand you communicating with it.

In the realm of multidimensionality and merging, animals are adepts. Animals move through dimensions. Have you ever seen an animal or a bird one minute, and then the next second it is gone? Animals are very concerned with the quality of life—much more so than you are. When the quality of life is in question, the animals automatically migrate toward a more sustaining reality. They remove themselves into other domains of existence, for they are programmed to survive.

Animals are intelligent and flexible and have many more adventures than humans do. Animals don't need to build shopping malls, graveyards, watch television and movies, and distract themselves with superficial forms of entertainment. Do you think animals are ever bored? Do you think animals ever wonder what to do? They have many, many adventures that you are not quite capable of understanding, though you will one day.

Insects and frogs, for example, open dimensional avenues with their sounds. Others may travel on sound. Everything dreams, journeying into many realities. You can best relate to the concept of dreaming knowing that, when you sleep, you go into another world that does exist. Everything exists because it is connected, whether memory is open or not. Beetles, earthworms, and frogs know they go from one reality to another. They go into other worlds, yet they are right here in this world.

Insects are represented in greater numbers than any other class of animals on your planet, and they take up less space. They keep a balance, for without the insects your planet could not be. Insects are multidimensional and act as unseen guardians for many worlds. Some of the creator gods are insectlike in appearance and character. There are people who have taken photographs and had encounters with beings who look partly human and partly like insects. The creator gods have duplicated themselves in many forms to be here as silent representatives of their own species.

Insects work with you in a way you cannot conceive at this time. You think they just accidently land or crawl on you, when in actuality they are checking out your electromagnetic frequency. You do not look like yourself to insects. You are a force field, and there are certain parts of you that are very attractive to insects because of pheromones you give off. Perhaps when they give you a little nip here and there you are getting used to their identity.

There are many forms of life that will come to awareness and existence. You will want to capture these forms of life and put them in a zoo. To them, you are in the zoo, like a prison, locked behind bars. They want to assist you and bring you back to interspecies communication. They are waiting to see if you can relate to particular animals or species. As you demonstrate your acknowledgment of intelligence in all forms of life, you begin to qualify as an ambassador or diplomatic representative of these various species. Life will become very strange indeed.

When a frog makes a croaking sound, it creates an opening to other dimensions for the animal kingdom—for insects in particular, but for many members of the animal kingdom. Frogs and insects keep frequency and have certain abilities. Frogs, when they croak in the stillness of the day or night, create a harmonic and a spinning momentum. Surrounding energies can move into this sound and experience what it is like to be other forms of life quite easily.

All animals are much more in tune with multiple realities than humans are, and they can teach you about these realities. Some people are able to merge with animals and explore the animal kingdom to discover what it is like to be in the Living Library.

Many very intelligent forms of life can manifest themselves by merging with the animal and plant kingdoms. In this way, they can come peek into your reality. Now these many intelligent forms of life want to merge with you, the library cards. The way they can access the library through you as humans is quite different from the way they can access the library by coming in as squirrels. You are complex. You have a tremendous amount of knowledge inside you.

And, as you prepare yourselves to merge with other forms of sentient existence, you will be able to bring peace to your planet. You will be able to bring a magnificent new upliftment, a new way of being, a new prayer. It will seem as if it is coming out of you, and yet you will know that it is more than you. Understand that there is great intelligence in all life forms, and the experience of all life is waiting for you. Open your emotional selves and employ the vital force of love as key to your own spiritual evolution.

Energy Exercise

Place yourself in comfort, take a few deep, centered breaths, relax, and slip into the moment. Visualize yourself with a group of people you love and trust. You are gathered together to open a light portal to meet other worlds. Imagine a pillar of light coming from above, penetrating your body and the group. On this pillar of light ride many energies that make an opening or doorway through which realities can meet.

Send your intent to the opening of this portal and make your presence known. Signal all energies and realities that, to merge with you, a vibrational match is required to meet your version of the love frequency as you presently understand it.

Picture yourself with others in the group making a ring around this opening, standing arm in arm and hand in hand. You are all filled with joy and laughing over what you have accomplished together, feeling the unity that allows you to go further.

Now, as a group, go through the opening in the portal of light. Go up and locate the place where your portal will connect you with other portals on your planet. Find yourself moving to other dimensional doorways and make rings of light. Take your light and weave it in as many portals as you can perceive. Broadcast the idea and imagine that in order for energies to enter onto Earth they must meet and match the frequency that you are discovering and holding, the frequency of love.

Picture yourself and the group all over the globe, being scattered by the winds, creating rings of light and feeling joined by other circles of light. You feel supported in the love frequency that you are now enamored of carrying.

As you travel around your globe forming these rings, feel the energies that support you in this. Feel beyond your planet. Feel who we are. Feel the Pleiadian energy infused and folded into your personal chakra system. Let our love match the love frequency that you presently understand. Allow yourself for a few moments to feel supported, nurtured, and cherished by energies that honor your existence. We love the essence of your being.

Image now a portal in your galaxy that we own and operate. As your Pleiadian friends, we act as gatekeepers for the frequency that would pass through. Let us hold that portal open for you at this time and let love from other systems filter through. As the portals open on your planet, feel that love filtering down. Picture rays of golden streaming light and feel all the cells in your body tingle. Feel embraced and surrounded by this light. Let this love enter the planet and remind all those who encounter it of an alternative way of living. Let it remind them of a new blueprint, a new ideal.

In your own identity, the one that you are seeking to discover and understand, picture yourself now standing before a mirror. See your physical body change. See the molecules move as love transforms you. Hold this love, for it is your wealth and your value. This love is you in living form. Love that you are destined to hold is the key to uniting various factions of energy—to bringing these energies to a new creative expression for your universe.

Imagine yourself weightless, moving through energy waves and opening doorways. Picture yourself, in human form, catapulted into the forefront of existence carrying a commitment of love. Take a breath, and as you breathe in, feel the love frequency all around you. It is being sent to every part of your body, and whatever you choose to do with it is up to you. Feel it fill you now with a rich calmness. Picture your planet encircled with love as it comes flooding through you while you hold your frequency over the portals around your planet.

Now, from wherever you are, picture yourself spiraling, spinning, and turning. As this spinning accelerates, moving faster and faster, unite that spinning with your physical body wherever you are. Feel that this love spins off you and touches every form of life—everything that is created. Feel it spinning off you, touching all things wherever you go. Picture that spinning getting faster and faster, and picture your knowledge becoming clearer and clearer.

Stay in that energy for a while. Feel that love—seek it, know it, share it, become curious about it, want it, and it shall be yours. We trust that you know you change your world by every thought you express. We thank you for so willingly donating thoughts of love and peace to Earth. It will affect all of existence.

EIGHT

The Gift of the Gods

The orgasmic experience sends energies of healing and reju-
venation into your body.

The Living Library's doorway in your body is your genitals, and if you learn how to use this doorway, it serves as an
opening into the records of time. Humans, in general, come
together and copulate in minutes. Often, humans don't take
the time to explore each other sexually because lustful pleasure is sometimes associated with deep emotional pain.
Many of you have been imprinted with shame around seeking that pleasure. Remember, as the story goes, you were
given the gift of the gods.

It is interesting to us how many of Earth's schools of
thought proclaim that the height of achievement is to move
beyond your sexuality. Be aware of ideas that steer you away
from the total essence of who you are. These ideas and concepts sound lofty; however, they take you away from the
earthiness and richness of your physical form. Your secretions and mysteries are gifts to be explored with dignity,
grace, reverence, and respect, through a committed, bonded
relationship.

It is our intention to inspire a reinterpretation of sexuality
within you. Please understand that as Earth goes through her

changes, you will be moved and realigned in all areas of consideration. You need not be afraid of being alone—you have the ability to manifest the deepest bonding of partnership that you desire.

Sexuality aligns your body into a state of healing and opens gateways to the stars. Sexuality in a bonded, loving relationship can be profound and take you into other worlds, revitalize your body, and remind your body of its most idealized patterns.

Sexual expression offers exploration of both the spiritual and physical realms. There is a balance that is needed. You dwell in a physical body that, in essence, came about through sexual expression by your parents. Have ease in your sexual energy; honor and accept that vital force that flows through you. We want to see you enlivened, enriched, and understanding of the vehicle you are.

You have been kept in ignorance about sex on your planet. To you it is a local event that ideally feels good, when in fact the event is quite cosmic. Whenever you have sex with another person, an energy pattern immediately connects you, and attracts invisible energies. The gods and goddesses are very infatuated with your hormones—so much so that they used to eat you alive when you were in a specific state of hormonal secretion. You may not like this data, because it makes you more responsible for yourself. It makes you look back on what you have done with your life. Ideally, you are not judging what you have done and where you have been, and ideally, you will learn from what you remember you have done—in this lifetime or another.

Using sexual expression to regenerate yourself rather than degenerate yourself is the ideal you will pursue. Dealing with sexuality involves dealing with hormones. Sex excites the very core of your cells—and the light-encoded filaments become entwined with one another. In a magnet, the energies all line up and face the same way. When you become sexual and do the dance that starts in your hormones, your whole body lines up in one direction. When you and another individual are lined up, you are like the north and south poles. Usually, the cells in your body are like a milling crowd in Grand Central Station or some other place where people are moving in all different directions. Then, during sexual activity, it is as if a whistle blows and everybody turns and looks in the same direction. When you reach states of true bonding with another person during sexual activity, you trigger each other off, and all your cells' energies line up in one direction. Your body turns into a magnet. When you and another individual achieve a heightened state of electromagnetic force, you pull on one another and create a balance between each other. When you get really good at this, you will not even have to touch each other. You can create this web of love between you, and it is through this force field that your inner bodies rise and go into other worlds.

Most of you are selective about what you eat. Be selective about how you want your body to be pleasured. Give yourself permission to discover pleasure, to talk about it, and to feel it. Look at your body—stand naked and see it in all positions to find the divinity in every crack and crevice that you have. Remember, when you drive a car, you don't say, "Oh, don't look in the trunk." You accept the whole thing. Every part of the car works together to give you a ride. It is the same thing with your body.

We think sexuality is one of the most exciting gifts you have been given, and we want to guide you further along this journey so that you can have a better time on Earth. Love yourself and love Earth because they are one and the same, and that means every part of your body. You need to talk about sex. Make a commitment to accept every area of your body and to draw a partner to yourself who will honor every area of your body. Know that your partner will be wanting and willing to pioneer this glorious part of your god/goddess force.

It is essential for us to speak to you about sex. Our ancestors were responsible for steering you away from your own sexuality and assisting you to misunderstand it. The healing that will come as you begin to understand your own priorities of life will occur through understanding this vital force that is called sexuality. It is one of the major key healings that needs to take place on the planet.

We have some suggestions for you. They have to do with how to come together with a partner and honor your body and the body of your partner as you explore the mysteries. Remember, you are exploring how much energy you can hold between yourself and your partner and how that energy will transport you somewhere.

As the hormones of attraction move, you experience exchanges of energy between all your chakras and those of your partner. Your energies become fused. If you raise the energy upward rather than keeping it in your genitals, you can increase the flow of energy and operate with a new consciousness. Learn to lift the energy up each other's spines and move it through your bodies, holding off orgasm. During the act of sex itself, you may find that you move into a collapse of time.

When you share sexual energy as a couple, you open yourselves up for other forces to merge with you. For outside energies, fusing with humans while you are having sex is a special and exciting part of the Living Library. At one time it was considered the ultimate honor to have a god or goddess merge with you and your partner during your sexual experience. The ultimate experience was to merge with highly evolved beings who honored you and carried the love vibration so that it became a multidimensional sexual experience. How many people do you know who draw high vibrations into themselves before they have sex? Some people get drunk or take drugs or do whatever they need to do to get the courage together to have sex. You have to set out values, standards, and conditions about your sexuality to the nonphysical realm so that only those who meet your standard come to you.

Be clear with these energies that want to work with you. Tell them to fit into what you are available for. You call the shots—to the Pleiadians, to all the extraterrestrials, to the gods and goddesses. You decide and say, "Hey, listen, I'm learning about you. I don't understand. I want to get to know you. These are my standards. I only have sex with someone I love. I honor my body. I honor Earth. Integrity is first and foremost with me. If you can fit into my values, I welcome you into my life to teach you about human sexuality." This is an approach.

You have learned how to recognize our Pleiadian vibration, yes? If something else were to come in and to pretend it was us, you would know. Yet, perhaps you have not learned how to recognize the other energies, so you don't know who they are. The higher realms are not beyond deception. How do you know when you make a friend on Earth that the friend is a good person? You have a feeling for the person. We want you to use the same perceptual abilities for the nonphysical realms.

We suggest that as you explore working and playing with entities who are looking for a human to help them come into form, you maintain your values and be very clear about what you are available for. Reiterate those values and your clarity over and over again. Honor your body, honor the body of your partner, and have sex only coupled with love—that is a key. The sexual energy in your body is your life force. It is the god or goddess force within you. It holds the secret of secrets—it is the creative force.

Most humans use their sexuality in a way that degenerates rather than regenerates them. A long time ago, the Goddess was so in tune with the forces of nature that she would create vibratory rates that these forces of nature would feed off of. Remember, all things are interlocked—nothing is separate, and everything is connected to everything else. What you do here today affects the whole globe.

You inherit the blueprint of every person with whom you have sex, so you not only have your stuff to deal with but theirs as well. When your body comes together with another's, your chakras are stirred and your kundalini is moved. If your kundalini is only moved in your lower two chakras and is not a full body infusion, you can have "hooks" in the other person's auric field, and they can have "hooks" in yours. This is why it is important to be very selective about who you are going to have sex with. Make sure if you are going to go for it that you have some kind of bond and commitment and that you plan on working things out, because in this day of accelerated time and sped-up energy, you can take everything on from someone else.

We advise you to clear all old attachments from your body. See your body cleansed and blessed and all sexual energy from previous attachments released. Do whatever you can to lovingly release former sexual relationships with a hold on your life. Stop talking about the past and energizing old partners. Let that stuff go. If you keep talking about people that you were involved with years ago, you keep energizing their thoughtforms in your auric field, especially if you've had a sexual connection with them. This prevents you from experiencing a new now.

This is similar to possession in that you put out a magnet or doormat for these people's energy even if you have not been in contact for twenty years. You cycle through their energy. They may not even be anything like what you remember, but you re-create your experience with them. These are very tricky times. Twenty years ago, things were nostalgic. You rode around with the radio on—Sunday afternoons cruising down the strip, Coca Colas, getting drunk, going to the beach, hanging out. Life was just one fast lane, one great party. Things have changed. You had the leisure then to daydream and fantasize. There was a huge gap of time between when you thought of something and when you eventually got it. It took eons to get what you wanted to manifest. Now, that is not so. Now, whenever you think of something, you bump into it when you cross the room. It comes to you that quickly. Be selective. Be in respect of this time capsule you are in. There is a collapse of time, and a shift in the way everyone is going to view reality.

When you use a Kleenex, you pick it up, you blow your nose, and you throw it away. People are not like that. The process is not that smooth and that quick. Whenever you have a sexual relationship with a person, you are bonded to that person. When two bodies come together, even for a one-night stand, you take on a merging of each other's auric fields. Perhaps until now you did not understand this.

Sex is wonderful. It is absolutely one of the most glorious gifts that you have as a human being to discover your identity. However, you must learn to use it. No one has educated you on the ramifications of the energy link that comes from having sex with people. You may want to do a number of ceremonies or rituals with the intention of releasing people's energy from your field. Smudging is a very good ritual to clear your energy field. Churches all use it. Many institutions use incense or smoke of some kind to clear energy. Smoke is multidimensional. When you smudge, it is an indication you are taking a step to cleanse, clear, and release the energy so that there are no attachments. You may want to smudge your body and smudge your home.

When you are disengaging from people, you need to invest energy in this process in the same way that you invested energy to come together. You can't do the Kleenex routine and toss them away; there must be an ending. How do you do this? Especially if the people are being uncooperative? You work with people's energy on the etheric level. With love, you bless them, release them, and ask them to move out of your field, giving thanks for the lessons you shared together.

It is more intense these days to have sex, in case you haven't noticed. And if you are not having sex, it is probably an appropriate stage of your development. However, if you have not had sex for a long, long time, we would say: What are you hiding from and what beliefs do you have about yourself that you believe you do not qualify to have sex anymore? The orgasmic experience sends energies of healing and rejuvenation into your body. Many times it can cause an intense emotional release, and you are flooded with feelings.

The endocrine system releases all kinds of hormones and chemical substances in your body. Some of these substances are meant to be disseminated, while some are meant to be held in your body. When they are held in your body, your body absorbs them and comes into a higher order. You become more autonomous, more all knowing. When the life force is consciously directed outward, in the form of semen, it is used to impregnate. Just as women have been sold the idea that they cannot prevent pregnancy if they do not wish to have children, men have been sold the idea that the ejaculation process is the only way to have an orgasm. It is a process that can be held, with the fluids distributed into the body. It is a higher form of sexuality that has been practiced in the East for eons. If men ejaculate every time they reach orgasm, they lose their life force, in one version of reality.

If you are a man, when you have sex you can learn to retain the sperm and not ejaculate. There are certain techniques to do this. Pressing on the perineum, the small area between the anus and the scrotum, holds the life force inside the body, and the orgasm changes. Humans have been tricked into having genital orgasms, which are localized experiences, rather than full-body, cosmic experiences. If you think about how many bodies you are, you will realize that you can experience orgasm in all of these bodies. So as you reconsider and redefine how you are pleasured, you begin to experience different ways of receiving pleasure, and you move out of the locality of the genital area.

Sperm is a catalytic force of existence, and every time a man releases sperm, he is to some extent depleting his body. In the ideal, a man will ejaculate by choice when there is a need for procreation, or the desire for the experience. You have been given ideas that keep you in a very low vibrational state that is degenerating rather than rejuvenating. First you were infused with the idea that sex is bad. Then institutions were created to forgive you for doing these bad things. You have this duality flipping backward and forward. Many men and women, especially in the Western world, do not understand how deeply infused they are with the idea that sex is bad. This is such an overlay of all of their behavior that they rush through the sexual experience, because if they are doing something bad, they don't want to get caught.

There is a balance, where you find the right place. You have no guilt or shame after you have come out of the sexual event. That is why we say it is essential to have a deep bonding of love with your partner. The love that you have with your partner prevents, in general, the shame and the guilt. Without love there is often too much shame and guilt, and the emotional destruction can be great.

There are so many things to explore in the genital area of the male and female. The orifices that you have as openings have different spots, or acupuncture points, that can be triggered. These have very little to do with genital penetration.

There is also tremendous excitement that can come from looking into each other's eyes, exchanging the strands of DNA. This is the heart connection into the eyes of the soul— the heart of the soul. Of course, you can close your eyes; however, a tremendous amount of eye contact changes the experience. You may also wish to work with your chakras, touching especially each other's heart chakras. Put your hand on the heart chakra of your partner and keep keep your hearts open.

As you stimulate with your eyes, and use the chakras, and activate the acupressure points in the genital area, these places come alive. As you touch these places, there is a chemical response that hooks you into an orgasm that moves outward into your many bodies. This allows you to climb the ladder to higher knowledge and come into your divinity. It also involves allowing yourselves to explore each other's bodies—to be completely free with the shape and expression of your bodies. This is the next avenue.

Explore who you are, make an intention of what you are after, and make your time of expressing your sexuality a time of joy. Sex is not about performance; it is about the most intimate bonding and sharing that can possibly be. It is not just about, "Yeah, you were great." It is about intimacy, about fusing with another as you maintain your own sovereignty. It is about being supported and supporting, because it is going to be essential as you maintain your own sovereignty and rediscover what pleasure and joy are. Your body will begin to remember.

Perhaps you can change your focus during intercourse to not reach climax immediately. Have fun and build to the point just before climax, then hold that frequency, subside to a point, and build it again and again. Take some time with it. When you honor the process, spend hours doing so, because this creates a deep intimacy and the experience will last you so much longer. The rejuvenation or regeneration of the life force occurs when there are hours and hours of intimacy, with your eyes open, and you learning to get your body to do what you want it to do.

An orgasm is not a local event. There are people who can have their ears tickled and have orgasms. There are people who can have their wrists tickled and have orgasms. You can have orgasms when you dream. You can have orgasms when you are out of your body. The orgasm is misunderstood. You think it is a local event of the genital area. It is not. It is a cosmic event that has been interpreted to be localized so that you would miss the point. It is an ongoing pulsation of godhood and goddesshood—of pleasure and of connecting to the pulse of existence. So it can occur anywhere. If you were really tuned into your sexuality, taking a bite of a delicious food could send an orgasm through you if you were that free. It is the height of appreciating the divinity in all things.

There is nothing wrong with masturbation. It is a fine practice if you learn to honor your body and the rightness of stimulating certain feelings within your body. Masturbate without projection, without shame, and without dragging varieties of unknowns into your body through thought. It is tricky, like everything. It is a fine art form, but it is not to be practiced solely as a form of release. If you are using masturbation to release tension, then you need to reconsider. If you have never masturbated, then how can you expect to have sex with someone else and expect them to know your body when you don't know it yourself?

When you feel drawn to expressing your sexual energy, you may feel, "Wow, if I decide to follow through and practice the art of masturbation, this time it would be simply that I want a release. I want to lessen the tension." If this is what you feel, then say to yourself, "All right, how am I going to handle this buildup of energy? Well, rather than using my old pattern of masturbating and releasing the energy and feeling good for a few moments, I think I will go for the gold and be a little out of comfort. I will hold this energy. Instead of practicing masturbation, I will sit somewhere, use crystals, do breathing techniques, and pull in the pillar of light." Pull the light up in your mind's eye, and feel it flood your body.

This will help you tremendously, because you want to come into knowledge and self value and know what your boundaries are. You want greater relaxation and a broader view, yet you are constantly only taking your energy to certain levels. By holding your sexual energies, you will start using your solar plexus, heart, throat, and third eye. Your crown chakra will open and you will go, "Aha, I am getting smarter here. How is it that I am becoming more intelligent?" The answer is, because you are using your life force in a variety of ways rather than simply using one recipe for it. You have one recipe for the energy that you call sexuality. It is your life force. There are many ways to use it.

It is one thing to explore your sensuality and have orgasmic experiences by wanting to feel good and understand your sexuality so that you know who you are. It is another thing to feel horny (to use your terms), to have all this sexual buildup, to simply masturbate to release the tension, and to have a climax. Sex is a sacred offering of the body, something private and sensual. It helps you understand this force within you that brings you pleasure.

Many people these days are practicing celibacy because they realize that the kind of sexual activity they were previously engaging in was draining their energy. Perhaps this occurred because they were sexual with others without love, without a commitment, and without a spiritual connection to bond together. As we have said, your electromagnetic bodies and auric fields get fused together. There is back-and-forth telepathy—"You own me." "I own you."—playing out on the etheric level.

If you are experiencing periods of celibacy, wonderful, because what you are doing is containing your energy. When you have a sexual experience and you are not fully integrated in your chakras, it is very draining. Even though it is exhilarating, the energy is only working with your first and second chakras, which work with strands number one and number two of your DNA.

When you stop having sex, you may still feel sexual. You want it, but you learn to contain that energy and let it infuse your body rather than simply having sex to release it. As you infuse that energy in your body, you value your body more because the energy all of a sudden shows you that you are worth more and can do more than you ever thought you could.

The ideal is not to avoid sex or transcend sex. The ideal is to revalue your sexuality—to revalue the very essence of what your physical body does when you have sex and experience orgasmic states. There is going to be a lot more leeway and experimentation with sexual expression. Remember the 1960s? Who could forget them? Women threw their bras away and breasts were in. Over the last fifteen to thirty years, women began to feel more comfortable with nude sunbathing and topless bathing. You explored yourselves sexually, and things of a sexual nature began to cultivate and develop.

In recent years, there has been a pulling back, a fear of sexuality. People are withdrawing from sexuality: "I don't understand this force. I come together with someone and in the moment it feels absolutely exhilarating. It feels as if I'm having a hundred hot fudge sundaes and not gaining a pound. Then afterward I don't feel so good." Intimacy and honesty and commitment are the essential parts of having good sexual experiences. You must be able to be vulnerable and open in each other's eyes; then sexual activity holds a higher vibration. Just as there was great experimentation as a result of the energy that was loosened in the 1960s, there will be great experimentation with sexuality in the 1990s, and for the most part, it will involve spiritual exploration.

Practicing celibacy is fine as long as it does not mean to you that sex is out. It is good if it means that the sexual experience is being contemplated and reconsidered. It is being put on the shelf for a while because sexuality is misunderstood, and by moving away from it, perhaps it can be observed. If you've ever climbed a mountain, you know that it is quite different to be on the mountain than on the plain looking at the mountain. This is what some people are going through. They are looking at the mountain and are not feeling deprived by not being on the mountain. They are setting up a reevaluation of what sexuality is, what love is, who they are, and what values they are establishing for themselves.

Sexuality is one of the most intimate aspects of your lives. Yet most people on this planet have sex with no intimacy whatsoever. It is a function, like putting oil in a car: "I need sex, roll over." Men and women alike. It has always been our contention that the reason you were steered away from your sexuality was because, if you started having sex without fear, you would discover that it is a doorway to higher consciousness. The very life force that you can use to create babies can also be used as a magic carpet ride into other realms of existence. Eventually, the strands of DNA will be read in the iris of the eye. When you are sexual with another person and you look into each other's eyes, you trigger one another into other realities. You can also use breath and imagery to start cycling energy. The energies are likened unto the force that sends the space shuttle into orbit around your planet—the energy that lifts the so-called space vehicles and sets them on journeys. The energy of sexual expression can release you and set you on a journey.

Sex is the ultimate event to make special and to plan around. It also needs to be very spontaneous but in the spontaneity of it, it has its own ritualistic appreciation and approach.

Love is the ingredient that brings bodies together, whether they be male and male, female and female, or male and female. The body was designed to have male and female mate. That is very obvious—the polarities meet. It is a matter of biology, although we will say that there is nothing wrong with those of like vibration being drawn together. That is what they are working on to learn about themselves; it does not pay to judge The ultimate experience comes when there is love, when the eyes are open, and when there is a commitment. Then you can begin to travel.

Sexuality will take on a whole different value and become one of the most powerful forces discussed as Earth changes become more pronounced. As your society disintegrates, you will want to reevaluate everything. You will want to be close, to be committed, and to have a partner you can count on. As you become aware of life extension, and understand about everything speeding up, you will eventually experience great movements of rejuvenation. The partners that you choose will be partners you know and have known for tens of thousands of years.

In most cases, opening to intimacy is easier for women than for men, simply because women are more comfortable with their emotions. As humans, you are forever searching for the vibration of ecstasy, love, and connection that comes through the expression of emotion. You cannot access the sexual frequency of ecstasy and love without feeling, for sexuality *is* feeling. Many people are in desperate search of this frequency, and they do not even know that they are searching for it. In their naive way, the only way they know is to seek sexual expression.

If you are female, you can help your male partner open up by accepting yourself and your own body and by creating for yourself a standard about the kind of man you are available for. You will magnetize this kind of man because he will be willing to learn and change. The male vibrations, in general, are very confused at this time, not knowing for certain what their identity is. They are going to find out that they need to draw to themselves those who will integrate them into these changes. The more you can be stabilized in your love for your body, and in your willingness to know what you want and what your intentions are, the easier it will be for men.

Too many women for too many years kept their mouths shut and were simply happy to have dates on Saturday night. Women did not create any standard for men to reach for. With the activation of the Goddess energy, and the understanding of the complete female form as it is designed to be, a new standard is created. Women must learn to speak about their feelings and desires in order to create a new standard of experience. Then it will be easier for men to open their feeling centers, experience their emotions, bring their sexual energy up through their chakras, and comfortably experience greater intimacy than they ever thought possible. These things will take time. Women have been so locked into not speaking and men into not feeling that these changes will not happen overnight. Be patient with each other. Have great compassion for all people and for what they are going through. You have many things to share and teach each other.

One of the big taboos in your society has been oral sex. We've said that women's substance of power is blood, while the substance of power for men is sperm. Sperm carries a tremendous amount of data, while blood can be likened to an elixir of healing, a source of life; both offer revitalization and rejuvenation. When you share these substances while in a bonded, loving relationship, it is the ultimate in sharing your secret power. It is the ultimate in blending in your identities so that you can remember who you are and why in this life-time you have come together.

As women become aware of the blood mysteries, many will do outrageously creative things with their blood. They will learn that it is not a horrible, smelly, ugly, bad thing, and that it has many mysteries. They will play creatively, respect-fully, and without shame with this substance to see what they can do with it. This will also be true for sperm.

When you ingest these substances, you create a very deep bonding. It is like drinking or infusing the secrets and sum total of the individuals from whom they came. Again, we will state here that without the ingredient of love, you will never reach this exalted state of achievement.

When you are in a state of love and trust, sharing, ingest-ing, and using these fluids opens the deepest gates of memo-ry, bonding, and intimacy. You go beyond what is called secret. Most people are incapable of sustaining this state for any length of time. They get close and may experience it; however, they are not able to carry the next phase of intimacy into completion, which goes beyond the physical.

The intimacy that comes from this sharing is profound. What you are experiencing and what is revealed is very deep. It takes love and much preparation to use these substances properly. Be of clear intent as you experiment with these things, and you will open yourself to new avenues of journeying.

We suggest that couples who have sex have an intention around their sexual activity. This does not take the spontaneity out of it. It does not mean that you have to get organized and structured and make appointments and have all this processing before you come together. As you develop intimacy, sexual activity does not take place only when your hormones are zinging. Sexual expression takes place continuously. As you walk into a market, you can carry on a conversation about your sexuality. You don't have to lock that experience into the bedroom or when you are having a drink or within certain little boxes of performance. You are going to be infused with this energy. It is part of what will train you about your divinity. It is essential.

You will not understand what it is to be gods or goddesses without your sexual experience, not completely, because you are humans and it is part of the way your bodies are designed. All the creatures on this planet have some sort of sexual expression—some method of titillating and reproducing themselves. You don't understand how two flies can simply touch antennae and titillate each other. Creatures on Earth—plants and animals—stimulate one another and bring themselves into heightened states of activity without reproducing.

Hold this image. It is needed for you to understand and not be afraid of your sexuality. Do not make your sexuality out of vogue because you fear the very life force you have.

As you come together in couples, there will be much more free talk and discovery of sexuality. In time, you will find that this will be very comfortable. No one will question the so-called moral view around it because you will not even qualify to attend that kind of teaching session if you do not understand what it is about. It is about spiritual sex.

You have many things to look forward to in the sexual arena. Stay open, evaluate your present beliefs around sexuality, and explore your boundaries. Sexuality is your birthright and your heritage as humans. It is your gift from the gods.

Energy Exercise

Take a deep breath and relax. Imagine light charged with particles filling your lungs and moving into your body. Find that place where you are in tune with your attention and find the part of yourself that observes who you are. Now ride the energy through your breath and into your body to a subatomic level. Fill that place with light.

Simultaneously, feel the energy around you as you sit quite still, holding your ideals. Picture twelve chakras blossoming with color and light, spinning inside your body and out. Sense the energy that flows between your chakras, and make an intention to open to the sexual codes, mysteries, and secrets stored within your being through the transformational qualities of gold.

Listen very closely to discern any sounds your body resonates with. Follow those sounds and picture yourself lying on a table that is made of twenty-four-carat gold. Whatever image comes to your mind, hold onto it. Look at the table in great detail. Feel your body lying on the gold table, absorbing the warmth of the gold. Gold is a premier conductor. Imagine the gold table conveying codes of electrical impulses into the very cells of your body. You are at peace as you lie on this table. Your guides and higher self stand around, supervising and watching you. You are very relaxed, in a place inside your body where there is deep space. In that space, you are feeling the gold light and seeing the pulsations of electricity as they move through a well-lit space in your body as you lie on the gold table.

The four corners of the table, rectangular in shape, act as anchor points through which energy enters. Keep yourself in this subatomic consciousness and experience the transference of electrical energy on a subatomic level. It is as if huge bolts of lightning move from planet to planet. These are electrical jolts that move between the atoms. You are warm and stimulated by a sound that calls you and keeps you in a lullaby-like state. You are enthralled watching this space in your body as if you are watching an electrical storm over the vast countryside.

The lights and flashings of this electrical energy recharge the smallest particles in your body, which begin to come alive and remember their identity, letting you know they have consciousness. Find yourself swirling throughout your body, excitedly meeting the atoms that are waking up. Feel your body decreeing to you willingness, intelligence, and desire to work in cooperation with any direction you set. Feel yourself excited with this discovery as new possibilities endlessly present themselves. Allow yourself to go deeper into relaxation and trust, surrendering to a process that will reorganize you and offer greater meaning and purpose to your sexual, sensual self. Drift into a soft pillow of memory, experiencing yourself as valued and mirroring your value and appreciation of others. At this moment of letting go, picture something that will bring you meaning in your life and that will be a contribution to the planet, stirring many people. Feel the ongoing gentle electrical stimulation, and when you sleep this evening, dream you are on the gold table and travel into the transformational vistas of sexual value.

NINE

Riding the Corridors of Time

The Living Library of Earth will ease you into a vibrational shift of sharing and flowing with energy. From nature, Earth's majestic playground, you will learn how to merge and emerge into the corridors of time.

Time is a construct. On Earth, you have been under the assumption that the present springs from the past. We suggest that the present springs from the future as well. Time has many doorways through it, and the past and future both have their own validity and importance. This is all part of the ever-expanding now. The past, in its now, continues to influence its ongoing now. These ongoing nows continue to grow and mature, the same as their future counterparts. The assignment you are on involves changing your past, as you spring from the future, in order to create a different present.

Time is collapsing in upon itself. Right now it seems to you that space implies distance—that it separates you. When you think of a friend in another part of the world, there is space between you. The collapse of time involves a disruption of the boundaries of frequency control that define the world you operate within. As cosmic rays are caught by your sun and energized into your solar system, everything is sped up. This brings more possibilities into the now and bursts the barriers of third-dimensional time that determine the stage on which events must be played out. The structure of third-dimensional time locks and isolates you from your psychic self, the self that moves beyond time. Your psychic self knows things that are beyond what is apparent in the time you are in.

You are ruled by cycles and rhythms. A main influence that designs the pulse of life is the moon. Through the moon's cycles, and by the revolving of Earth on her axis and Earth's rotation around the sun, you make and define time. The moon, of course, in orbit around Earth, acts as Earth's celestial companion on the cyclical journeys. Until the advent of electricity, these were the rhythms through which life was lived and defined for thousands of years. People could watch time pass. Day turned into night, and night turned into day. Time had distinctions. People could *watch* the seasons pass, and time was based on something that could be verified. With electricity came the breaking of these rhythms, for there could be light past dark. People began to use time differently, for functioning with light while it was dark heralded a radically different approach to the twenty-four-hour day, because electric light provided more moments to expand into.

With the advent of the computer, there was another complete change in perception. Time became condensed to such an extent that, within nanoseconds, billions of separated segments of time were experienced by a machine. The second could not be divided by the human eye. More and more people worked around computers, and computers began to speed up.

When people first worked around computers, their concepts of time completely changed, and they could only handle so much of a distortion. Now that people are trained in computers, their altered time perception is passed on through the generations, and time is more sped up. However, the computer is a third-dimensional manifestation mirroring the collapse and distortion of time, and people fed the results of this into the mass psyche. This permits people like you to weave things together and perceive reality from a significant psychic viewpoint—a different point in time. The splitting of the second and the infusion of the computer heralded the technological boom of this century, completely changing everything and speeding your consciousness toward untold probabilities. The second and the moment continuously hold more events.

Because time is collapsing, the third-dimensional structure is not in place anymore. More events happen per moment, preparing you for psychic breakthroughs. To a large degree, everything is very playful right now. There are many, many energies around you in your daily lives, enticing you to meet them and reinterpret your basic beliefs about reality.

You all share the idea that time can be clocked. Everyone agrees that time is in existence. We say it is a construct. As a matter of fact, every few years you have to make adjustments in your Greenwich Mean Time because of the missing time, or extra time that you are off. One of the things each of you can shift to your advantage is your entire perception of time. Stop letting other people define your time and let go of this business of "I don't have enough time." As time collapses, it may feel like you are running out of time. When you send the message to your body that you are running out of time, your body starts to run out of time, as if you had set a stop watch. Many people rush madly these days because they sense the collapse of time, and they don't know how to interpret it. Remember to go into the moment, the ever-expanding now, to discover yourselves and maintain your balance. This is the direction the cosmic rays provide—an initial chaotic scrambling, rearranging your perceptions and concepts about the world in which you dwell.

Time has a variable now. It cannot be measured and clocked any longer. You can change, bend, and move time. As time collapses, new concepts, ideas, inventions, and alternatives are bombarding the mass psyche of the planet every few moments. Probabilities of the moment are awakening and expanding through your experience of self-realization. Because you have mastered an affinity to connect with intelligence outside the planet, collectively the planet is beginning to qualify for a higher rate of intelligence and responsibility. Though it may appear your world is reeking with corruption, please be aware that both polarities are going on at the same time. Those who carry light are becoming very empowered, and in a few years you will be amazed at the force of these people, for they are you. One belief you have in common is your belief in a new version of reality in which people express their freedom with respect, harmony, and cooperation, and in which Earth and each form of life—animal, plant, mineral, and human—is valued.

Remember, the Keepers of Time steer your universe along a certain course and are able to move through what would be called the barriers of time. They create slices or segments of your universe that allow your universe to be connected. Energies move from one segment to another, and certain segments are kept separated—this is time as you know it. Remember that energy is in all things and that you are part of Prime Creator. Prime Creator is on a journey of separation so that it can come to a greater understanding of itself. So the Keepers of Time keep the universe alive by keeping it separated.

The Maya called themselves Day Keepers. We call them Keepers of Time. They are associated, of course, with the Pleiades system. They are masters at going into and out of time events. They also are masters at creating time locks— they cordon things off so that events can be directly in front of you and, because of the time locks, you do not see them. Time locks keep your consciousness from perceiving simultaneous time.

The Maya laid the groundwork, timewise, for events that are to transpire today. The Egyptians laid another type of groundwork, the Incas and Native Americans each laid another. Each civilization played its part to create the time-locked events that are ready to open now in this kernel or this segment of existence where you are. Atlantis is another civilization that layered a grid of information for this present time frame. Remember, everything is ongoing, and civilizations never end. You think Atlantis was destroyed and exists no longer, so it must be in the past. That is one version of reality. In actuality, there is an Atlantean civilization that was never destroyed—an Atlantean civilization that solved its own dilemmas, found solutions, and did not need to terminate itself because of a misuse of energy. Similarly, versions of your world will find solutions and move into the Golden Age, just as versions of your world will be destroyed.

This is how Atlantis, or any other civilization, can be in the future. Civilizations are ongoing—outside of the constrictions of time. So, in effect, the Atlantean version of the future that found its own solutions wishes to assist the Atlantean energy of the past, because it is all the same energy and it is all reincarnational versions of the self. The purpose of going back to the past is to heal and make whole and teach the proper use of energy. Civilizations that are quite successful in all versions of themselves always go back—if you want to call it that—to assist the versions of themselves that did not have the same opportunities or did not find the solutions. A successful civilization can be conceived of as a conscious collective aware of its purpose and effect on the great web of existence.

The Keepers of Time that orchestrate events are like balls of light with rays that travel into many different realities and directions. The Mayan Keepers of Time were able to anchor on Earth the data that would make sense to future generations, because they were multidimensional. They could travel backward, forward, and sideways in time, and their civilization was based upon time travel. They left many clues to this story buried throughout the land of Mexico. Their *now* became more meaningful because it was their purpose to grow a now that would benefit nows outside of their now. The Maya meant to create the paradigm, the description of what is going to occur, the cycles that your Earth goes through, and the cycles of time that are based on cosmic doorways. Earth's cycles with the sun, moon, and planets within your solar system have a significant effect on your physical electromagnetic body. The Maya understood that Earth is involved in a larger system of rotation than just the solar system. That system of rotation was based on different numerical divisions. The Maya created and defined time in your system based upon their knowing that you were part of much larger cycles.

There were many versions of Maya—many different groups of Time Keepers who came in at different junctures to work and play with third-dimensional time. The Maya certainly did not make their first appearance in the time period that you are led to believe they existed. They were on your Earth many times prior to that, thousands and thousands of years ago. In actuality, they can move to the completion of the universe as easily as they can move to the beginning of the universe. It is their task to make certain that all the pieces of the universe work and come to collapse when the time is right. They also make certain there is not a premature collapse. Feel your connection to these Mayan Time Keepers and open yourself to the keys they prepared for your discovery.

Time locks around realities work in the same way that mechanisms adjust the lighting in your home to go on and off when you want it to. Electromagnetically, consciousness has a pulsation, offering an indication of its presence, no matter where it is. Consciousness is in all things, and according to how it is bundled, it gives off a unique, definitive signal.

There are those who know how to time lock consciousness. They change the modulating frequency so that if others scan existence to see where or how certain energies have combined and bundled themselves they would not find them. Because of the time locks that were put upon the portals here, and because the corridors of time are owned, those out in the cosmos are not able to find Earth. Its light of existence was erased. A different electromagnetic spectrum, a harmless one that does not register the kind of consciousness Earth has, was put here so that Earth could not be found. Earth was covered up—quarantined.

The purpose of the Maya was to come onto the planet to establish a paradigm for the future. Different civilizations hold open portals of energy through collective consciousness. Energies that support or sustain other types of realities can, in limited number, be pulled onto the planet. However, a civilization must be prepared and trained to anchor this pillar of light. When there is light, there is information.

The Mayan civilization was one of these civilizations. Today, the Balinese culture is one of these civilizations. These cultures exist in pockets around the world. They can be communities within states or areas of cities, where there is great harmony, cooperation, reciprocity of support, and creativity. The Maya were an experiment to affect the future and seed this planet, which was very dark for a very long period of time.

The Maya knew what their purpose was. They knew when their demise would be, just as the Tibetans foresaw the invasion of their country and hid many of their most important documents and artifacts years before the Chinese came in and created a seemingly outrageous slaughter. Because the Maya were Keepers of Time, they were able to evacuate Earth, knowing that their purpose was done. This is one of the deepest secrets of the Maya—they knew the date and the time.

The Mayan calendar precisely indicates the cycles of the heavens and the hells. The Maya knew their day of departure, and they prepared for that closure. From their point of view, they were transported to another physical dimension. In actuality, the Maya still very much exist; they flourish.

The Maya knew that one day their time would come and they would leave the planet. And they knew that one day their knowledge, their keys, would be uncovered and discovered by the Family of Light—by you. We suggest that there are some people who have discovered these keys already. The Maya knew the whole story of their purpose and why they came here to seed clues for a future that is now.

Your keys of consciousness are moving through the time locks that the Maya are lifting for you. Because they are the Keepers of Time, the Maya are opening many time locks all over the planet.

You may wonder how these secrets have been kept from you—how you could have been so controlled and kept so isolated. If all of these other creatures and realities exist, why is it that you have not bumped into them? It is because of the web and the time locks around the web where you are located. Your civilization has been locked for the most part in the primary web that owns the corridors of time. Your corridor has been locked in 3D.

There are many other ways that this particular corridor could be developed: only one main trunk line could be built, or various smaller routes could be explored, like the numerous roads that lead to your cities, towns, and neighborhoods. If only one road exists in and out, and it is locked, then commerce is forbidden from entering this time corridor, and it is cut off completely from all other influences. In your reality, governments issue sanctions against other countries, most often as a punitive measure, creating isolation and boycott in the same fashion as the time players along the corridor of time.

When the road is opened—when the time locks are lifted—realities will merge and blend and change, and you will be very connected with your higher identity. Over the next number of years, you must prepare yourself for that infusion of knowledge. You are on an accelerated journey, preparing you for the opening of the time locks and the fusion of your identity.

Time locks keep civilizations or realities from blending together. As the time locks are opened and you come into this birthing of the new world, there will be a merging of many realities. If this is done with maturity and understanding of the use of light, it can be quite an uplifting period.

All time is simultaneous. A planet has layers of energy grids around it that allow it to be experienced from its various time frames. In order to enter a planetary body, you must discover the portals or openings that take you to the realities of the planet where sentient life exists. You can land on a world and it can look completely empty to you if you don't go through a portal. By going through a portal, you access all of the different realities and time frames and corridors that run off this portal. So someone can come back to an Earth that existed two hundred or five hundred years ago—these realities exist.

Layer upon layer of gridworks surround worlds. As these gridworks are shifted and moved, they create different realities and different energies. When you move or shift the grids and pass through a portal, you are able to enter worlds of past, present, and future simultaneously.

Portals are protective devices that are put around planets. The ownership, creation, or making of a portal is an awesome task. There is a frequency energy that must be maintained to hold that portal open. There are many portals on Earth. We will speak of a few. There is one in the Mexico/Central America area. There is one in the Sinai, and there is one over Tibet. These are three major portals through which energies come and depart the planet. Ancient crystal skulls are often discovered or kept in portal areas. When people maintain guardianship and ownership of a portal, they also have the ability to access the corridors of time. Those in Tibet could look into the future and see that they were to be invaded, so they made preparations for the times that were coming. They could see what their very seeds—the sperm of the Tibetan monks—would be used for. They could also see why their artifacts had to be hidden, and that they would have to go into exile.

The portal in the Middle East has been one of the main openings onto the planet. The Bermuda Triangle, the portal of the old Atlantean area, also served as a major gateway onto the planet. However, now the energies are chaotic and confused there, and that portal is not safe to access. You can get stuck or lost because of the conflict and chaos that took place there. Other portal areas include Easter Island, Mount Fuji, Mount Shasta, Lake Titicaca, the Nazca lines, and Uluru.

There are those who can read and travel the corridors of time, and there are those who cannot. Empires of consciousness are forming to take over different factions of existence throughout the cosmos and universe. If they have the ability to ride the corridors of time, they have incredible knowledge about probabilities and how to insert themselves into the variable of electromagnetic portals. If the corridors of time are not traveled with knowledge, many events can blindly trample through what is called time, moving from one place to another like tidal waves pulverizing existence. These events seem not to care which portal or probability they enter; they strike them all without aim. And yet, you know that all events are synchronistically tied to a deep order and meaningful plan—a Goddess-staged show, indeed.

In order to establish a new time line and a whole new web, the event that anchors the web must be a primary event of such profound implosion that it affects all of existence. Otherwise the web has nowhere to go. Those who own the time line to Earth have been keeping Earth segregated, not allowing free commerce to come and go on the time line. There are those in the future constructing secondary and tertiary webs. A secondary web is a second fabric to reroute energy around the main corridor of time. A tertiary web is a third, a catchweb in case the second web doesn't work.

Time lines, the fabric of time, and the tubes that run on this fabric of time are all hooked into primary events. Without a primary event, you cannot hook into a time line. In other words, the secondary and tertiary webs need to be hooked into a primary event, so that other time lines can use it as an anchor. The splitting of the atom was a primary event. So was the splitting of the second. Harmonic Convergence was a primary event. Primary events can be public or private events, and are events through which the course of history is affected drastically. So, in order to anchor a new time line onto the planet, there has to be a mass event taking place.

Your time corridor is being penetrated from outside— from the future—by these webs. When you build secondary and tertiary webs and you want to go into a locked corridor, you must find a primary event. If you do not find a primary event, then you do not have something to hook into. It is like catching a fish. You can throw a hook into the pond. If nothing bites it, you don't have a primary event.

A primary event is an occurrence that is registered within the prime webwork in the corridors of time as a pivotal juncture around which all of reality transits. It can be considered an event that is a turning point for the domain in which it transpires. Harmonic Convergence was an orchestrated event impulsed from the future. It was sent from the future into the past and then reorganized into the present to create a hole through which the secondary and tertiary nets could be built and find a link onto the planet. What was the link? If these webs needed a primary event to link onto, what was it 'n the primary event that gave them the hold? The consciousness of the people.

There are those who specialize in studying primary events in certain sectors of existence. They know the leeway with which a specific time can be changed without altering all of time—because of changing sub-times around the event. There are those who specialize in parallel events happening in different worlds. They create geometric vortexes, taking primary events from various stellar systems and galaxies, hooking them up and creating new highways of communication. It is a magnificent realization, once you liberate yourself from Earth "time."

The prime corridors are currently being reconstructed in order to offer a greater influx of energy onto your planet. In the future we help build the underlying networks so that when a primary event is orchestrated, the webs can be connected, and everything will change on Earth. This will change all of time. It will, to some extent, rip a gigantic hole in the fabric in which you dwell.

A long time ago, when these corridors were discovered and developed in other civilizations, there were millions of worlds that did not use wisdom. There are areas of space that function as balls of chaos because too many holes were ripped in the fabric that made their reality. It is the same lesson you are learning regarding your environment—misuse it, pollute it, and it becomes tarnished and fades from its original vitality. All of existence is vital, and it becomes a major task to exist within all that is and enhance it, rather than use it and destroy it. There are whole universes like this being worked on and cleaned up. You think you have pollution on Earth? Can you image an entire universe polluted in chaos because all the time lines are not connected? You could leave your house to go to the store and when you returned, your house would be gone because it slipped through a hole. Another reality now exists there. It's insanity.

One day these will be integrated. This is our challenge: How do we integrate the consciousness of those who created the entrapment in the first place out of disrespect for creation? They didn't honor the fabric, went through the time corridors, and did whatever they wanted to. We play a dangerous game, yet, as we see it, it is quite necessary to change events. Not that we are completely in charge of this. We operate under the guidance of our teachers, the Keepers of Time. From a grander perspective, we reflect to you the tremendous responsibility of claiming consciousness. The task to juggle the laws of cause and effect among the time corridors is indeed awesome.

The libraries are on a version of the primary web that is closed down and inactivated. The libraries are guarded. It is not easy to get into a library these days, especially from the future. So the underlying time corridors are being constructed. Many, in order to own certain territories or to have greater influence over them, route specific time lines together. They have as many time lines link onto each other as possible, or they avoid as many as they can, depending on what the purpose is.

From a certain point of view, there are those who own the corridors of time, or believe they do. They are reconstructing the prime corridors and organizing new eras of existence. Once these corridors are built, many forms of intelligence will be able to move back and forth, with the so-called owners of these corridors determining which forces are allowed to enter. This is the problem that Earth is headed for, and is connected to why there has been a great influx of life forms who have been using the human species for experimentation. There are secondary and tertiary time lines built so that if the secondary one is raided there will be another time line still open.

When the secondary and tertiary events are established and built, it means that there will be a major opening in the corridor of time. This opening will allow many to come through the so-called officially approved channels. They will find an underground movement and doorways that simultaneously open in many other directions.

The Maya, those master tricksters of time, have left you a number of clues with which to play this game. The Mayan calendar is well worth considering, as it marks a time of ending and closure at the winter solstice in December 2012. The Game Masters watch and wonder what you'll do as the speculations fly! The concept of the end of your time means that a cycle is coming to completion. It does not mean Earth is going to be finished. A particular theme, essential to spiritual growth, is being played out like a long-running Broadway show, and you have less than twenty years to complete the agreed-upon performance.

When that last stretch of time is completed, there will be a dimensional shift upon this planet. Those who are able to accommodate the dimensional shift now are already moving in and out of the fourth and even the fifth dimension. During the next twenty years, the new frequency will become so predominant on the planet that it will catapult one version of your world into a new cycle, and another version into a complete ending and destruction.

In the new cycle, there will be a bursting forth of energy from the Living Library, triggering a unique blossoming of all life forms. You cannot access the other Living Libraries until you are able to assimilate this one. You will feel a portion of yourself reaching, stretching, and peeking in, to see how you are handling your newly acquired awareness. You may also peek to see how others are handling their creations, though you may not understand the life form of another Living Library. The worlds could be very different in another Living Library, with knowledge stored as geometric shapes, looking to your eyes like a vacated cosmic playground. Remember, a playground is only brought to life by players. The Living Library of Earth will ease you into a vibrational shift of sharing and flowing with energy. From nature, Earth's majestic playground, you will learn how to merge and emerge into the corridors of time.

We discovered that events are coming from the future. Events can spring out of the future, as well as the past. This is the ongoing game. We are here to facilitate changing the past, in order to alter our present in the Pleiades, our version of now. It is being done to reroute and reorganize a tyrannical takeover that exists far in the future. In actuality, your past is racing toward our present, and yet we went into the future to change it.

Eventually, you will perceive a very different set of memories because you will change the past of your universe. This is how things are. We have told you that we come from your future and that we came back to change the past. We are very clever. We are changing the history of the entire universe by making a parallel universe. This is what parallel universes are—plans that shift the mechanisms of time from one point by changing the memory and changing the event. You can do the same thing in your own personal life. You can change your past as well. Be flexible as you learn to play the game.

Energy Exercise

Place your attention on your breath and follow it into your body, picturing your lungs filling with light. See your bloodstream absorbing this charged energy and distributing it throughout your body. With each exhalation, feel your body relax and let go. As you continue to breathe, imagine yourself surrounded by twelve energies that assist in your well-being. Experience a feeling of safety and comfort as you examine their presence. Look deep into the eyes of each energy, then shift your vision and read the surrounding energy field.

Imagine fibers and rays of light dancing from your body as you experience a familiar tug from your belly and heart. Your body vibrates with recognition as the twelve guides offer you a peek into another now. Allow yourself to see into the time and reality that each of the guides represents, experiencing all twelve in full vitality. Let your memories soar, and feel lines of time, like roadmaps to realities, available to point the way. Follow the light fibers from your chakra centers as they move into the energy field of each guide. Where do you find yourself? Experience and observe.

Perhaps you hear the sweet sound of a gentle rain falling, or the howl of a cold wind along a desolate road. There may be jungle, rain forest, snow-covered peaks, deserts, rivers, oceans, and plains. Every corner of Earth holds memories and mysterious clues about yourself. Let the lines of time carry you deep into another now. Experience Earth from twelve lines of time, and ask to be shown that which is most significant toward understanding yourself and your link to the stars.

Feel the web of light that is the vital grid connecting existence, which is everywhere alive. Now, imagine the web lines transporting intelligence, as life seeks out life. Imagine Earth, a blue-and-white jewel suspended in space, holding court in her own realm of time, a gem of a stop along these great light corridors. Look at Earth from space, and feel a tug from times that beckon you to remember. Are they past events you recall? Wonder about this as your concepts of time, space, and Earth become scrambled on the web of light.

Now look through the lines of energy that intersect in space a bit beyond the moon. What do the signposts read? And to what stellar byways do your trusty guides point? Let your spirit absorb the vitality of the moment, honoring Earth and yourself for the unbounded opportunities to express and explore. Pay special tribute to the web of light, that great force of existence with which we all learn to play the game.

TEN

The Heavens Speak

You yourself selected a moment and a lineage, a bloodline that you were born to, to give you the opportunities that you assessed would be ideal for you to experience in this lifetime.

Before you came into this reality, you applied for a slice of time—the moment you were born. At the precise time of your birth, the stars, planets, moon, and sun were in a specific configuration. When you emerged from your mother's womb, the energy from the stars and planets imprinted your flesh, no matter where you were, because the energy was touching Earth at that time as well. Within that moment were written certain probabilities, specific opportunities, and distinct challenges. The language of the stars explains your world in a way that is helpful for you to understand the bigger picture. Everything is in geometric relationship to everything else, creating energetic patterns. You yourself selected a moment and a lineage, a bloodline that you were born to, to give you the opportunities that you assessed would be ideal for you to experience in this lifetime. You determined these experiences according to what you needed to learn, based on what you had created, will create, and are creating simultaneously in other places.

The heavens speak to you of your own majestic splendor,

playing out their story through you. The planets broadcast their life force as electromagnetic waves that create cycles within which significant achievements, designed as challenges and victories, define specific epochs or ages. These cycles, if understood, will automatically benefit the planet. The cycles have been ignored and trivialized to keep you in ignorance, causing you to miss the tremendous self-realization that accompanies the meaning of life. One of the ways the teachings of the cycles became lost was through the disputing and refuting of astrology. You have been told that astrology is a meaningless study, when in actuality astrology and astronomy are the languages of the universe. In its truest form, knowledge of the heavens translates the macrocosm into the microcosm, acknowledging you within a significant slice of existence.

In 1993, you experienced what we refer to as the Galactic Tidal Wave of Light, which was translated through a planetary lineup that created a pathway of energies. Each planet within your solar system has its own field of consciousness that pulsates and radiates rays of energies, like highways of data. When planets align in specific geometric relationships, they create energetic complexities as their independent forces merge. When two planets move into conjunction, it appears from your point of view on Earth that they are on top of each other. In actuality, while still quite distant in the depths of space, their energy highways are merged. The energy that moves from one planet is connected with the energy moving from the other planet.

The Galactic Tidal Wave of Light can be understood through the two planets Uranus and Neptune, which came into conjunction on three separate occasions, in February, August, and October 1993, aligning and energizing the sign of Capricorn at 18 to 19 degrees. Each planet has its own identity, its domain of influence. Each planet is a sentient being, an intelligent force of its own. As these two forms of intelligence came together in the sky, they transmitted a combined beam onto Earth, affecting those portions of Earth influenced by Capricorn. Capricorn is ruled by Saturn, which represents form, structure, authority, limitations, and time. Among other things, Saturn has to do with rocks, stones, and crystals. Because these two planets joined in Capricorn, they mystified, electrified, energized, and changed the stone of Earth herself.

On a planetary scale, the energy of this conjunction is leading you toward an opening of the feeling center, offering a solution to the building chaos. Therefore, when systems go down, use your feelings to move ahead. Without feelings, especially those of love, you are doomed. You will experience soul-stirring feelings in the solar plexus. Once these feelings are connected by threads of compassion to the heart, you will be able to determine reality through a source other than the logical mind. You will begin to feel your way into reality. This will release energy that is locked in the lower chakras as unrecognized and unresolved memories. The released energy will rise to the heart, the throat, the third eye, and the crown—the fourth, fifth, sixth, and seventh points of distribution in the body. This process will connect humanity, and you will see that you have things in common, rather than the opposite. You will remember past lives by experiencing them as ongoing and simultaneously occurring. This will throw many of you into confusion as you are challenged to process the memories and realizations that are flooding into your consciousness.

This opening of the energy centers is meant to serve as a solution. In the ideal, it will create a chaotic vortex that scrambles your reality, so you will not know for certain any longer what is real. You will doubt the blind allegiance you have had for various institutions as uncertainty and confusion take hold. Some of you will experience a depression accompanying this doubt. Others of you will say, "Wow, I am unburdened. I am free. This is magnificent."

Those of you interested in alternate versions of reality

will grow to numbers you would not believe possible. You may find that when you are shopping at the local store, your casual comments turn to conversation of a deep metaphysical nature, or involving the presence of extraterrestrials. Spirit will impulse you to say things that you would never, ever have said before. Be open to this, and to the opening of people in every avenue of life. Members of your families may be making 180-degree turns. Not all, though some, will begin to see the light. Perhaps you used to think about certain people, "Oh, there is no hope for them." This will no longer be the case.

You will be amazed by which of you will shed cloaks and be activated, for it has nothing to do with the amount of time you have spent, the tapes you have listened to, or the books you have read. When spirit comes knocking on your doors, and your codes are fired, the awakening happens quickly. What took some of you twenty, thirty, or five years to learn, others of you will know in a flash. You won't learn it, you will simply know it. So, be prepared to offer and seek counseling, and to learn, for you learn the most when you teach. People mirror for you, and as you teach them and explain to them, they teach you in turn about yourself, your patterns, and about how people learn. The momentum of the awakening energy is a tsunami-like experience, growing in magnitude with each passing moment.

This flood of cyclic energy is responsible for the rapid mutation that will take place within the human species. You, as you exist here in this very moment, are changing or mutating through this energy, and your cells are becoming something different than they were. An alteration on a cellular level will catapult you to a metamorphosis in the spiritual dimensions. The Earth changes that occur as a result will finalize the shift in consciousness that is needed to restore sanity, purpose of living, and meaningful existence to dimensions that are to be home here on Earth.

There are a number of natural cycles in the lifetime of

humans in which the kundalini rises. As humans, you run off a current of energy that lies coiled at the base of your spines, called the serpent energy. It is the closest thing that you have to the energy of Prime Creator. You use your kundalini energy to reproduce yourselves, and do not have a clue that it can be used to change the way you view reality. In the Western world, you have not come to this realization, because there are those in power who do not want you to change the status quo of your consumer society.

Kundalini most often moves from the base of the spine to the second chakra—from identity and survival up to creativity and sexual expression—and goes no further. Around the age of forty, at Uranus opposition, or mid-life crisis as it's called, the energy is pulled upward by the planet Uranus. With Uranus having such a powerful affect on the global collective at this time, there will be an ongoing series of mass kundalini risings, no matter the age. The status quo of electromagnetic cosmic energy must become greater within the human race.

Before you agree to enter the physical plane, you go over in great detail the parameters of your most outrageous probabilities. You set up blueprints, and then you wait for the gap, the perfect electromagnetic window into physical reality. This window is a lineup of energies, directed by the heavenly bodies, that allows you to travel a road into your genetic code. One day the reading of astrological charts will reveal a correspondence between the alignment of planets and the arrangement of DNA. Currently, there are twelve houses in the zodiac, and there are twelve strands of DNA. The twelve strands of DNA are eventually going to show themselves in the iris of the eye, and you will be able to read the genetic purpose within the iris. If you divide the iris into twelve houses, like the wheel in a birthchart, each house will correspond to its own place in the body, much as it corresponds to a person's astrological imprinting of planetary and stellar energies at birth. Through a reflection in the eye, the twelve strands of DNA will eventually reveal their genetic codes of purpose and intent as stored in the blood. Many so-called mysteries will be revealed, liberating you from further deceit. It is through the eyes that you peek into the window of the soul, and where the deepest imprinting and exchange occurs among all species.

Long ago, astrology and astronomy were one. When the left brain came into great activity and the plan surfaced to create a false ego or scientific mind to steer humans away from themselves, the truths became ridiculed. Ancient laws became a mockery, and you were sent back onto the planet to honor and reawaken these truths.

The moon is a satellite that was constructed. It was built and anchored outside Earth's atmosphere as a mediating and monitoring device, a supercomputer or eye in the sky. It affects all life forms on this planet, beyond what you can currently grasp. In your history, there are references to two moons around Earth. You don't hear of this often, but there are those who know.

Earth must be owned by those who dwell here; however, it is not. You have outside gods, creator energies, who prevent you, as a species, from having free rein with your kundalini. The influence of the moon, as a main satellite computer, affects all of Earth. At this time, powerful cosmic rays are crossing space as photonic waves and being transduced through Uranus, Neptune, and other forces. This is creating an overloaded circuitry around the control that has kept you from understanding that you, as human beings, must take stewardship of your planet.

Why are you locked into a prescribed formula of time that is irrelevant in every other place? What is the significance of twelve in this marking and dividing process? Who would you be without this? These are the questions we wish you to ponder. The answers have, of course, to do with control of your life span and kundalini. You see, in the ideal, your life span would be much longer than it is, and your society would honor the process of gathering wisdom through experience. In the ideal, the kundalini experience at forty, in a society structured and nurtured to bring it about, would create the maturation of the individual. Right now, you consider yourself to come into maturation at the age of twenty-one. Please be aware that you experience numerous cycles of energy that come through the body to teach you new vistas of maturation. Awareness of this process is key to your development. It challenges you to continually take on more responsibility, and not to feel burdened by it.

There have been many, many battles over the moon. Parts of the moon are owned, and parts are utilized. There is a plan to gradually insert different programs of influence on Earth when the moon becomes occupied by forces that would assist you in your growth, rather than limit you. The moon's programs have, for eons, been of great limitation toward human beings. The tales about the full moon and insanity, madness, and heightened bleeding are all quite true. There are repetitive cycles that the moon creates, to which you respond. You know that television influences you to a great degree. The moon is the same way. You simply have not been able to tune into the moon's programs and learn how to turn them off. You cannot. Others must turn the moon off for you, or reprogram the moon, which is what is taking place now.

At this time, the moon is quite controlled. Some people are gravely affected by mania and craziness from the moon. Extraterrestrials and others have many bases on the moon, and those from Earth have little influence, when it comes down to it. It is the extraterrestrials who really operate it all. Your technology, though rapidly advancing, cannot begin to compare with the biotechnology of sentient space travelers.

You are newcomers to the game, and you miss a vital key, for your senses and the essence of your physical world structure reality in *a particular way*. You constantly translate data, and, like interpreting a dream, condense the experience into physical boundaries, where you find you can explain less and less. All is thought—a mental architecture—with a construction crew in many realities.

The sun is the governor of your solar system and is the seat of intelligence that rules this particular locale you occupy. The sun reaches into your domain and reads the vibrations as it touches your skin. It is intimately connected with every aspect of life as you know it. It is a force of intelligence that fuels your very existence and creates the environment under which you can evolve. The sun is very interested in your evolution, for as you evolve, you feed everything that you do back to the sun as it touches you.

In many cultures, the sun is revered as the intelligent force that governs this world, like a god. You would be amazed at who and what dwells in the sun. The sun is an illusion. Highly advanced worlds can disguise themselves as suns to protect themselves from invasion and penetration through the force of light. For some, the sun is a place of great learning, while for others it is simply an initiation they pass through to get beyond and behind the sun. It is not, as your scientists say, simply burning forms of gas.

Science, to a large degree, has ruined your interpretations of life. It has taken all of the fun, vitality, excitement, and mystery out of life. Life has been made very mundane and boring, as if it is meaningless. Can you imagine the sun being meaningless? Contemplate this for a moment. Yet today there is a campaign of fear and negativity against the sun. People no longer feel connected to nature because science has said that nature is not safe. The suspicion of the sun, nature, and Earth has contributed to your current crisis: your lack of respect in honoring and cherishing your home. There is a deep crisis of conflicting beliefs in the scientific community at this time—thank goodness, and thank Goddess.

The sun and the moon are the luminaries within your system by which you are most profoundly influenced and affected. The sun generates its own light. The sun, in turn, illuminates the moon. The moon is a sub-satellite of the sun, orbiting as a computer around Earth, built and maintained by many generations of gods. Heavenly bodies are constructed in the shapes of asteroids, moons, and planets, and it is through these luminaries that rays of intelligence, radio waves, and gamma rays are transmitted from star to sun and sent to Earth. It is through these rays that your actions are also read and taken back into the sun, the moon, and the beaming system—in this case, the Pleiades.

When you are able to move to another location and view the solar system and sky from a different point of reference, you will see that Earth and the stars and everything shift quite dramatically. One of the systems with which you rotate is the system of the Pleiades, whose central sun is called Alcyone. Your solar system is located on the fringe of the galactic spiral.

Imagine that you draw a line from Earth to Alcyone, intending to connect to the central sun. Then, once you get to Alcyone, someone says, "There is another central sun around which we rotate here as well." So you draw a line over there. Then someone else says, "There are many central suns over here." So you go here and there, drawing these lines. Your universe houses billions of galaxies, and you are located in one galaxy. A geometric form comes into being when you draw these lines. We are making this very simple. This is not how it is; however, we are creating an image for you that will help you understand. When you draw lines and energetically connect one central sun to another, you connect a collective of intelligence. That collective of intelligence can be likened to what you call a location of Prime Creator, though it is not. It might be a location of one of the creator gods or representatives, or home to a Game Master experiment. Imagine that an intelligent being, operating through many dimensions of existence, is made up of central suns peppered throughout its so-called body from all over your universe.

It is through the suns that all worlds are governed. Growth is oriented toward these suns. It is your sun that allows you to have light, and light is what permits you to see reflections of yourselves in the outside world. Without light, what could you mirror for yourselves? What would you see?

The sun is the governor, the ruler of your particular system as it appears to you. It is the sensitive spot of your particular arena of space. The sun reads its creations and in turn feeds the creations what they need. So when you carry love of yourselves and Earth, the solar rays completely understand the consciousness you carry. When you carry fear of Earth, the solar rays understand, and they nudge you into those experiences.

When the intensity on your planet speeds up and broadcasts itself as misuse of energy, the sun reads this. The sun is the feeling heart center. It permits and activates life, because it touches and reads all things. You cannot hide who you are, for the sun's rays read your vibration. Some people attempt to hide from the sun by going underground to keep their activities secret.

Think about the consciousness of the sun as it peeks out on its domain. It touches all points with varying cycles of light, checking to see what is happening in every nook and cranny. It feels and brings the energy back to itself, and then makes decisions about its own expression. It learns how to correct balances and imbalances within its own creations. The sun is changing. The sun and its many forces are brewing phenomenal shifts and sending them to every aspect of your being. There are plans within plans within plans. Understand that always the highest plan of opportunity is available to you, if you so choose.

There will be a tremendous increase in solar flares; the energy of the sun will burst and burn, sending out massive amounts of gamma rays. Sometimes the sun is quite docile and gentle, like a little baby. Other times it has volatile periods with activity like a million volcanoes going off at once. Yet if you have the appropriately tuned consciousness, you can move right through this activity into the domain that exists behind that particular illusion. The form of the sun is an illusion that is deeply imbedded in the essence of every facet of this solar system, and in every part of the DNA of the universe. Within the overall blueprint and design of core beliefs, it is decreed that certain illusions will be perceived and others will not. The sun is an agreed-upon root assumption that emerges into many realities and actually allows realities to merge.

As the rays from the sun change, activated by the consciousness of the inhabitants of Earth, and as the sun releases solar bursts, the polar regions of Earth are affected. The flares sent forth are like atomic explosions or jolts of electricity that go millions of miles deep into space. Earth's poles, which are magnets, catch this energy. They grab energy that comes from space to the planet. Because of the magnetic force, they arc it either around the equator or inward to the core of Earth. Each pole grabs the solar energy, drives it in, and creates a huge cylinder of vibrational energy. As that vibrational energy jolts and jiggles to fit, it has to align with the energy gridwork of Earth that is connected from the poles. This gridwork is decreed by you, and to some extent, all energies merging or emerging through your version of Earth conform to this grid of beliefs.

Of course, many things are not in balance, which is why you are going to have a relocation of the poles so that the gridwork will be more able to catch the energy. Right now, the particular pole alignment cannot serve as the electrical ground or lightning rod that is required to avoid burnout. The poles create a lightning rod through Earth, though the current setup will short circuit everything. So, in order to avoid complete destruction, there will be a shift. The poles will move someplace else, as they have numerous times before when the balance of Earth was at stake. There will only be a minor shift from a space perspective. From your perspective, however, the shift will seem quite major.

The solar energy is creating a new vibration with which disturbing and disruptive energies will not be able to fit. In order to qualify and join the club, energies will have to lay claim to a certain vibration of love. The sun is saying, "Enough. We are going to put you back into alignment. See what you can do this time around."

Only those with uncluttered consciousness will be able to house this energy in their bodies. Those with negative thoughts feel it as a direct poison; their thoughts will return and potentially cause havoc in their bodies. The solution is to have clear thoughts and uncluttered bodies that are able to take this energy in completely without fear. Each time you expose yourself to these fantastic doses of energy, you increase your intuition, your psychic potential, and your ability to decode the DNA. All of these abilities are magnified thousands and thousands of times. This is part of the way that the sun is responding to who you are, so trust that the sun reads you. Have honest, open, and agreeable energy with the sun and with all the elements around you.

Intelligence designs itself as light. We will say that again: Intelligence designs itself as light. It is the intelligence of your sun that holds your solar system in its energetic field. At this time, effects are coming to you from beyond your sun. It is almost as if the effects of your sun have been unable to penetrate what has happened here on Earth, so other suns are coming to be assistants to your sun. Your sun makes the solar flares that draw the cosmic rays, grounding them into this solar system. Think of the sun as a gigantic magnet. Its solar flares send out tentacles to reach and grab for the cosmic rays. The cosmic rays are solar flares from a central sun at a distant place in your galaxy.

Imagery: This is the whole means of control in your world. There exists a select group not necessarily aligned with the upliftment of humanity. There are some who understand that there is a mutation going on in humanity at this time, and that the sun is responsible for much of it. In order to counteract this mutation or changing within the human race, they create an image by which you become afraid of the sun. So masses of people are obediently following the suggestions of authority. There are people who so readily accept the imagery fed to them that they can create skin cancer dashing through the sun's rays from the garage to their car.

There has been a conspiracy against the sun, as if the designers of your world were flawed and made a mistake when they put the sun in your solar system. That is the idea that is foisted upon you as humans. And as humans—just to show how foolish you are and how controlled you can be— you believe everything you read. Because it is in print, you believe it.

If plants are smart enough to work with the sun and provide the canopy of energy, prana, and oxygen that keeps you in existence, don't you think the sun is also good for humans? Do you think the sun is only good for plants, and that it hurts humans?

We say the sun is grand. Studies have shown that when sunscreen was introduced, the rate of skin cancer began to rise. There is nothing wrong with the sun. In fact, the removal of the ozone layer allows you to have even greater receptivity to the rays of the sun. There are those who say, "Don't look at the sun. It is bad. It will burn out your eyes." We say you will have a change in your eye structure. There will be a mutation within the optic nerve that will allow a new type of vision and unlock what has been holding you to 3D. Trust that no one made a mistake when they put the sun in the sky.

In the past, some of these holes in the ozone layer have been bigger than they are today. The holes fluctuate; however, this fluctuation is not caused by what your scientists attribute it to. These holes in the ozone allow a different quality and experience of the spectrum of light and radiation to penetrate Earth's atmosphere. When the difference in spectrum is experienced by the masses, a chemical response takes place deep inside the human body, which begins to change. The human body is affected by the radiated light. In actuality, the radiation of this light alters the body on a subatomic level. Those of you who understand this are able to be in balance with this natural shift. Some of it is not natural; however, for the large part, it is orchestrated to be an event that will benefit you. There can be an increase in the evolutionary intelligence in the species in a very short period of time whereby the species becomes stronger.

Holes in the ozone allow radiated energy to come in to speed up the process. When you encounter cosmic, celestial events in your future, you will already have been exposed to the energy. So what you are being given now is like a homeopathic dose.

The main force of any system dwells within the sun of that system, where the sun's collective consciousness is demonstrated by its solar rays. So, as a form of intelligence travels to the various star systems, the light rays can be read. Once energies become capable of emitting the frequency of light from their home, that light is read by everyone because it is transmitted in a certain spectrum of rays. From vast distances in space, others can translate and read certain spectrums. They can understand who lives inside of which sun, and what their predilections and specialties of existence are.

There are many, many benefits that can come from the sun. It contains the ultimate in shamanic knowledge.

As each of you moves through life's challenges of judgment and separation, ideally you come into a greater understanding of your own impact upon life and you are able to carry more light. That light, which you are earning individually, creates by the very essence of its existence a fusion with similar energies within the mass consciousness that will appear to others as a star or a sun. Your planet will radiate its shift in consciousness and awareness of spirit as light. That is how Earth will become a star on the horizon of other worlds. That in itself will magnetize other worlds to you. They will read the energy of your Earth light, and they will know who you are.

In the beginning there was sound. Sound began the whole thing, and in sound resides tremendous power. It opens doorways to other realities, for with the production of sound, an energy can move from one system to another. When you utilize sound, it is quite easy to bypass the logical mind, shifting the channel by intending and being clear.

The development of the rebundled DNA expresses itself beyond logic through sound. Sound allows matter, as information that is formulating itself inside the body, to find a proclamation of knowing outside the body. You can move into a state of bliss when you surrender to expressing sound, particularly through toning and chanting. To various degrees, that bliss is based on the feeling and knowing that you are not limited and that you exist as unbounded beings of light.

Allow sounds to come through your bodies, not just by singing specific notes, rather by allowing combinations of sound to play your bodies as if they are instruments. These sounds go beyond the logical mind. Sometimes you may fight or struggle because you have intellectualized a concept yet cannot anchor it in its entirety into your emotional experience. By toning, your intelligent intent is transmitted on sound, on carrier waves. Many forms of intelligence can communicate to the cells of your beings, bypassing the resistance of your logical minds, and going directly through your bodies to your higher minds.

When you tone, there is a nonverbal transmission that is communicated outward. It is beyond words. Toning can throw you into a collective of information, where things suddenly become clear. It can also activate your creativity—your drive to do something or to act. Or, you can feel, all of a sudden, that you are releasing big burdens. Most people feel very invigorated after toning. They feel light, as if something has been lifted from them. You automatically are impulsed to make the sounds and tones most needed for your bodies' balance and alignment.

No one gets offended by the messages in toning. People don't take toning personally, yet their bodies receive the personal messages. For example, if our words offered something directly to you, you might say, "Oh, wow, I'm under the gun here. I'm getting fired at." Yet, through toning, the same energy could be sent to you and you could integrate it because it is more neutral. The logical mind does not overlay its own interpretation of the energy because the logical mind cannot translate it as criticism or error. The logical mind says, "I don't know what this is. I'll just relax." The intuitive side absorbs the energy and message through sound.

We suggest that you hold weekly group tonings. Let this become part of your rituals and entertainment, and part of the process of joining together. Toning is very beneficial to release pent-up energy. You feel light and uplifted afterward. It lines you up and gets your bodies in balance.

Tones themselves correspond with and affect specific areas of the body. Some sounds affect your eyesight, or taste buds, or hearing. They affect all of the various senses, and the organs as well. The ancients understood that a simple sound could reorganize the body's structure. The body automatically makes the most appropriate sounds that you need in a given moment. Trust.

Many bodyworkers are beginning to have the courage to tone over their clients as they are working on them. For some people, this is too much. We would say to bodyworkers: Follow your impulses. When you are working on an area of a person's body, and the energy is simply not moving or cannot be penetrated, then tone into that area of the body to get entry to the issues. The person lying on the table is not necessarily saying, "I won't let you in my body." The patterns of the energy fields are so intense that parts of the body won't let your hands or new energy in. The sound makes an opening.

There is sound around you all the time. If you want to hear the sound of your bodies, for example, take your fingers and plug up your ears and remain quiet for a few minutes. You will hear your inner sound. In the high Himalayas, lamas and monks receive training in sensory deprivation. They are placed in stone caverns with no light, and completely isolated from outside sounds. In isolation, they use their senses to develop abilities to see in the dark, to manifest, and to hear and know the specific songs and sounds of each other. Each chakra has its own sound, and these sounds correspond to the universe that is inside of you.

If you listen very carefully, you will find you are being vibrated continuously by sound. You have nonstop inner chatter, always planning what's next with yourselves. You have external noise with your families as distractions. You don't have enough silent time to notice that sound is continuously being directed at you to alter your bodies. When you make the sound yourself by instrumentation or toning, you balance the adjustment because you work from the inside, not just from the outside. This is how you are being adjusted at this time.

Cultures were given different ranges of sound in which to operate in order to hold the frequency of balance on the planet. Extraterrestrial or off-planet intelligences visited and established native civilizations in various parts of the globe. Very often the same teachers had two or three experiments at different times. They might operate in three or four locales around the globe, offering each of their seedling civilizations a slightly different set of beliefs, and then let the seedlings evolve with those beliefs to see where they could take them. Instruments and creative crafts were offered to set the paradigms for what sounds would be expressed in that particular civilization.

Specific energy rides on specific tonalities. You know, when you sing a song, that different notes combine to express the completeness of the song. Earth resonates at a frequency of 7.8 hertz. When the human body is able to vibrate at the same rate, there is an incredible psychic opening and awareness. The resonance of Earth, this electromagnetic energy, is based on the complete tonality of available sound anchored on the planet. The combined sound of all cultures, anchored on the planet for eons, held the planet in existence and created the electromagnetic frequency of balance. Now that you are being blasted with these incredible cosmic rays, and now that the native cultures are no longer practicing sound for the most part, Earth is going through tremendous changes. It is being realigned, and new patterns of electromagnetic tonalities are being expressed.

There are sounds that can stimulate deterioration or regeneration of organs in the body. Sounds that are harmonious activate the body and create healing. Healing can come through intention; however, there are certain sound frequencies that remind the liver to organize into its native geometric blueprint. Geometry is the form of intelligence that takes shape after sound moves away from Prime Creator. Your bodies are filled with geometry, for everything is made up of a geometric essence.

Combinations of sounds, as notes and chords, will be played for enhancement of the liver, thyroid, and heart, and for regeneration. The entire body will be mapped and tuned, much like a piano. You see, the body functions on a blueprint, and it absorbs the sounds. It has an idealized blueprint, which it automatically grows toward. You yourself do not have to know how your body grows from the infant stage to the adult stage. Within the blueprint of being, part of the purpose is to grow and maintain a healthy body.

The blueprint of the body is changing, altering the purpose of the body. There will be reversals in health and numerous regenerative experiences as sound is utilized to remind the body to move in an ever-uplifting fashion. A great reversal is at hand concerning your beliefs about the degeneration of the body.

When you participate in mass events where you may find yourself in a large crowd, pay close attention to how the sound affects you. Many of you avoid crowds because you get headaches when you go into them. You are much more sensitive. You can read energies and feel what they do. People often attend events where enormous crowds gather for entertainment of one form or another; they participate in contributing to uncomfortable waves of sound, not realizing what the sound is doing to their bodies. They are creating thoughtforms, through sound and emotion, that are set into being.

What about the sound of a battle cry? Have you done a firewalk? When you walk on the coals, you are encouraged to let out a huge yell. The sound is used to open doorways that you then move through. The marching forces that brought down the walls of Jericho used sound to create a standing columnar wave, invisible to the eye, yet like a sonic boom in effect. Sound is much more important than you currently understand. Sound creates life or death, health or disease.

Most people have not discovered that sharing sound during sexual activity is a deep key. When you tone together, you feel the spinning and opening of the chakras. During sex, sharing sound with each other beyond the usual moans can lead to greater distribution of sexual energy. Sound moves energy beyond the genitals, dispersing it throughout the cells of the body and triggering memory that unites you with more of who you are. Remember, the totality of your being contains both the shadow and the light. Please, do not be distressed with the shadow; it adds beauty and understanding to the light. Move out of judgment, yet stay in comfort.

Through sound and a willingness to experiment with sexual energy, you can meet your partner in his or her various multidimensional forms. Clear individuals, playing with energy and properly understanding it, will unpeel their multidimensional selves, revealing simultaneous sexual experiences from many, many realities coming into this now.

There will be new, exciting experimentation with your sexual expression. It takes a bit of surrendering to allow your partner to tone into your vagina. We say that it is a real step. Think about it. A tremendous releasing and letting go is needed for both partners. One of you says, "Hey, I've got this idea. How about toning?" When kids do crazy things, do you think they talk them over first? No. They are silly, and they do them. They play, and then afterward they giggle over what they did. It is essential to take these innocent, playful, creative, and trusting qualities into the sexual experience. Your heart must be opened to fully explore sexuality, for the deepest connection to your sexual identity is through your heart.

A time will come when the children will gather and, using their unique telepathy, make silent sound. They will use their minds to create symphonies on other dimensions of existence. They will use sound internally and externally to create harmonics as light shields all over the planet. The children will gather in the hundreds and then the thousands, and they will be led into this collective image-making process. It will be a ritual, set into motion as a very sacred event. While the children are doing this type of silent sounding, they will anchor and establish huge geometric identities that will eventually protect and govern Earth as psychic forces of thought. These geometric identities will be perhaps the higher selves of what you call the reptiles—the higher selves of *many* of the extraterrestrials or god forms that appear to be physical and etheric. Beyond them is geometry, and beyond that, sound. Sound is the governor of existence. The Game Masters employ sound, light, and geometry as basic tools for operation, and they wonder what you will do as you discover the tools of truth.

Many will awaken to the use of sound. There will be major discoveries and energy impacts using sound. If one hundred thousand individuals are impulsed to harmonize, and allow themselves to be played harmoniously as instruments of consciousness—imagine! Everything comes from sound. Sound is the primal energy that is used to create. Sound came first.

Energy Exercise

Place yourself in comfort. Adjust your spine and sit with your body erect, as if you are being suspended from above by a string. Allow yourself to become still. Take a few deep breaths and picture your twelve chakras spinning like planets radiating light. With your imagination, reach to other portions of your universe where you can feel a version of yourself on the same assignment.

Feel your consciousness climb your chakra system, picturing twelve suns making a ladder through yourself. Move up this ladder of light and send out what you know now to any other portion of yourself. Send your essence of awakening, cama-raderie, commitment, and love.

Climb those twelve suns into the universe. Picture in your mind a collection of cosmic planetary beings and formations of geometries. As you climb higher, feel other portions of yourself broadcast to you. What is being sent? What do you feel and hear? Be open to receive love and support from other portions of yourself, and see the twelve suns as a slide of light, bringing this knowledge to you. Let go of your version of self and become a receiver, allowing the effect of this light and energy to be realized by you. Feel it make a difference in your awareness. For a few moments, release the image of your body and allow your molecules to blend and merge with your surroundings.

You are being utilized as a transducer as this energy flows through the collective self and into Earth. It moves along the gridwork to bring about necessary changes. The energy travels deep into Earth. Picture ancient keepers of information, as crystalline structures hundreds of feet in height, receiving a huge spiral of energy from you.

Then, from within that gigantic spiral, spin yourself off, forming your own spiral of identity. Keep yourself completely still as you feel this spiral spinning around and around. Feel a revitalization and rejuvenation in your body. Feel the spinning from the tips of your toes to the very ends of your hair. Feel the new molecules that have been mixed with your body.

Take a deep breath and feel your twelve chakras lined up, ready to operate with full capacity. Then take another deep breath and say your name to yourself, feeling the sound of who you are in this reality. Translate the sound of your being unique and alive. Love who you have created; honor and cherish yourself. Act as if your physical being is the most valuable thing you will ever own. Now, place a gentle smile over your lips as you realize your unlimited potential, and commit to live it.

ELEVEN

Earth's Initiation

This present-day epoch involves the fall of global civilization and a reawakening of a brand new form of consciousness. This is unheralded in your history.

We have emphasized your value as well as that of Earth. She is your mother, she feels you, and she knows your name. In her quest for understanding, she has allowed a grave misuse of energy and has even allowed herself to lose her true identity by being raped and abused by humankind. In order for Earth to make the necessary leap that will affect all of this universe, a cleansing and healing—an initiation—must take place.

In an initiation, you must pass through the bowels of hell—through that which appears to want to destroy you and limit you. Actually, you face that which you fear. If you find yourself immersed in what you fear, hold the image of who you are as a whole and happy being and transmute the energy of fear by learning about yourself. You energize fearful thoughtforms into being. When your energy field no longer holds the fear, what you fear no longer has the life to destroy you. Initiation concludes a series of tests that bring you to mastery within a part of existence. Earth is going through an initiation and will guide you through the process as well.

Earth is on the crux of an identity crisis. There have been summits and meetings by environmental organizations that act as if Band-Aids will fix things in time. No. There is no fixing the dam as the bricks crack, crumble, and fall. What is this dam? It is all of the ideas, structures, and belief systems that hold the waters of consciousness together. You are made from water, dear friends.

Earth is going to go through tumultuous changes. After studying the records of Earth and of many worlds, we see this probability as being inevitable because of the extensive polarity on your planet. Rest assured that the more you pollute and destroy Earth, the more energy will go into shifting and shaking to clean things up. Humans who do not operate with love of self and love of the planet will be departing in vast numbers very quickly after exposure to the rays entering Earth. This is part of the electromagnetic change of the civilization. In death, the human vehicle moves consciousness into another realm.

You must become aware of yourselves as spiritual beings, and ground this knowledge into practical application of your now. As Earth moves forward into her own experiences, there will be multitudes sitting on etheric bleachers without physical bodies, watching the laws of cause and effect play themselves out. That is the only way they can get the lessons about valuing themselves and planetary existence. These watchers will feel the collective emotions of the participants on Earth. In this way, they will both participate and perhaps infuse you with compassion as comrades of all that is.

Some of you want to pretend that the Earth changes are not occurring. However, they *are* occurring, and there is nothing to fear, for they are part of the process of the great shift. Each of you creates your own reality and an opportunity to evolve. On some level of awareness, all of you who are on the planet at this time know of the agenda because this potentiality of Earth is stored in all blueprints. Though many of you will be surprised to find yourselves in this place of turmoil and transformation, and wonder how you ended up here, you are all choosing to be here. Whether you stay on the planet and alter your vibration, or you check out and sit in the bleachers to watch the show, doesn't really matter. On some level, in some avenue of existence, you will participate and you will learn.

Have compassion and neutrality, and understand pain can be a powerful teacher. If you are in pain today, you do not need to be in pain tomorrow. Certainly you do not need to be in pain a week or two weeks from now, because the cells in your body keep changing. It is *you* that tells your cells how to be every time they change. It is you who replicates yourself time after time through your thoughts, beliefs, and imaginations.

The healing crisis has just begun, and the fever is building. Between the years 1994 and 1999, you will move into peak chaos. During that time, there will be a great movement to create fear and confusion on the planet. Concurrently, there will be a great merging of the multidimensional self because energy fields from space will have been opened to allow sources of intelligence to travel quite easily along these pathways. They will travel through to you and emerge in your domain.

This present-day epoch involves the fall of global civilization and a reawakening of a brand-new form of consciousness. This is unheralded in your history. Registered in some people's memory and on the planet's surface itself is the shifting of the land masses—the sinking of what you call the Atlantean continent, through a cataclysm. In its time period, that land mass called Atlantis was an entity unto itself.

The state of global community and global effectiveness that you have today is very different from what existed during Atlantean times. Societies, of course, were all touched by the shifting of the Atlantean land mass in one way or another. However, the effects today will be far different. You have telecommunications networks, continuous traveling and exchanging of ideas from one land mass to another, and an interweaving of peoples and intermarrying of the various continents and cultures. These things will make the effects of the changes far grander than the effects of the sinking of the Atlantean land mass. Atlantis was not as completely integrated and linked to the rest of the planet as your continents are. There is much less isolation now, so you affect one another more.

There will be no continent untouched, and no people unmoved by what takes place. There will be few of you who will not have to migrate, for all of you basically will relocate yourselves at some point. For some of you, this is unheard of. Yet, by relocating yourselves, there will be a major shift in consciousness.

Few of you in the next ten years will move only once. Someone said to us recently, "This is shocking to me. You are really disturbing me." We said, "Good, we want to disturb you." He said, "I have a dozen monkeys. I have goats. I have this. What am I to do? I don't know what to save, what to pack up, and what to give away." We said, "Listen, the first time you move, take a big truck and cram all of your stuff into it and save everything you can and drive away. The next time, you might have time to fit it all in your car and drive away. The next time you move, you might only walk away with everything you can carry on your back. And the final time you move, you might take only what you hold in your hands." Do you get that? There is a need to mentally let go of attachments and be in the peace and clarity of the moment. Perhaps for you, those are the big moves.

Eventually, your fixation on material goods will become meaningless to you. You will be moved to take care of your life, not to take care of your goods. You will learn to trust your feeling center and let spirit guide you to a new home if need be. To energize your new location, you can say, "All right, I'm getting an impulse to move. I don't know where to go." Then, there are a number of ways you can go about energizing the new direction. Every night before you go to sleep, you can say to yourself, "I intend to activate the location of my new home in my dreams. I intend to dream of my new home. I intend to remember the new home and I intend with clarity to recognize it in 3D."

Using a pendulum and dowsing are other ways that you can check, verify, and discover your location. There are individuals who are delineating quite clearly through prophecy where the safer areas are going to be. There are a number of ways you can do this yourselves. Your lives will be, out of necessity, simplified. The more you can prepare for this simplification, the easier it will be on you. Unclutter your lives by letting go of the unnecessary things that would drag you down with responsibilities—the things you don't need. Lighten up. Sit on the ground, feel Earth, communicate with Earth, and trust Earth. Trust that when Earth moves, you will move in sync. Trust that Earth will love you, warn you, and inform you, in some way. Trust that the insects will speak to you, along with the cats, the dogs, and the birds. If you have this communication and deep love and appreciation for the energy of Earth's vibration, Earth will work with you. Remember, she knows you. No matter where you are, she knows your feelings and intentions, and responds accordingly.

As you learn to trust that Earth works with you, you deepen the trust of yourself. If at some point you find you are without food, we suggest that you remember something you do have, which is your most valuable resource—your imagination. It has been proven that people can imagine themselves eating and feel nourished. Can you embrace that idea? This would take great discipline; however, you can imagine food before you and yourself sitting and eating it. Imagine it moving through your body, and imagine yourself tasting it and feeling full. That is a suggestion if you find yourself really, really pushed to the limit.

As the changes take place, many of Earth's animals will

leave the planet. The vibrations that come about will be quite different, as people process pain. There is a collective pain stored inside everyone, and this must be brought to the surface to detoxify yourselves.

Your environment is so toxic you cannot escape it. You have no idea. Yet, many of you feel great every day and will continue to feel great every day, because you create what your cells do. Others can create toxic situations for you. You can be subjugated by these situations and spiral downward. Or, you can say, "I create my reality, and while I'm creating my reality, I'm learning how much I'm creating around me."

Earth changes are equated with death, yes? On your planet you know next to nothing about death. There is a tremendous opportunity in all of these shifts to learn about death. It appears to some of you that as people leave, or die, there is a mishap taking place. It appears that there is failure and that something was done wrong. We see the opposite. We see people leaving the planet with a new point of view. They are so gifted because many of you have your hearts open and are transmitting unity of purpose, allowing others to know and realize what they came for. Not everyone came here to see a new Earth. Can you realize that some people came to this planet to die in peace, without torture and pain, and to die with a consciousness of liberation?

There are multitudes of death walkers on the planet at this time. They are capable and willing to follow the dead into the realms of the unknown. They create peace for those who cross over. A great commerce between the living and the dead will revive. Those who cross over to die will not lose a thing. They will gain consciousness. One of them might say, "I have completed a cycle. I no longer need to carry a painful body, and I do not ever need to die in fear again." Many people have come to Earth at this time so that death will be understood. They have been held here through lower astral entrapments and frequency control.

It is a challenge for each and every one of you to assist

others in leaving the planet. This does not mean the taking of life. The vital force that you are has a purpose and agenda, and the more you communicate and stay with your body, the easier your transition will be. In the ideal, you will learn how to consciously die and deactivate your bodily functions. There is nothing to fear in death, except the things you imagine about it. It is all set on your own decree, or the decree of those you choose to follow. Trust yourself and design your own experience. Dare to create the ideal.

When you are afraid of death or pain, and you have an opportunity to assist someone pass over, your heart may want to close down. You may think, "I can't do this. I can't look at death. It is too frightening." Keep your heart open. Let the Goddess do it, and you will find that there is a ripeness and timeliness in every person's exit. Yes, events are being orchestrated; however, they cannot be orchestrated without the consciousness to match them. As you are clearing the last dregs of fear and misunderstanding, many of you will be called upon to work with the dead and help release them. When this happens on a large scale, you will find that those who have passed over will periodically return.

When you become a death walker, you are able to make the death experience with another and walk back from it—to go to the other side and come back. You find that there are many different energies accompanying each person's journey. Ask for a knowledgeable, uplifted, wise, and benevolent being to blend with you and help you understand the best way to create the highest opportunity for the death. Ask to have the ability to walk through the death experience and see people over to the other side, as they once did in ancient Egypt. Take the departed on a boat and journey to the other side, then come back and tell everyone where they went. For some of you, this is essential to master in this decade on your Earth plane.

When you are helping someone die, let yourself become a huge cloak and allow your molecules to be dispersed. As you become this huge cape, become one with the being who is dying and go with him or her. Create a pillar of light, let the light move upward, then go with it and see what takes place. It will be very, very profound. There are many recognized near-death experiences that have taken place over the last fifteen or twenty years. Knowledge from those who have gone over and come back is essential to peace on your planet. Time after time, those who have died come back to the loved ones they left behind and tell where they are and verify where you took them. There will also be many who appear to die; they will experience the portal of death, then return to life altered. This is known as a near-death experience.

When people move from one dimension to another—when they die, as you call it on your Earth plane—the process can be greatly facilitated through the use of sound. You may want to experiment with different kinds of sound. You may want to tone, make sound through instruments, or sing. You will discover what is most appropriate. Ask for guidance and impulses. You need to make an agreement to trust your impulses. They are what will save your bodies. When you get an impulse that says, "Leave," something is telling you to move; something is telling you to go, so do it. Learn to recognize your impulses and to respond to them.

One of the greatest gifts you can give to your parents is to assist them off the Earth plane, much as they assisted your presence onto Earth with the gift of life. They brought you into being, and there is a cycle to be felt. Understand the release of karma, the letting go. They said to you, "Here you are. I give you life." You say to them, "Here you are. I help you out of life." People have children to complete and fulfill a cycle. Seek to discover joy in all phases of existence.

Many of you may be contacted by dead people telling you they are stuck and need help getting over to the other side. They may have been dead for a number of months or years. This involves another kind of death walking. You can say, "Go to the light. Go and look for some friends." You will learn how to do this, because it is in your cells. It is not something you will necessarily take courses in. You will remember how.

It can be considered a privilege to be with people as they exit the Earth plane. You may not be able, in your conscious mind, to journey with them into death, for this takes a certain ability. Also, if you are very attached to people, you may not be permitted to venture over with them, because you might not want to come back. However, if you think you are going to avoid death because it is unsanitary, we have some news for you. There will be no avoiding death in the years to come. It is a privilege—remember this throughout all time—it is a privilege to assist people to die.

The death walker's job is to assist people into a place of forgiveness, allowing the death release to occur without any attachments to blame, judgments, or victimhood. There is an art to this because, often, in the final moments, people open to forgiveness. As dying people get close to their Maker, time collapses, moments elongate into poignant lessons of life, and a great opportunity is at hand. The greatest act of forgiveness is ultimately to yourself, because *you* passed all judgments and made forgiveness necessary.

You can assist the dying to find peace in their lives, to exit in serenity and love, with smiles on their faces. Help them by asking them to look for friends or relatives or others they would recognize to beckon them onward. This is a pivotal key in assisting and death walking.

Part of this experience involves your being able to say to a person who is dying, "You are loved. You are beautiful. You are like a newborn babe, going into another realm. Release now anyone, and everything, that is a burden to you. Release everything and know that you have lived your life to the fullest. There is no judgment on you. Go in peace, put a smile on your face, and release any judgments you hold. Relax, and allow your life to have meaning as you embark on the next phase of your identity."

There is healing in death, because there is life on the other side of death. As you send your energy to these individuals in transition, transmit it also to Earth. Support Earth in her process, and let her know that you want to be here to participate in the transformation. It is a true form of allowing when you surrender to the process and allow Earth to do what is necessary.

As Earth continues her dance of purification and the shaking and moving intensifies, you will be impulsed to cluster together to enhance existing communities or form new communities. Each community will grow and flourish based on its members' abilities to feel and to create thoughtforms together. Each community will need to energize a cooperative codicil so that everyone can come together to contribute food, shelter, music, movement, and sound. This system of communities will go back to the old way of living in which you need each other. It will reestablish the ancient blueprint of relationships by which you experience interconnected living. There will be disagreements; however, in general, all of you must want to work to energize similar thoughtforms. These thoughtforms will create energetic fields around the areas you dwell, and those who come to your doors will be drawn there, your thoughtforms acting as magnets. If your thoughtforms and the community are strong, and your bond with one another is established and readily energized and strengthened, you will draw to yourselves those of like intention. You will not wonder who these hundred people are who want to join your community. You will know that if a hundred people show up to be integrated in your community that your established thoughtforms drew these people to you, rather than to another community.

If your community is out of balance and in great dissension, you will create all kinds of chaotic energy. You must learn to work together, and if someone cannot work in a group and creates a descending force in the community, then the community will have to seek to heal that person. The person will have to be available to be healed, and to be responsible for whatever is creating the disharmony. Or, if the person continues with the disharmony, he or she may have to face leaving the community. You will not be able to have warring factions in the days ahead. A lot of your work will involve healing, being very tolerant and compassionate, and reading the signs and symbols. You will need to allow other people and yourselves to act out whatever is needed for you to come to deep realizations and move through them.

Each person that is a part of the community must contribute to the whole of the community, so that everyone adds their talent. Communities will specialize in certain products, talents, and abilities, which will be determined by the collection of consciousness of the people. You might ask, "How will I know what collection of consciousness of people I will end up with?" An invisible hand will move you to the community that you can serve and that can serve you, according to your intentions, beliefs, and desires.

You will feel relief when you belong to a community and live closer to the land, breathe fresh air, and feel alive. There will be a new vitality in food. There will be deeper laughter and relationships, and a greater value to every moment of life. Eventually, you will come to the conclusion that life is to be played, and that only in playing life can you succeed in work. If you do not play properly, you cannot have successful work. The work needs always to benefit the community. Many healings will take place. Communities will be inspired to build, and a renaissance of the temple culture will occur.

All over this land, sites will be marked and sacred buildings of beauty brought forth. Earth changes will open many secrets from deep in Earth herself. The pyramids that dot this land and are covered over will be uncovered, and many cracks and crevices will reveal ancient sites long buried.

A community that can meld its thoughtforms, move beyond personal ego battles, and come up with a viable purpose and quality to life will be successful. In some communities, vegetation can be grown around meditation, sound, and intent as an ongoing communication with nature. Members of communities can tone together, and make dreams and music together. These will be the most sought-out communities, the ones that play the best. This does not mean you will move into a hedonism in which you forget, eat, take drugs, drink to forget, and then think that is play. When you play you will *consciously play* with energy, freeing it and directing it in a childlike fashion. Then you will have the duty, responsibility, and dedication to want to make your community a magnificent place. There is great power in interacting with a group.

Many of your talents that will contribute to community are undiscovered and unrecognized at this moment. These talents will come from inside you.

Your energy fields will be based on a cooperative codicil that the core group of the community will agree to establish. This core group will not do this in secret, for there will be no secrets; the days of secrets will be over. A code of behavior will be needed, which everyone who lives in the community will take an oath to uphold. Fields of energy will surround everyone, creating wisdom and fairness. Everyone from the tiniest baby to the oldest member to the animals will live in these fields. As founders, you must get very clear about what you know works. If you adopt very basic ideas to harmonize, cooperate, and dream together, you will be a success. Dreaming must become an essential part of community life, because it is through dreams that people reveal who they are.

Through dreams, you can discover off-balance energy and seek to return to balance. Those who have problems in waking life play them out in dream life. People who have grave difficulty in the waking world have more difficulty in the dream world. Listening to dreams will give you clues about who people are. Learn to listen and observe without judgment, allowing your intuition to guide you.

You will pool resources and share your ideas about food, education, barter, business, leisure time, and places of meditation. Prioritize and agree that a strong community comes first, knowing that each person is a valuable asset to the whole community. As you do these things, you establish a field of ideas, or a field of thought. You will create huge thoughtforms over the community. Those who have a predilection for reading thoughtforms will be able to view your community and know by reading the energy in the thoughtforms who you are, and what you are about. Your thoughtforms will be a new sort of etheric telegraph.

No one person will be in charge of your community. You will all contribute your own common sense, impulses, and spontaneity. You cannot look to one person to come up with all of the ideas. It is essential that you all value yourselves on this journey.

As you design your community or place to live, you must be able to speak with the plants and animals. This is essential. It sounds a little farfetched, yet it is not, because right now you just don't take the time to do it. How many of you have sat down lately and had a chat with your dog or cat? This develops your sensitivity and takes you to a new level with decision making and advice, because animals and plants receive their knowledge directly from Earth. They are tuned in and patiently waiting for you to recognize that they can help you and advise you. They can tell you all their healing secrets, and show you where all the energy places are. They can show you everything. They know. Do you know why they know? Because they don't exploit nature and Earth.

Because you as humans exploit as a species, things are hidden from you.

The animals and plants will be your way-showers to the devic and elemental kingdoms, the natural kingdoms that are governed by those forces whose reality is unrecognized by yours. Take the time to find intelligence in the chrysanthemums, the grasshoppers, the ants—in all these things. The experience will implode everywhere, for anyone who wants to become connected to Earth. The healing of Earth will come about because of the conversing and exchanging with all of Earth's occupants.

The rights of birth are going to change. The value of birth and what women do to bring children into this world will come into the highest honor. A man will be honored to stand next to a mother and child and say, "It is my child," reclaiming the pride and responsibility that goes with fathering a child. Women will no longer experience shame with childbirth. Why do so many women not have fathers for their children? Because they are ashamed of the process and not connected to the honor of what they are doing. There will come a time when a man will truly seek the favor of a woman. He will want to be in her vibration, to bond more than anything else, to be a part of the miracle of life, and to deliver children. It will be completely changed. Your current era will be looked upon as a most barbaric time, when the darkest of darkness was at hand and when women themselves did not even know that they were playing out the patriarchal game of birth.

Your communities will be oriented toward children— toward what you can do for children to create a safe, loving, nurturing environment. You will learn from the children, as they become your teachers. They will instruct you and share with you what they know and what is going on from their perspective. There will be a series of children born this decade whom we call the Family of Love. They will teach you about the energy of the Goddess and about love as a force of creation. They will carry the epitome of creative energy. They will be born to those who know how to honor their sexuality. When a couple unites in the highest vibration of spiritual energy, with complete chakra opening and intention to invite an energy to life, this allows the Family of Love individuals to be born.

Many of these children will be highly evolved, speaking eloquently within a few days or months of birth. They will know and remember many things; they will say, "I have returned." They will walk, talk, perform tasks, and speak other languages. They will look different. The period you carry these children will be shortened. Everything in your bodies will speed up, so the gestation period will be less. These children will experience ecstatic births, and will transfer to their mothers the same experience and take away the pain of birth. They will not drain their mothers; they will enhance them. Their consciousness will depend upon the consciousness of their fathers and how highly evolved the male vibration on the planet can demonstrate itself to be. It is in the hands of the men at this time on your planet to demonstrate what kind of consciousness you can welcome from space.

These children will be looked upon as prized members of every community, as lucky omens. They will be in telepathic linkup with one another all over the planet. Whatever room they walk into, they will be able to maintain the same flow of creativity through their hearts, for their presence will stimulate and raise the vibration of all they come in contact with. They will not be large in stature. They will be blue. They will be from the blue ray, for they will be Pleiadian consciousness and will have specific tasks to do. They will be a part of every community, born on every continent and in every tribe. They will come here to bring the love vibration and to teach you.

These children will be a telepathic link with the Goddess.

They will be in direct communication with the Goddess because they will carry the love creation frequency. They will speed up everyone's telepathic communication so that you will hear and feel what other people are thinking. This will discipline you to be more in alignment and selective with your thinking. This is the biggest challenge to the planet at this time. You need to comprehend that *what you think has an effect on reality.* Now, many of you believe this concept based on trust. However, it shortly will be demonstrated as living proof in existence, and all people will see it.

These children will be phenomenal. They will be treasured because their consciousness will be so valuable. They will be like having walking gold among you. They will change the vibration of all people, and the flow of creativity will change. As they emerge as valuable members of families and societies, all communities will consider themselves to be in the highest of fortune to have these members in their midst. These love avatars will return. They will lead the way and link you with all the other communities around the world.

These children will create telepathic linkups with their potential parents so choices can be made. We wish to communicate to each of you that you do have a choice. Will you exercise that choice? Or will you slip into disempowerment and think that you have no effect on what your body can do? This teaching is crucial to the days that are coming. Each of you, as a female or male embodying the Goddess or God energy in all phases, needs to embrace the idea that you have power over your body, over the life-giving process, over the distribution of your kundalini, and that you decide when a child can enter through you.

Not all of you will have these unique children. These children will seek out those with appropriate consciousness and bloodlines. They will be born in every village and community. They will help change the planetary vibration, and will be born to parents who have a spiritual and psychic experience of sexuality. These children will be the embodiment of the vibration of love and will willingly decide to carry a mark of difference within them. They will be engineered in the very DNA of your bodies and your bloodstreams.

Depending upon the choices of consciousness, there is presently the potential for many, many places to no longer exist. You will take your children first to safety before yourselves, and spirit will gather up children from all over the world. The children are indeed your treasured resource, your lineage in form, seeking to live in a vital world. Make it a priority to provide them with a safe world. In the later years of this decade, much of your work will be with and for children.

Soon you will not recognize life on the planet because what you now experience as routine and take for granted will not be here. There is nothing to be afraid of. Many of you will go through experiences to discover where your power lies and where your energy is, and you will discover that it all lies within you. You are all qualified to surf through these times that are coming—to ride these waves and rise above the churning and the undertows. You all have the knowledge to stay on the crests of the waves; therefore, you do not need to fear anything that is coming.

We want to ask something of you. No matter where you are, no matter what is going on, no matter how severe events may seem to get, we want you to promise to always bring fun, love, and laughter to every day of your life. Take time out to say, "Hey, listen, we're too freaked out over this. Let's laugh for a little bit. Let's stop and have tea. Let's energize the pleasure frequency."

These are the most brilliant and uplifting of times. They are magnificent. It is just that you do not have daily reminders of this. There are unique sound and light technologies that are energizing new opportunities for effortlessness and cooperation. There are many, many solutions that are being born.

The new civilizations may desire to advance to a high degree of technological skill and experimentation. They will only be successful when their creations are ruled by the mind in connection with the heart and spirit. When creations are co-ruled by the mind and heart, they are a living technology. The differentiation we are making is that technology will become alive. It will be run in cooperation with the minds of those who created it. Then it can appear as hardware, though it will be living hardware. This is the phase you will go into. Understand that all you create and bring life to, you do with your mind. What you do with your mind, and how you invest it, is a key to your survival and the survival of planet Earth.

Energy Exercise

Willing your body into stillness, feel the pillar of light energizing, cleansing, and reminding your body of its idealized functions. Intend that the pillar of light fill your body, and intend that health and well-being pulsate through the cells and essence of who you are.

As you feel this energy come through your body, combine the energy that is yours with your surroundings in a way that all can benefit. Relax, and with rays of light, reach inside yourself in the area of your solar plexus, a place of will, feeling, and power. Imagine you are pulling something out: a piece of gold, a diamond, a gem that is beyond price. Hold in your hands the object you consider to be of priceless value that you have discovered inside yourself. Marvel at the majestic beauty of your treasure.

Imagine now that you are with a large group of people, and each of you is holding an inner gem of priceless value. One by one, you walk up to a green and gold cloth and, with great gentleness and great reverence, lay your treasure down. It is a symbol of the value you have inside yourself that you are willing to contribute so the whole of humanity can benefit. Your gift may be as large or small as you select. Once you have laid it down, step back and stand in the circle, observing the gems and treasures representing the collection of your group's contributions. Sense our presence as well. Feel the results of combining your wealth with that of the others in the group.

Now, imagine what you would like this collection of wealth to contribute to Earth, as well as to your own heart's desire. As your wealth is acknowledged, feel the pillar of light energizing you. What do you imagine that will make a difference for Earth?

Hold your vision as clearly as you can. Feel the energy move around the circle of consciousness. Let the energy spiral and spin, moving quickly from one person to another, reminding you to invest yourself, with mind and heart, in the future of Earth.

TWELVE

Awaken, Dear Friends, Within This Dream

As a species of life, you are poised at that moment when you are required to make a leap of faith.

We tell you stories from which you can evolve. You can choose whether to believe them or not. However, if you believe them, be willing to let go of them and recognize when they no longer serve you. Our entire approach and purpose at this point in time is to confound you into clarity and create unsolvable contradictions within the patterns of thought that occupy the cells of your beings. By considering our words, you change. The days before you will be filled with majestic splendor in the same way that your physical world once offered pristine beauty for you to explore. You are creating an opportunity to transcend third-dimensional reality and to enter the corridors of time, where worlds and realities have more variety and flexibility. Your task is to heal yourselves on a treasure hunt through the corridors of time. We have shared many keys with you, and left as many unannounced. You must transform yourselves as the sum total of the force of existence, poised in your moment of the ever-expanding now.

We speak to you as evolving humans—as ambassadors of

light. You are, at this moment in time, poised on unprecedented discovery. You are ripe, through your own exposure and your own seeking, to make a choice. When we journey into your reality, we learn as we watch the processes through which you resist, learn, and create life. You can consider yourselves, at this moment in time, at a summation point of life's journey. Whenever you reach this very moment that draws you to our words, it is indicative of an ending.

Everything we have shared with you throughout the previous eleven chapters has been designed to take you deeper into yourselves. You have viewed the beliefs and ideas around which the self is structured—by choice, by overt and covert influence on Earth, and from the heavens. What does it matter? Do not begrudge reality. You have created an opportunity now. You are poised at this ending to give thanks for what you know and what you have journeyed into. You have learned more of who you are in the story of twelve.

The idea of twelve is deeply imprinted and embedded in your physical being. Twelve is a code that has been used by numerous sentient beings to enter your reality. You live in your world today according to certain mathematical agreements about reality. There are numerous mathematical bases for which numbers and interpretations can be pursued. Most of you simply agree on the one that is most commonly taught and used, and you believe that this is the only one. The idea of twelve coincides with the most commonly held mathematical base and point of view. The story of twelve is grander than that base; however, it fits well within it. Through this structure you can be influenced, and a way can be established so you can be guided to approach reality.

Can you imagine, as you go through life and all of existence, wherever you travel, there is always a road? Say you are in an automobile on Earth driving down the highways, never veering or venturing off the paved way. You can see what is off to the sides of the road, but your vehicle only operates on the road, so you are only able to go where the roads are, and you never get out to walk. Understand that the imprint of twelve is like the road—whether it is twelve signs of the zodiac, twelve hours in the clock, twelve chapters in this book, or twelve imprints of your identity as strands of DNA or chakra energy centers. All of these things are roads through the cosmos around which you have traveled as an intelligent being.

Our intention is to have you become more fully aware that you are on a highway of twelve energy forms. If you can truly conceive of this grand mapping of twelve, then perhaps you can have some idea of where the cosmic roads will take you. You are tooled to fit twelve roads as models of universal thought. This is part of the teaching that is coded throughout this book. There is a very deep creation in the understanding of the twelve roads of energy that take you to separate places within existence that unify you. When you understand that these roads take you to the great shifts in consciousness you are now accumulating and experiencing as a mass consciousness, it will catapult an ending to reality as you currently know it. However, endings are completed moments when you gather, suspended, before a new, unseen beginning. As a species of life, you are poised at that moment when you are required to make a leap of faith.

You may ask yourself, "What is the point of what I know? What good does it do me to know that I am a member of the Family of Light? That perhaps I am Pleiadian? That Earth is valuable, that I am valuable, and that if I walk Earth and search Earth, I can find her secrets in her unbounded majesty, her sacred sites, and her symphonies of silently speaking circles? What do I need to know about the Lizzies and the Goddess and my body? And, how is it that my body can have room within it to have others merge with me and peek out from my eyes? And, if others merge with me, do they see the same world I do? Or is it through their merging with my being that other worlds *emerge*, and that I myself emerge into those other worlds? What is possession? What is merging and emerging in late twentieth-century Earth? What do my glands have to do with this and my body? And, where does sex take me through all of this?" Now, as you ponder these points, we in turn ask you: What great depths of surprise are you discovering as you learn to open your personal sacred sites to the secrets of your own loops of consciousness? What do you find when you meet brick walls and get to know the deepest mysteries of yourself?

If you can learn to transform energy, and move beyond judgment, you will come to an exalted place that takes you beyond the moment into a grander aspect of time—a time that is structured in a different fashion from yours. Time for you is ruled by numbers. There again, you find the story of twelve, encapsulated in time, defining who you are within a circle. So, as you complete the cycle of twelve in this book, consider a new way of viewing time. Realize that it is a structure through which other forms of existence use mathematical heritage as a language to express geometry.

Consider the geometry of time, which connects the cycles that you believe exist outside yourself—the rotations of the planets and the moon. Is the moon a computer? An eye in the sky? The Mother Goddess? A home of secret bases? A refueling station? A cosmic library, storehouse of ancient knowledge? The moon is the magic maker and cycle rotator, the energizer of your own inner tides and Great Mother water deity. Who is the moon in relationship to the sun? You must explore this on your journey of self-discovery.

The sun is the great master ruler, the governor of your solar system—for who are you without light? Who *owns* light? And, who, indeed, *are* light? And who are the surrounding energy forms, the stately planets that you believe exist in your solar system, which are spread like pearls throughout cosmic space—jewels equally as beautiful as Earth herself? There are those who would scoff at the idea that each of these forms glittering in space has intelligence.

We, in turn, who exist many times on these glittering rocks in space, marvel at those who shut themselves off from the grandiose ideas that are bombarding your planet at this time. Be not fooled by those in authority who want to bring you limitation. Be uplifted. You are reaching an exalted state by deciding to choose a more expanded version of reality. You are giving everything in your life a greater role and finding yourself at the inner core of your own authority.

As you journey to this point that is the sum total of who you are, knowing all these things, you arrive at a moment when it is time to share your knowledge with your family, society, and culture. Many of you are poised in this moment. You have a duty to share what you know—not to preach or sow seeds of fear or plant the field for another, but to vibrate in the wholeness that you are. You need to understand and encompass all the things that make up society—life, death, birth, children, and all society's members, young and old, not simply those whom you consider to be productive. Radical change will occur. Have compassion as you put the things you have learned to work.

As a mass consciousness, you are facing a collective total of karma as this Piscean Age completes its final act and point of purpose. Karma is being played out as determined by the universal laws of cause and effect. Through a grand gesture of generosity, karma is allowing for the creations of existence to return to their maker. *This means you.* You are facing a personal return of what you have created. That is now crucial for you to learn. We stated in the very beginning of this journal that we are here, experiencing Earth, because of our karma. In your own way, you are at this point realizing this as well. So, there is a need to look at your lives, to step outside yourselves and become the watchers, the great observers of your journey through twelve. Who is it that you are, and how have you employed your own selves as you have journeyed on this board of consciousness—this game of twelve cycles of life, or twelve influences that go around and around and come full circle again and again? Can you get off the circle? What do you know? And, what are you going to do with what you know?

We exist in a place in time that is beyond where you can be at this moment, and yet the place we exist occupies the same moment that you do. You are going to learn how to go deeper into your moments of time and how to discover that there is an unending enchanting melody that entices you forward. We want you to understand that what you seek in some way is always just ahead of you. Do not be burdened by that idea. Understand that, in the seeking, you ignite yourselves and inspire yourselves with your own imaginations. It is our intention to offer you an idea of purpose, to further inspire you to live. We cannot *make* you live. Only you, yourselves, can.

By using the power of your kundalini and directing that force into the ever-expanding vision of paradise and the vibration of ecstasy, you are led onward, moving from one moment to the next. Paradise exists. Indeed it does. You are all in search of it, and furthermore, you will find it. You will recognize it as a moment of bliss. It is not an ongoing place where you dwell forever and get bored; it is a *moment* of bliss. Often you seek it ahead of yourselves, always wondering when it is coming. When you are fully in the moment, you can realize that you are in a moment of bliss. Or, you can look back and reflect on many moments of bliss. You can dwell in the frequency of bliss, knowing that time and time again you have created that ever-expanding, spontaneous, synchronistic moment, and that it is ever beckoning you to move further along.

When you reach the point of closure and completion, in the twelfth sector, it is indeed a place of karma. It is a gathering of lessons, when the sum total of what you have set into motion returns to you as a completion of the cycle. There are a few ways to handle this realization. You can feel entrapped and enslaved by it, and create suffering, which is the victim idea: "I am powerless. I can do nothing about this. I am stuck in the loop. I have no idea how this happens to me." If that is your stance, you can trust that you'll create it again. Or, you can use the sum total of the journey of twelve to say, "What is it that I have learned on this journey of twelve? I take responsibility for everything in my life, for it was of my own design and creation. I have, on this journey, come to see why I selected certain things, even though I was unaware of them. They served me by showing me that my thoughts do create my own reality, and now I understand how the journey of twelve has served me. I am not saddened or enslaved by what I have discovered. I can now set myself free."

All of you are looping through this particular aspect, experiencing the ending of the Piscean Age, staged as an event on a cosmic calendar. In the near future, the bottom will drop out. You are at that point of ending, processing, and realizing the loops through which you have traveled as patterns and ideas connecting all aspects of being. Some of you who have processed the loops of the exterior system are now understanding the loops in your own systems, deep in your bodies. Some of you are discovering that you are like prisoners, trapped in your own Eiffel Towers. Resolve your confinement. Visualize when you go to sleep tonight that there are keys on the walls of the towers in which you dwell. If you imagine yourselves as prisoners, in whatever isolated aspects of reality you favor, you can also imagine that there are keys to walk out and new suits of clothes as well. Be uplifted, and know that you can resolve that which appears to be a karmic burden.

If the karma is squeezing you at this time, it is because you need to release yourselves from the prisons you have created by your own need to punish, or feel shame or blame. You are all poised at the grand moment of letting go. Imagine that you are ambassadors of light, feeling space and vibrancy within yourselves, knowing that your thoughts have designed the energy that moves you. A new frontier and vista of the world await you if you visualize and imagine it. You must visualize that moment of bliss; it cannot exist without you.

Initiation is the test through which you learn to trust, let go, and change. When you are very young and your legs are small, you learn to ride a tricycle. When you can sit on it without help, you are proud. And when you can move those little legs and get it going, and learn how to stay on it, you are quite accomplished for a three- or four- or five-year- old. Then, there is an initiation. Your legs grow longer, and you no longer fit on that little tricycle. The world today is full of those in positions of authority on tricycles. They never moved beyond the moment of knowledge they experienced. They force reality and their long legs to fit in that one moment only. The initiation is to allow yourself to go into the ever-expanding moment—to get on a bigger bike and move with your body's growing needs. Understand that your body grows more than physically. It grows mentally, spiritually, and emotionally into a multidimensional existence. The key is to trust the process of growth and change, in all dimensions of reality, with all versions of yourself. The crisis you confront is one in which world leaders and authority figures are on tricycles, riding around the block, lost in a loop of anachronistic beliefs.

The initiation is to get on with something that is vast and unknown, and to master it. The accumulation of everything you learn through the point of twelve often takes you to a place of crisis. Why does it reach crisis? Because you are stubborn beings. Because you like to say, "I am expanded. I am uplifted. I am open. I make space in my body. I am ready for change." And then the brakes go on: "Not here, spirit. Oh, no. Not here, spirit. I'm not changing. I'm staying the same." You do not make room for the energy to pass through you, and you clog up the sieve of yourselves. Then there is a big backlash.

If you've ever seen a dam break, you know there is a

great mess to deal with. You will see this soon. Some of your dams will break in your world because, as people, you have dammed-up consciousness. Rather than go through the initiation, you stay on your tricycles. You are afraid to get on bikes that are bigger and fall off. Let go. Realize that there is a great love for who you are. Reality is designed by you, and you can design it to benefit yourselves. The force of existence moves in your direction as you call it. So make a grand, beautiful symphony of how you want the world to be. You are unlimited, and this is what the initiation teaches you. You can get off the tricycles and get on bigger bikes and ride them faster and see another world. You are growing now as a collective to ride something bigger, a vehicle you are just beginning to imagine. Have compassion for those who are afraid to get off the trikes of life. Have compassion, open your hearts, and invite them. Show them the way, those of you who have the courage to be the ambassadors of light, for you ride on invisible vehicles.

Do not be attached to what we have shared with you. Do not proclaim new bibles of truth through our stories. We are here to entertain you and, as we have said, to create new images to give you a stepladder to what's out there. It's a gigantic universe, so do not limit yourself and force everything to fit into one recipe to bake a pie. There are many ways to look at life.

The embodiment of twelve will give you a sum total of yourselves. Take it, and realize that with the completion of twelve a whole new journey begins. It is this moment upon which you are now poised. Enjoy every moment as a moment of bliss. Keep yourselves in the ever-expanding opportunity that the goddesses and the gods and all the versions of yourselves are funneling your way. Accept the mantle of your own creation.

The sum total of twelve also relates to the idea of the twelve libraries. This you cannot conceive of at this moment in time. However, as we offer you a vision and an idea, some of you will begin to create these libraries in your own artistic forms, first in your imaginations and then through different mediums on your planet. However you bring these images into form is your freedom to choose. We want you to hold the idea that twelve unique centers, including Earth, are coming alive. In this very moment that moves out in every direction, as you enhance your now and explore, and dare to have the courage to climb a new peak of existence—to insist that there is more—this reverberates into every aspect of twelve as well.

When these twelve centers of knowledge are once again reconnected as an energetic laser grid of light, there will be a new mandala—a new highway of energy within the universe you find yourselves within. The story of twelve fits within a circle, and as reality stretches to fulfill more moments, it also fits within a spiral as well. When you complete a cycle of twelve, it creates a larger sphere or circle of consciousness into which you evolve. You have difficulty imagining the unbounded, so you bind yourselves with a circle. You divide that circle into twelve, whether you call it the zodiac, the calendar, or the clock. You find yourselves within that aspect of geometry because you are comfortable within it. You can move without it; however, at this stage of your development, it is where you learn the cycles of yourselves, and so we teach you within that arena. All geometry is contained within the circle, and the circle is a key to the spiral. It helps the spiral understand itself by capturing the moment.

We want to remind you that you are in two worlds. Even though you drive your cars, go to the bathroom, sleep, eat, and do all of the things that all humans do, you do not dwell in the same world. You reside in a world of knowledge, and you have gained access to the rules to bridge both of these worlds.

We also want to remind you to energize the idea of a safe world. Much will happen, bringing change through tumultuous, shocking, and surprising events as things that have been prophesied begin to occur. It would be wise for all of you to seek the wisdom of the elders, the indigenous peoples in all cultures, and to listen to the teachings they share. They speak of these times, and their teachers have been our teachers. They understand, as Earth speaks.

We are friends from many, many creations of existence, reminding you that the Game Masters have a good time intertwining and orchestrating realities as they create from afar and dwell within. Awaken, dear friends, within this dream and realize that it is your duty and responsibility as human beings, based on what you now know, to imagine and visualize a safe world. It will be as you decree, and your own experience will thus reflect it.

We salute you for the courage to kindle the flame of faith as the spark of life in the core of your beings and to pioneer the frontier to blissful living where meaning and purpose thrive. See that flame grow and allow it to serve as the fuel for a safe and unique adventure into grand arenas of experience.

Energy Exercise

Imagine yourself standing under the open sky. The air is fresh and alive, and the ground feels firm and solid beneath your feet. Take a deep breath and say to yourself, "I am alive!" Focus on your vitality and travel into the moment of your imagination, as the painter of your inner vision.

Picture an ancient stone circle before you, and for a few moments open yourself to the vibrations of the twelve majestic megaliths as they stand erect and dignified under the canopy of time. Feel the stones speak as they convey the experience of their commitment as consciousness. They have been alive and aware for grand epochs of existence, encased as the bone of Earth. Walk up to a stone, place your hand on the cool surface, and listen with your cells as golden spirals dance their way through the stone into your now. Walk from giant to giant, experiencing the twelve and sensing the task and monumental energy each stone preserves. Take that energy and transfer it to yourself so that the bones of your being are filled with golden spirals.

Step now to the center of this ring of stone and plant a seed that holds a resplendent and glorious version of Earth, in which she is honored and crowned by her people. Using your knowledge of light and intent, create a spark of life to activate this seed. See the center of the circle expand and the seed grow as golden spirals spin off in all directions, passing through the avenues of twelve, seeding a new Earth.

Now, a voice speaks, familiar in tone and form, saying,"We are you, on the golden spirals of time, cycling the epochs of existence, calling to ourselves. Be uplifted. May your journey begin anew. Be yourselves."

EPILOGUE

Dear Ambassadors of Light,

Be aware that even within the new concepts you grasp lie structure and limitation. However, each new "daring" you pursue takes you to a new vista, where you scale the peaks of existence as divine teachings play themselves out today in your very own version of life. Ask yourselves what chapter closes as you view this segment of your lives, this moment of the ever-expanding now. What have you pursued to steer you to this very moment in time in order to further experience life? Inspire yourselves to move further into the moment by letting go of old discoveries, and trust to the core of your beings that a new cycle of learning awaits. Go forward, friends, and be uplifted. Learn in your own way to go into the past through the ever-expanding, spontaneous, synchronistic moment. A new cycle of existence awaits you. Use the tools of thought to guide yourselves on the new superhighway of consciousness. No technology will ever surpass the magnificence of your own biological/spiritual beings. For many of you, these days may be filled with sadness as the letting go becomes more and more challenging. The keys of consciousness for living through these tumultuous times on Earth have been given to you to the best of our ability and yours at this time. May you grow in wisdom and flourish.

Your invisible friends and colleagues in the unknown,

The Pleiadians

ABOUT THE AUTHOR

The Pleiadians are a collective of extraterrestrials from the star system the Pleiades. They have been speaking through Barbara Marciniak since May 18, 1988.

The Pleiadian teachings can be likened to those of shamanism, the ancient body of consciousness that has served as intermediary between the realms of the physical and the spiritual, leading people to self-discovery in the worlds of paradox, paradigm shifting, and spirituality.

Barbara Marciniak is an internationally known trance channel from North Carolina. She began channeling in May of 1988 in Athens, Greece, at the conclusion of a three-week journey through ancient Egypt and Greece. On this trip, Barbara was impulsed to reexperience specific temples and power sites in this lifetime—the Great Pyramid at Giza, the temples along the Nile, the Acropolis in Athens, and Delphi.

Since that time, Barbara has coonducted class sessions and workshops throughout the United States and has facilitated tours to sacred power sites in Great Britian, Peru, Bolivia, Mexico, Egypt, Greece, Bali, and Australia. She feels that the sites themselves are connections to energy vortexes that hold knowledge of the higher mind, the higher idea that Earth is presently seeking to re-create.

Barbara feels that her experience with the Pleiadians has

been a gift of priceless value. Her work has connected her with opportunities for personal, global, and cosmic transformation, and for this she holds tremendous gratitude.

For information on audio tapes, transcripts, and a quarterly newsletter, please send a self-addressed stamped envelope to:

Bold Connections
P.O. Box 782
Apex, NC 27502